The Religions of the
American Indians

HERMENEUTICS
Studies in the History of Religions

GENERAL EDITOR

Kees W. Bolle
UCLA

ADVISORY BOARD

Robert N. Bellah
California, Berkeley

Thorkild Jacobsen
Harvard

Giorgio Buccellati
UCLA

Gerhart Ladner
UCLA

Wilhelm Dupré
Nijmegen

Jaan Puhvel
UCLA

Mircea Eliade
Chicago

William R. Schoedel
Illinois

Amos Funkenstein
UCLA

Guy R. Welbon
Pennsylvania

Hellmut Wilhelm
Washington

The Religions of the American Indians

Åke Hultkrantz

Translated by
Monica Setterwall

University of California Press
Berkeley   Los Angeles   London

Originally published as
De Amerikanska Indianernas Religioner
© 1967 Åke Hultkrantz and Esselte Studium AB.
University of California Press
Berkeley and Los Angeles, California
University of California Press, Ltd.
London, England
This translation copyright © 1979 by
The Regents of the University of California

ISBN 0-520-02653-5
Library of Congress Catalog Card Number: 73-90661
Printed in the United States of America

1 2 3 4 5 6 7 8 9

Contents

List of Plates

Preface to the American Edition

The literature on the religions of the American Indians is almost beyond reckoning in its quantity, yet it is easy to enumerate those works which provide a systematic or historical survey of particular complexes of belief or of the various branches of religion.[1] Native America is still in large measure a terra incognita where scholarship in the field of history of religions and religious ethnography is confronted with great and basic tasks; consistent theoretical descriptions of the history of the religions of the Indians are yet to be formulated. To be sure, H. B. Alexander's two works on Indian mythology provide considerable material on cult and religion, but they are primarily concerned with epic narrative. Daniel Brinton's careful (for his time) analyses of Indian beliefs and myths can

1. General surveys of American Indian religions, in chronological order: Müller 1855, Brinton 1868, Spence 1914, Radin 1915, Boas 1915, Alexander 1916, 1920, Karsten 1926, Métraux 1949, Alexander 1953, Underhill 1957, Krickeberg 1961, Trimborn 1961, Müller 1961, Zerries 1961, Hultkrantz 1963, Karsten 1964, Underhill 1965, Métraux 1967.

Regional surveys of American Indian religions exist for the high cultures (see Chapters 11 to 14) and for North America: Loewenthal 1913 (the east Algonkian area), Müller 1956 (the eastern woodlands), Dorsey 1894 and Hultkrantz 1973b (the prairie and plains areas), Parsons 1939 and Underhill 1948 (the southwest), Kroeber 1907 (California), Lantis 1950 and Hultkrantz 1962 (the Arctic Coast).

hardly be said to give a balanced survey of Indian religions. Three relatively recent works, while useful in themselves, do not answer the need for a general description. North America's religions have been presented in popular form by Ruth Underhill, and the religions of the South American Indians have been treated, from special points of departure, by Rafael Karsten. A volume in the series *Die Religionen der Menschheit* [*The Religions of Man*], edited by Walter Krickeberg, gathers within its covers much of the religious history of Indian America, but the various sections have the character of independent essays.

Only one well-thought-out work exists which deals with the entire history of Indian religion. J. G. Müller's 700-page classic *Geschichte der Amerikanischen Urreligionen* [*History of the Primal Religions of America*] was printed in Basel in 1855. Müller, who was Professor of Theology at Basel and at the same time taught Latin, published the result of years of research in what he called "American archaeology." The first major portion of his book treats the "savages" of North and South America, and its second half the "civilized peoples" in Peru and Mexico. The work is naturally out of date, both with respect to its material and its theories, but it does provide many surprisingly fresh and fruitful points of view.

More than a century has passed since Müller wrote his survey, and the time may now be ripe for a new attempt. The present work, more limited in its extent than its classic predecessor, claims only to supply the most basic of the knowledge we now have of the Indian religions. In a number of cases the author builds his argument upon special investigations which, for lack of space, cannot be reproduced here. The interested reader is directed to the bibliography, in which some of the author's published accounts of his investigations are listed. In order to avoid confusion between what may be considered established facts and sheer hypotheses particular care has been taken to point out hypotheses where they occur. It scarcely needs emphasizing that hypotheses are sometimes helpful in integrating facts.

Part I of this book treats the religions of the tribal Indians and was originally written for French readers. In contrast to the conditions prevailing in the Old World, where the high cultures at the time of the great European discoveries had extended their influence to the most distant places, the New World has in large measure been characterized by cultures which were "primitive" in the sense that they lacked writing, the use of metal, cities, and state-forms. The religions of these cultures, which we may appropriately call "tribal," include an enormous mass of myths, rites, and religious conceptions which in large part are still not published or even recorded. The material accessible in print is already overwhelming enough, and could not be surveyed by any single scholar. If in the following pages North American religions dominate the discussion, that is a result of the author's greatest acquaintance with the ethnography and history of the religions of the North American continent.

It is not always easy to systematize large amounts of religious data within the framework of the field of "primitive" religions, particularly since the familiar principles of classification applied by historians of religion are of only limited use in such a context. It is only for the post-Columbian centuries in America that we possess documents which illuminate the religious situation of some of the tribes. There are several good descriptions of Indian religions in tribal monographs, most of which discuss North American Indians. However, in recent years South American Indians have also been portrayed in some praiseworthy publications. I can imagine that an anthropologist, working with a comprehensive presentation of native American religions, would have chosen to portray selected religions within the framework of their cultural systems. His reasons for doing so would probably have been the same as those put forward by L. M. Fruzzetti-Ostor in the following pronouncement:

In the field of social anthropology, the most significant and meaningful studies of religion have been those that link beliefs and rituals to the social organization, social structure, and social morphology of society, tying religion as an ideological system to society in a holistic approach. [*American Anthropologist* 78 (3), 1976, p. 652.]

I would agree that this is a possible way of approaching the subject, although I should have dedicated my attention to a broader ecological view rather than a narrow sociological interpretation. Again, we do not achieve much more than a disparate bundle of social systems demonstrated by certain religious connotations. The rationale of this approach is clearly given by the same author:

From this point of view, religion cannot be divorced from society as a separate reality nor can it or need it be comprehended in terms of a separate method and a unique kind of understanding. [Ibid.]

This is a very outspoken statement by a member of the "reductionistic" social-anthropological school, and a student of the American religions will not find this approach very promising. First of all, he will question the ideological premises, which are highly arbitrary. Second, he will argue that only selected parts of a people's religion are accessible by the methods described, for there are religious concepts, myths, and personal religious feelings which do not always fit the social context or which derive from foreign sources. Thus, lofty concepts of God exist in the most varied native cultures in America, the myth of the Earth Diver in North America has close counterparts in the Old World, from which it originated, and the religious experiences of medicine men often take us far outside any cultural frame. Indeed, even complex ceremonies like the Sun Dance of the plains Indians may be traced to details in the annual tribal rite among the Tungus of Siberia.

It is, I think, appropriate that a book devised to give a comprehensive survey of indigenous American religions should bring together those features characteristic of these religions. The perspective in this work, therefore, must be mainly typological and phenomenological. The author restricts himself to providing representative examples of conceptions and rites which characterize the "tribal" Indian religions, and to discussing the elements in these religions which receive attention in the scholarship in history of religions, folklore, ethnology, and sociology. Historical reconstructions are attempted, and the main lines of the development of tribal Indian religions are sketched.

Part II treats the so-called high religions, i.e., the religions which in pre-Columbian times were part of the high culture of America. In their organization and their forms these religions diverge in many respects from the tribal Indian religions. They are in part so-called scripture religions, and that fact makes it frequently possible for us to follow their historical development. The high religions are represented here by the Inca religion in Peru and the religions of the Mayans and Aztecs in Mexico. In an introductory section the author has sought to set forth the common terrain from which these "peaks" shoot up. Earlier scholarship has to too large an extent tended to see them isolated from one another and from the development of culture in America, and this in turn has led to speculations about the non-American origin of these religions. In certain circles assumptions were made of direct stimulation from Southeast-Asian Buddhism, assumptions which are in large measure unrealistic. The author has striven to present the American background for religious development, and has thereby been able to build on the scholarly results attained by modern archaeology and ethnology.

In the description of the three high religions attention has been given to cultural, social, and ecological factors. Each religion's profile is drawn against the background of its culture patterns. At the same time a detailed description is presented of each of these religions. Doubtless the tribal religions could have been treated in the same way, but space has not permitted this. By selecting for special treatment the three high religions the author believes he can make some contribution toward knowledge of those religions in the Indians' America which are of greatest interest in the general history of religions.

This book was originally published for the Swedish public in 1967. In its present form, revised for American readers, new facts have been added and some earlier perspectives have been changed. As it stands it should mirror the facts but, of course, also the personal view of its author.

Professor Birger Pearson of the University of California, Santa Barbara, first suggested that this book should be published in the United States and took the necessary steps toward this end. Monica Setterwall has skillfully translated the original Swedish manuscript into English. Finally, the chapters on the high religions have received the friendly scrutiny of Professor Sigvald Linné, formerly curator of the Ethnographical Museum in Stockholm. The author tenders his warm thanks to them all.

Åke Hultkrantz
Stockholm, June 1, 1977

Introduction

The time is scarcely remote when white people thought there were tribes without religion in America. In the days of Darwinism and unlimited evolutionism the assumption was prevalent that the most "barbarian" peoples were also the least developed spiritually. It was Charles Darwin himself who said that the inhabitants of Tierra del Fuego lacked more lofty religious concepts. Darwin had visited the primitive Indians on the windy southern point of South America, and he was thus a direct eyewitness and did not remodel other observers' information. During the nineteenth century reports on Indians without religion continued to pour in, and not only from little-known South America. The merchant agent John McLean, who at the beginning of the last century lived for a long time among the Carrier Indians of western Canada, assures us in his notes that the language of these Indians "has not a term to express the name of Deity, spirit or soul." As late as 1928 the German student Tessmann asserted in his work *Menschen ohne Gott* (*Men without God*) that the Indians of the Ucayali river in Brazil lacked developed concepts of god.[1]

1. Darwin 1890 (1839), pp. 218f., 226f.; McLean 1849 (1), p. 165; Tessmann 1928, p. 183. Cf. Müller 1855, pp. 251f.

Such information could be accepted in earnest during a time when the knowledge of American Indian life was faulty and existing ethnographical data often derived from occasional travellers, ignorant government officials, or other superficial observers who had not penetrated the spiritual world of the Indians. Darwin's observations have in fact been thoroughly repudiated by the Austrian ethnologists Gusinde and Koppers, whose meticulous field research was performed in the 1920s. Gusinde has published two gigantic volumes primarily treating the high-god beliefs of the Indians of Tierra del Fuego! Although we may rightly suspect that missionary influences have partly changed the traditional religion of these Indians the fact remains that, in pre-Christian days, there existed among the Yahgan (or Yamana) of Tierra del Fuego a most comprehensive concept of God, among other things associated with primitive rites of initiation. In the same way all other assertions on tribes without religion have, one by one, been banished to the world of fancy.

As a matter of fact, we do not know of any Indian tribe that lacked a variety of religious conceptions. In their entirety the religions of the tribal Indians offer an image that is both comprehensive and richly faceted. As was the case in the primal societies of the Old World, the lives of both the group and the individual were surrounded by religious ideas and rites. Indeed, the religion is today often all that is left of the culture of the North American Indians. Religion was furthermore the first sign of cultural life the European intruders experienced: Pizarro's conquerors were acknowledged as the Peruvian god Viracocha and his men come back from the Western islands of the sun; Cortez was greeted by Moctezuma as the returning culture hero Quetzalcoatl; and Francis Drake and his sailors, landing in the bay of San Francisco, were worshipped by the Miwok Indians as their ancestors risen from the dead.[2] Early documents, such as the meritorious reports of the French Jesuit Fathers from Nouvelle France (eastern Canada) during the course of the seventeenth century, testify in an excellent

2. Heizer 1947, pp. 259ff. On the idea of the returning culture hero, see Hultkrantz 1977.

way to the central position held by religion in Indian life.[3] We need here only recollect Father Fremin's vivid description of the dream as the supernatural factor that regulated both private and general enterprises among the Iroquois Indians. Similar, although not so expressive, information may be had from other parts of North and South America.

It is only from a superficial perspective that the American Indian religions constitute a unity. They do not evince specific traits that set them apart from the tribal religions of the Old World, unless that strength of mind should be mentioned which has been expressed in severe asceticism and individualism.[4] Furthermore, Indian religions form such a changing mosaic that it is difficult to discern a common background. We must never forget that America is a spacious double continent and that it once housed hundreds of languages and thousands of ethnic groups whose religious peculiarities varied as much as European religions before the introduction of Christianity. It is easy to illustrate this by adducing some examples from North America: the simple hunting religion of the Naskapi Indians of Labrador contrasts sharply with the intricate horticultural religion of the Pueblo Indians of New Mexico and Arizona, and the simple structure of the Californian Indian religions bears little resemblance to the religion of sacred kingship represented by the Natchez on the lower Mississippi. Even among tribal religions of the same type the nature of conceptions and rites has varied. The more our research is concerned with taking stock of tribal Indian religions the richer and more complicated becomes our picture of their total outcome.

In scientific debates on religion attention has been paid to American Indians because of a series of religious phenomena and complexes that have been found in a more pronounced form among them than among other peoples. Comparative research concerning the North American Indian religions has dedicated itself particularly to the following themes: in religious beliefs, to guardian-spirit conceptions and the visionary

3. See Thwaites 1896–1901.
4. Cf., for example, Blumensohn 1933. Cf., however, also Benedict 1932.

quests closely allied to them; in ritual, to intricate ceremonialism and secret societies; and in mythology, to such myths as
those concerning the trickster and the culture hero. The
South American Indians, whose religious life is in many respects imperfectly known outside the domineering high cultures and their circum-Caribbean offshoots, have perhaps
less pronounced religious features, and consequently they
have been less appealing to scholars of religion. Nevertheless, even here research has found stimulating facts: in the
field of beliefs, the profusely ramified conceptions of spirits;
in ritual, the cult of vegetational goddesses and funeral customs; and in mythology, the—perhaps somewhat too
strongly emphasized—astral myths. In works on the sociology of religion the tribal religions of South America tend to
achieve the same importance as North American indigenous
religions have had for decades.

Added to this is all that religio-scientific theories have been
able to scoop from the rich treasures of Indian religions during different times.[5] The well-known British ethnologist Ed-
ward B. Tylor (who was a specialist on the Indians of Mexico)
based his animistic theory on materials he could adduce from
American Indian beliefs in souls and spirits. In a more restricted form, one documented with American materials, the
same theory was later upheld by the Finlander Rafael
Karsten, known for his South American investigations. Sir
James G. Frazer and his followers brought numerous examples of magic and totemism from America, in particular North
America. Paul Ehrenreich and other German ethnologists
worked on South American myths and reduced them to nature mythology of a solar or lunar kind. Marcel Mauss of
France examined the religious organizations of the North
Pacific Coast, and his fellow countryman Lucien Lévy-Bruhl
collected instances of "primitive mentality" from American
ethnological literature. A belief in power of the Melanesian
type (the conception of *mana*) was recognized by J. N. B.

5. Cf. also the classic scholar in the subject of civilization and culture, J. F.
Lafitau (d. 1746), who was the author of the first scientific work on North
American Indians (Lafitau 1724).

Hewitt among the Iroquois and by William Jones among the Fox Indians. It was repeatedly discussed by Konrad Th. Preuss, Alice Fletcher, and Paul Radin. The idea of primeval monotheism (*Urmonotheismus*), was finally vindicated by Father Wilhelm Schmidt and his disciples. Among the latter were Father Martin Gusinde, who conducted field work among the inhabitants of Tierra del Fuego and the Cheyenne Indians of North America, and Josef Haekel, who arranged American religious data in cultural-historical surveys.

It would transcend the frame of our main subject to discuss in detail here the long line of European and American scholars who have been engaged with problems of American Indian religion.[6] To the extent that their dealings with these problems have had importance for our account they will be mentioned in the course of our discussion.

6. See the following research reviews for North America: Hultkrantz 1966–67, 1965a; cf. Hultkrantz 1976.

Tribal Religions

1

The Supernatural

Like other so-called "primitive" peoples, the American Indians lack a word to denote what we call religion. Of course, nothing else is to be expected in environments where religious attitudes and values permeate cultural life in its entirety and are not isolated from other cultural manifestations. In some places, however, there is a term for the traditional, inherited cult practices, as among the Zuni Indians in New Mexico, whose *tewusu* includes all ritual, "each sacred custom, each urgent request."[1] But the rites are generally mingled with other, profane manners and customs, something like the Latin *ritus*. To the extent that Indian languages use an expression for exclusively religious customs there is often reason to suspect influences from Christian preaching and Christian practice. This is presumably the case with the expression of the Wind River Shoshoni (in Wyoming), *tivizi-togwei-shúenchaint*, "much in that fashion they believe."

There is, however, another expression found among many Indian peoples which clearly and concisely delimits the separation of religious reality from the profane: the supernatural.

1. Bunzel 1932, p. 489.

The basic dichotomy between sacred and profane, supernatural and natural, is not merely an abstraction coined for
scientific purposes by Durkheim, Marett, Otto, Söderblom,
and other sociologists and scholars of religion, but a living
reality experienced by the Indians themselves. The continuous, expected process of everyday reality is disrupted by the
supernatural reality with its discontinuous, unexpected, and,
above all, incomprehensible course of events. At times the
two realities are distant from each other, as when the spiritual
beings of one's dreams vanish at the moment of awakening
and are replaced by the living beings of one's home and
vicinity, but just as often supernatural reality interrupts the
natural. There are glimpses of the spirits in the surrounding
landscape, in weather transitions, and in the movements of
the stars, and they perform more concretely in the masked
dances of the cult societies. What was long considered by
some to be established fact, namely that "primitive" people
merely experience the dynamic, unforeseen aspect of the
mysterious, is hardly true. American Indians have not necessarily associated striking, exceptional phenomena and violent
or overwhelming experiences with the supernatural. Events
and processes of a superficially trivial, everyday nature have
often been regarded as manifestations of a supernatural reality. In essence it is the cultural tradition which determines the
borderline between the natural and the supernatural.[2]

Historians of religion and ethnologists have spent much
effort on investigating and delineating the concepts of the
supernatural among tribal peoples, especially in North
America. During the first decades of this century, when terms

2. Several authors have, for various reasons, doubted the reality of a
demarcation line between natural and supernatural in American Indian
thought (cf., for example, Albers and Parker 1971, p. 207n). Others consider
the dichotomy basic (cf. Lamphere 1969, pp. 279, 282). If we keep in mind
that we are facing not an absolutely drawn distinction but a general perspective the dichotomy seems understandable (cf. Momaday 1976, p. 81). It is
therefore never sharply expressed, as Boas has stated for the Kwakiutl (Boas
1966, p. 162). Indeed, on the Northwest Coast most phenomena of life could
be drawn into the supernatural sphere (Boas 1966, pp. 156–60). Perhaps a
similar case could be made for the Navajo (Toelken 1976, p. 11). Other Indian
tribes have particular names for the supernatural (cf. below).

like dynamism, preanimism, and animatism were catchwords in the debate on the science of religion, many scholars sought among North American Indians for correspondences to the well-known *mana* of the Melanesians (sometimes interpreted as an individual power, at other times regarded as a pantheistic omnipotence). The discussion was carried to the *manitou* of the Algonkin, the *orenda* of the Iroquois, and the *wakan* and *wakanda* of the Sioux Indians, concepts that were all considered more or less correlative. At the same time they were defined in accordance with specific scholars' personal theories of religion. Thus Boas found the concept of an impersonal *mana*-power to be paramount, whereas Fletcher, Hewitt, and Jones proceeded from a theory of an omnipotence penetrating all of the universe.[3]

The Algonkin *manitou* has been discussed at length by W. Jones, who obtained his material primarily from the Fox Indians.[4] Although Jones, in accordance with religio-scientific theories fashionable in his time, wished to present this concept as a variant of *mana*, little of what is known about it supports such an interpretation. The famous ethnologist Paul Radin maintained in a polemic against Jones that the concept of *manitou* refers to the spirit world, that the word *manitou* may be understood as "sacred" but lacks the significance of "inherent power."[5] Radin is no doubt right in that it is a general designation of spirit, referring to lesser vision spirits, higher powers of nature, or the Supreme Being. But humans could also come under this term, for example the transvestites among the Illinois Indians (according to Father Marquette). Since this latter is not a case of possession, we are brought to the conclusion that *manitou* is a manifestation of the supernatural world and that the word is properly rendered by "supernatural," "mysterious." The concept of supernatural power is not necessarily included but is sometimes a natural characteristic of *manitou*-beings. Among

3. South American Indians also have concepts that correspond to the *mana*: cf. the *tsaruma* of the Jívaro or the *nandé* of the Nambicuara. As to the latter, see Lévi-Strauss 1948, pp. 95ff.

4. Jones 1905.   5. Radin 1915.

the Fox Indians, for example, a *manitou* with great supernatural capacity is called "a very great *manitou*."[6]

The Iroquois *orenda*, conceived by J. N. B. Hewitt (himself
an Iroquois) primarily as a pantheistic omnipotence, provides
even less reason for this designation than did the previous
concept. Hewitt's thorough analysis of the *orenda* concept
leads instead to the opposite conclusion—that this is a notion
of supernatural power which is impersonal (i.e., not personified), individual, and local (i.e., not a general power
manifested in various objects); its modus operandi is mysterious.[7] We are told that the world is full of beings with various
degrees of *orenda*. The possession of *orenda*, says Hewitt, is
the distinctive feature of the gods. (Radin's objection that
Hewitt here makes a false distinction between the power and
its bearer is unreasonable.) A fetish with supernatural power,
however, is called *otkon*, which is also the name of a malevolent demon. This seems to indicate a sharp distinction between the impersonal power and its bearer, which latter in
any case might be conceived of as a personal being. Whereas
other peoples easily regard the supernatural power as personified, the Iroquois do not. In contrast to other Indian
tribes, they make a distinction between the supernatural
power, *orenda*, and man's individual guardian spirit, which
they call *oyaron*. It is obvious that for theorists *orenda* quite
adequately represents belief in an impersonal supernatural
power. Thus a German scholar, Pfister, has coined the term
"orendism" to cover all analogous occurrences in the history
of religions, and has replaced the technical term *mana* with
orenda.[8]

The Sioux terms *wakanda, wakonda, wakan*, etc., have been
subjected to the most diverse attempts at interpretation.
Partly they go beyond our present discussion in that they
refer to the Supreme Being. Partly they pertain to denotations
of supernaturalness and supernatural power. One should,
however, disassociate the term *wakanda* (*wakonda*) used by the

6. Jones 1939, p. 11.   7. Hewitt 1902.   8. Pfister 1927.

southern Sioux (Chiwere, Dhegiha) from the *wakan* of the northern Sioux or the Dakota.

According to A. Fletcher the concept of *wakonda*, as it exists among the Omaha, the Osage, and the Ponca Indians, implies on one hand mystic omnipotence, conceived as semi-anthropomorphic, and on the other hand every phenomenon with a mystic or sacred significance—one might say, every phenomenon that corresponds in nature to the great mysterious *wakonda*.[9] A closer investigation shows that the concept of a pantheistic, mystical omnipotence is not correlative to the concept of *wakonda*. We must rather distinguish between a Supreme Being, Wakonda, vaguely perceived and essentially anthropomorphic, and *wakonda*, a concept denoting something sacred or, more exactly, supernatural—a distinction Radin has also pointed out. *Wakonda* is the property which characterizes the divinities as well as a collective designation of the divine powers, that is, the bearers of *wakonda*-essence. Not only gods appear in this context, however. As Fletcher observes, all (supernatural) power is *wakonda* (she writes "of *wakonda*"), whether it manifests itself in thunder or hurricane, among animals or human beings.

In the religions of the Dakota and the Winnebago the related word *wakan* signifies, according to our authorities, sacred, mysterious, wondrous. The following definition (more or less inspired by the Dakota missionary Riggs) may be more to the point: *wakan* has the twofold meaning of being supernatural in origin and of being supernatural as a result of miraculous activity, that is, supernatural power. *Wakan* will accordingly coincide with *wakonda* in its more general aspect, whereas the theistic Wakonda corresponds to Wakan Tanka, "the great wakan." *Wakan* might properly be rendered "bearer of supernatural influence, especially supernatural power," for the medicine men are said to possess much *wakan*. In addition, the word has possibly had a more profane meaning, presumably a secondary one, of "remarkable," "marvelous":

9. Fletcher 1910; Fletcher and La Flesche 1911.

the horse is called *wakan*-dog, liquor ("fire-water") *wakan*-water. *Wakan* should be distinguished from *sicun*—the name of the guardian spirit as well as the medicine bundle—which is mysteriously active because it is a bearer of *wakan*. [10]

The preceding exposition suggests that *manitou*, *wakan*, and *wakanda* are most accurately rendered "supernatural," whereas the more precise meaning of *orenda* is "supernatural power," a significance which in a secondary sense pertains to the former concepts as well. A study of corresponding terms among other North American peoples indicates that most of them express the concept "supernatural" with the secondary meaning "supernatural power." In some cases there is, however, a special term for supernatural power, particularly, it seems, if the power concept coincides with the guardian spirit, as among the Dakota. A proper term for "holy" in the meaning of divine or pertaining to the gods I have not been able to find. The concept is expressed by the word for "supernatural." The Shoshoni render the English "holy" with *nanasuigaint*, "marvelous." Persons who have shown a faculty for the miraculous or who possess efficient guardian spirits are given the same designation.

Consequently, the Indian religious perspective centers around the supernatural world, populated by gods and spirits but also by human beings, animals, plants, and inanimate objects, for the supernatural breaks through into the everyday world. Its foremost means of expression is supernatural power, at times perceived as a specific, defined potency, at times merely experienced as a psychological reality underlying supernatural occurrences.

10. Cf. my analyses in Hultkrantz 1953, pp. 193–99, and 1971, pp. 70–74.

2

The Concept of the High God

In the Indian world of religious conceptualization the supreme position is held by a divinity who surveys the course of events from his high abode in heaven. This is a being who many times appears only vaguely outlined and, as a result of his remoteness and the rarity of his interference in the immediate concerns of mortals, recalls a *deus otiosus* created by philosophical speculation and not inherently linked to religious belief. Neither cult nor mythology seems to give him much attention. Nor is this concept of god a universal one. In some tropical tribes he vanishes altogether; in other tribes he plays an obscure role as a god among other gods. Furthermore, scholars are by no means in agreement about his original primacy. Some scholars maintain that he is very old (Schmidt, Haekel, Cooper, Eliade). Others interpret him as a deity of secondary origin, an extension of a theriomorphic demiurge (Kroeber, Radin, Pettazzoni, Kock). Some see in him a result of a process which is continually renewable (Benedict, Kluckhohn), or stimulated by Christianity (Karsten).

In this context we may set aside the intricate question of the origin of this Supreme Being. The determining factor is that he exists in various places throughout America, and is frequently found among the marginal hunting groups known for their primitive cultural structure. Moreover, he recurs in different manifestations among primitive peoples in the Old World as well. It is undoubtedly true that his appearance in later times has been modified by Christian teachings, but in essence he represents an archaic belief, the origin of which is certainly open to divergent opinions.[1]

It is as true for the Supreme Being as for other religious concepts that ecological and social environments have contributed both to form and to content: thus it is difficult to isolate the constituent features of the conceptualization. Nevertheless, we shall here make an attempt at defining them, having first considered some typical examples of American high god belief, all of them subjects of intense debate in the scholarship of religion.

The concept of god among the three primitive tribes in Tierra del Fuego and its vicinity, the Ona (or Selknam), the Yahgan (or Yamana), and the Alakuluf (or Halakwulup), was investigated in the field in the early 1920s by the Austrian ethnologists M. Gusinde and W. Koppers. Their scholarly findings have been contested by many. The facts of the matter are as follows.

After his visit to Tierra del Fuego in 1832 Darwin maintained that the Indians there were without religion, that is, they lacked a religion in the Western, Christian sense. This view was generally accepted and not noticeably altered by the records compiled by the first Christian (Anglican) missionaries (the Yahgan mission was begun in 1856, the Ona mission in 1889). According to the missionary Thomas Bridges, who published a number of articles on the culture and religion of the Yahgan during the forty years that he lived with them,

1. Kluckhohn thinks it possible to state that the concept of a Supreme Being was formed among the Navajo at a very recent time. He refers to the fact that a transvestite should have told the ancient myths in such a way that an hermaphroditic spirit, *be'gočidí*, was given the first place. There are, however, several earlier pieces of information which make us believe that this spirit had been interpreted in this manner in former days. See Kluckhohn 1942, p. 63, and cf. Reichard 1950 (2), p. 389.

their religion lacked a belief in a Supreme Being.[2] Other missionaries made the same observation. Consequently, the information from the Austrian ethnologists about a distinct, even predominant, high god belief seems improbable at first and raises the question of whether indeed Christian influence prepared the way for this belief. Upon examination, this suggestion appears unlikely. The high god of the Yahgan is well integrated into tribal existence and shows little affinity with the Christian concept of God (for example, he is not a creator). The prayers addressed to him mostly constitute archaic formulas of pre-Christian provenance. Finally, mention should be made of three Yahgan Indians who were brought to London in 1830. In the reports of the proceedings two of them (the third to a lesser degree) showed "a strong feeling for a Supreme Being."

The Christian mission may nonetheless have had a secondary influence on this concept of god. Métraux states that "Gusinde and Koppers undoubtedly are right in insisting that the Fuegian belief in a High God was independent of any Christian religious teaching, but many details and traditions concerning him may have been lost and the data gleaned at the last moment perhaps give us the illusion of a more philosophical and abstract deity than he actually was."[3] Here Christian influence must have been active.

If the Fuegian high god does in fact represent a pre-Christian concept, this circumstance, in light of the general situation of the Fuegian culture, is of great significance for the history of religions. These tribes are obviously bearers of a culture which in structure is quite archaic (especially that of the Yahgan and the Alakuluf, with their shellfish diet and

2. In Bridges's dictionary on the Yahgan language we actually find the word that indicates the Supreme Being: Watauinaiwa, Watauinaiwōn. It is translated there as "the Ancient One, the one who does not change." According to Bridges's commentaries it is an adequate term for God. Karsten in interpreting this remark attributes the term to Bridges himself, who would have applied it to the Christian God. It would be more reasonable to think that Bridges had discovered and noted the name of the Yahgan god without knowing who exactly was the being he portrayed.

3. Métraux 1949, p. 561.

their social groupings in family clans), a culture which according to archaeological investigations has undergone few material changes during the last 8000 years. It appears, moreover, that the range of this culture was far more extensive prior to historical times. Even if an exact correlation can never be obtained between a type of culture and a type of religion, the more recent religious structure of the Fuegian tribes should give us at least a vague idea of the religious behavior of the primeval hunters and gatherers.[4]

Characteristic of the Fuegian religion is the position of the Supreme Being, which is in many respects a central one. Among the Yahgan he is called Watauniéwa, "the old, eternal, unchangeable one." He is an invisible, lonely being who rules all the world. It is true he is no creator, but he grants life and death and provides for man's sustenance by apportioning food (primarily animals). He is not present in mythology, but he is in some degree associated with cult practice and he has established the tribal ethics. Consequently, he presides over the initiation rites by which young boys and girls are accepted into the fellowship of the tribe. Moreover, he is the ruler of existence and accordingly receives the prayers of the people. Some of these prayers are clearly spontaneous in nature; others are archaic formulae. Sometimes they are worded as indignant and accusing complaints concerning hunger, storm, sickness, and death, and at other times they contain humble requests for calm weather, daily food, good hunting, and good health. In still other prayers the god is given thanks for these gifts. There is never any sacrifice to the Lord of Life, the reason being that he owns everything, including anything which humans might offer him.

The situation is different among the Ona, whose Supreme Being Temáukl receives firstling offerings. This divinity resides farther away from humans and is also perceived as a creator. In both respects he resembles Xolas, the absolute,

---

4. For a closer presentation of my religio-ecological theories and the concept "type of religion," see Hultkrantz 1974.

high "master" of the Alakuluf, who is inaccessible to all human prayers.[5]

Similar to the situation in Tierra del Fuego, we find rather well-defined concepts of a Supreme Being in the simple cultural milieu of the Indian tribes in north-central California. The origin of these concepts has been subject to dispute. The Austrian scholar W. Schmidt argued that on ethnological grounds the central Californians as well as the Fuegians must be included among the so-called Urkultur or primeval peoples; consequently, their concept of god would belong to the earliest expressions of mankind.[6] No "Urkultur" has truly been preserved to our time, however, since all cultural life inevitably undergoes continuous transformation. In addition, the central Californian culture presents a far-reaching specification of the gatherers' culture adapted to particular geographical conditions (among other characteristics were the gathering of acorns and nuts and the storing of supplies).

Other scholars have maintained that the Californian image of a deity reflects missionary influence. This too is certainly incorrect. Birket-Smith has correctly pointed out that within the range of the Franciscan missions the California Indians lack the high-god concept, which exists only among Indians well outside the mission sphere.[7] And there seems to be no justification for Loeb's proposition attributing Mexican origins to the Californian notion of god.[8] It is no doubt autochthonous, but possibly representative of a late development in California closely connected with the Kuksu cult.

The California high god is well known through J. Curtin's records of the Wintu Indians.[9] His account of Olelbis, the creator-on-high of the Wintu, "sitting in the above," "he who is in heaven," has drawn remarkable attention in the scholar-

5. Gusinde 1931–37. The South American high gods have been investigated by Eliade in a series of articles (Eliade 1969–71). He dedicates much space to the Fuegian data but also covers other tribes' high divinities.

6. Schmidt 1933. See also the more detailed discussion in Schmidt 1929, 1934, 1935.

7. Birket-Smith 1943 (2), pp. 467f.

8. Loeb 1931, p. 538.   9. Curtin 1899.

ship of religion. Recently, though, ethnographers have been able to point to an abysmal difference between Curtin's report on a noble Supreme Being and the actual circumstances. Curtin obtained his material from a single informant with a particular aptitude for mythological combinations. Later he adjusted this data to fit his journalistic viewpoint. The mythology makes it evident, however, that Olelbis had been an anthropomorphic Supreme Being, neither omniscient nor omnipotent, neither enacting laws nor supervising them. In the religious beliefs of more recent times his image was greatly affected by Christian doctrines. In this context he appears as a creator more distinctly than in the mythology. In earlier times prayers were evidently directed to Olelbis at sunrise and he was perceived as a deity regulating ethics (a characteristic which the mythology is quite unable to substantiate).[10]

Some of the north-central California high gods are distinctly creator figures, and their creative process may furthermore be described as *creatio ex nihilo*. The high god of the Maidu is Kō'dōyanpĕ ("the earth-namer"). After prolonged, intense thought he constructed the canoe in which he and his antagonist, the Coyote, floated about on the primeval sea at the beginning of time. Among the northern Pomo it is said of Dasan, a peculiar hybrid of high god and ancestral father, that he "came out on the ocean and turned into a man. He intended to build the world. He talked, and by the power of his words, the world came into being. After this he made the first people." This "biblical" notion of cosmogony was certainly not very common. Some eastern Pomo Indians have even objected to the Christian doctrine, saying that it lacks common sense since its divinity created the world from nothing whereas the indigenous creators had materials from which to create.

If, nevertheless, the notion of a *creatio ex nihilo* has occurred in some places, Christianity has not been the source since it has never been able to reshape inherent, sacred myths. The

10. Du Bois 1935, pp. 72f.

abstract notion of creation from nothing or, more correctly, through the holy word, is naturally explained if we adduce the parallel with the magic power of the medicine man to evoke, bind, and destroy through the word.[11] Here more than anywhere Radin's thesis may profitably be referred to: it is in the medicine man, the religiously gifted one, that the highest forms of religious conceptions among primitive peoples are crystallized.

The California high gods are not essentially different from other divine beings. They are linked to nature as is the thunder god of the Yuki, they coincide with the culture hero as among the Maidu, or with the primal man as among the Pomo. Sometimes, as among the Patwin, the Supreme Being or the creator is identical to the ethically inferior Coyote, who appears elsewhere as the defective assistant or direct antipode of the Supreme Being. But the primary feature of the California high god is for the most part his marked distance from other divinities, his sovereignty.

The suggestion has been made, by Kroeber especially, that the high god belief of these tribes has evolved in direct correlation to the Kuksu cult; the areas of expansion for the two complexes are roughly the same.

The Kuksu cult is actually nameless but is called by scholars after the deity or primeval man represented in the cult. Its enactment is in a secret society into which boys at puberty are initiated and in which future shamans are trained for their vocation. Here, as in other religious puberty festivals of very primitive tribes, the bull-roarer or whiner is used, an instrument whose whining sound imitates the voices of the spirits, Kuksu, or the Supreme Being. The initiated, wearing feathered masks, perform as Kuksu or as spirits of the dead, and

11. Concerning the above see Dixon 1905, p. 335, Loeb 1932, pp. 3f., and 1926a, p. 305. We find some initial elements of an active creator of the same character in other Indian groups, for instance, among the Uitoto of Colombia. According to their creation myth nothing existed in the beginning, there was only "the appearance," and the creator Nainuema, "the one who is only appearance," seized this spectre in a dream and pressed it against his breast. Through his dream he managed to guard it and then transformed it into earth. See Preuss 1921–23 (1), pp. 27, 166ff.

apparently go through rites of death and resurrection. Certain of the ritual dances (the so-called *hesi* of the Maidu and the Patwin) symbolize the rebirth of vegetation or have such rebirth as a consequence of the dance.

Through a fine analysis Kroeber has made the likely assumption that in its recent form the Kuksu cult developed later than certain annual rites with which it shares several characteristics. It is then reasonable to assume that the high-god belief associated with the Kuksu rites is likewise a relatively late creation, at least in its extreme forms. However, neither Kroeber nor Pettazzoni has drawn the right conclusion in giving the Coyote priority as creator and ruler. Such a development is not deducible from our source material.[12]

The research of W. Schmidt, Michelson, and Cooper has gradually illuminated the older structure of the Algonkin religions and has consequently made more tangible the nature of the high god among these Indians. The central concept here is *manitou*, which was translated above as "a supernatural" and which may be freely rendered by the word "spirit." However, the Algonkin single out one of these spirits as "the Great Spirit" (Kitshi Manitou) or simply "the Spirit" (Manitou), specifying the Supreme Being. Thus we find a well-known theme from the history of religions: the highest god is called merely "God" or "the God." Algonkin theism is undoubtedly pre-Christian—the first missionaries in New France mention it—and it is presumably archaic, even if influences from the Mexican high culture and its northern extensions did transfigure much of the older concept of god in late pre-Columbian times. Certainly we must not forget that at least south of the Great Lakes the Algonkin tribes were exposed to the resplendence of the Mississippi culture with its temple mounds and plazas.

The Algonkin concepts of the high god are exceedingly diverse. They seem to have been most primitive furthest north, where the Supreme Being comes close to being identified as the master of animals. The Mascouten used to pray to the Great Spirit both before and after the hunt, and they gave

---

12. Concerning the above see Dangel 1927, Loeb 1926b, and Kroeber 1925, pp. 365ff. and passim.

him first-fruit sacrifices. The Supreme Being of the Montagnais, called by them Manitou, was the protector of the caribou and ruler of the world. But he was not, as Cooper particularly emphasizes, lord of the dead. (It should be noted, however, that the caribou have an additional, more specific, master.)[13]

The situation is essentially different with regard to a southern Algonkin tribe, the Lenape (the Delaware). The primacy of Lenape religion is controversial. Not totally to be disregarded are influences from the "formative" cultures further south and west and from the adjacent, dominant Iroquois, but on the whole this religion seems to have preserved a genuinely Algonkin character. According to the famous creation myth "Walam Olum"—recorded in the beginning of the nineteenth century, its authenticity contested by some scholars—the Supreme Being is the creator of all good things. His name is Gicelamu'kaong, "He who created us through his thought," another reminder of the mystical nature of the act of creation. Various sources confirm that this high god is a remote *deus otiosus* who has entrusted his divine tasks to a number of lesser deities: the sun, moon, thunder gods, four winds, earth mother, and master of animals. His supervising position is made manifest in the concept that the central pole in the cult house reaches up to his abode in the twelfth heaven, where it is grasped by his hand.[14]

Here we meet with a notion which is closely related to the Supreme Being for other American Indians as well: the cosmic pillar, perceived by numerous tribes to be the world tree as well, and symbolized in the cult system by the sacred pole. (The cosmic pillar may be an Arctic rendering of the world tree, a likely assumption considering its range of distribution in the Old as well as the New World.) This idea, so central to the high-god concept in America, will be discussed here at some length.

The cosmic pillar which upholds the vault of heaven is a notion of circum-Polar range, in America best exemplified among the plateau and coastal Indians in western Canada.[15] The Bella Coola, for example, imagine on the western horizon

13. Cooper 1933. 14. Harrington 1921; Speck 1931.
15. Haekel 1958.

a mighty pole, which supports the sky and prevents the sun from falling down on the earth. On top of this pole, which was erected by the highest god, is seated an eagle. The Flathead Indians vary the motif: there is a great world tree with its roots running deep into the earth, where lives the wicked chief Amtep. The treetop reaches all the way to heaven and in its uppermost branches Amotken resides, "the old one," the benevolent creator. In this and other similar myths may be traced a fundamental dualism between the powers of heaven and the underworld. The former are often perceived in the shape of birds (especially eagles), the latter imagined as quadrupeds or snakes, or incarnated in a female being to all appearances identical with Mother Earth.

The concept of the world tree is seemingly more prevalent than the concept of the cosmic pillar.[16] It is widespread in North America, not least among the agrarian peoples. Related to the world tree or the tree of life are presumably the tree of heaven, from the root of which the Iroquois mother goddess falls down to earth, and the plant on which men at the dawn of time, according to certain southwestern tribes, climbed up from the underworld to the earth's surface. Furthermore, the world tree exists in the beliefs of hunting and fishing Indians, as we have seen, and is then at times represented by the Milky Way (as is the case among the Tlingit in northwest America).

The sacred tree recurs in a specific sense in the Mayan high culture (the famous tomb relief in Palenque) and in large parts of South America, especially in the north.[17] Its function is then that of the "tree of life," that is, the prototype or source of plants and even human beings, but only to a lesser degree is it the upholder of heaven. Consequently, among the Acawai, Cuna, Choc, and other tribes there is the notion that the world tree sustained all the culture plants; it was cut down by the culture hero and his brother so that the plants

16. It is possible that the cosmic pillar is an Arctic interpretation of the cosmic tree, as one could assume from the diffusion of the two concepts through both the Old and the New World.

17. There are writings on this subject by H. Wassén (article in Swedish published in Ymer 1934, pp. 249ff.) and G. Hatt (Hatt 1951, pp. 895f.).

were scattered across the world and the water which had been enclosed in the trunk poured out over the earth (the flood myth). One is here reminded of the Delaware concept that humans sprouted on the branches of the world tree. Parallels to these ideas may also be found in the Old World in the "soul trees" of east Siberian peoples and of the Batak on Sumatra.

The cosmic pillar or world tree is not merely a mythical concept linked to occurrences in primordial cosmogony. It is an expression of the thought that the divine being is still keeping watch over the course of events; it is a guarantee for man's daily existence. It is small wonder, then, that it is represented in the ritual, primarily in the annual festivals associated with the Supreme Being but also in shamanic rites, where it is understood as a connecting link—and a passageway for the shaman—between humans and the gods and the land of the dead. Among the Bella Coola on the American Northwest Coast the cosmic pillar seems to have become differentiated into a number of life pillars, one for each human being as a guarantee of his or her life. Possibly a cultic correspondence to this differentiation is expressed, as suggested by Haekel, in the heraldic poles-of-arms, the so-called totem poles.[18] Such concepts are, however, secondary. In the cult the cosmic pillar is a symbol of the cosmos, indeed of the Supreme Being himself, as in the Sun Dance of the prairie and plains Indians. In any case, it is an expression of the deity's inherent power, as among the Lenape.

The Supreme Being is elevated above other beings but not necessarily perceived as lord of the other gods. As soon as the Indian analyzes his position closely, however, there is a tendency to regard him as a sovereign of gods and spirits. In sole majesty, he exists remote from humans but not indifferent to their fate. He supervises the course of events, provides food, and occasionally controls the tribal ethics, or, rather, the ritual observances. Due to his distance from mankind, his immutability, and the rarity of his direct interference in human affairs, he is readily apparent as a *deus otiosus*, although this

18. Haekel 1958, p. 41.

designation is naturally only superficially relevant. Not much is ever known about his nature. He is generally invisible, but there are those who have heard his voice, which is often referred to as thunder. Research has paid much respect to the fact that he is at times represented as a figure of white radiance, although other supernatural beings may also be perceived in this fashion, depending on their associations with the luminous sky, the sun, the moon, the stars, or the lights of visions. Two basic features may be observed in the being of the high god: the connection with food, which among the hunting peoples brings him close to the functions of the master of animals, and the connection with heaven, which manifests his eminence and authority and perhaps also his remoteness from daily existence.

From a cultic viewpoint the Supreme Being plays an inconspicuous part. This is particularly true among the very primitive tribes, from whom he often receives sacrifices in particularly critical situations. The cult system of the hunting tribes is on the whole, as we shall find, weakly developed, and many primitive Indian tribes refer their needs primarily to lesser deities who are directly associated with various areas of everyday life.[19]

The Supreme Being is equally intangible as a mythological reality. With the exception of certain creation stories and some other cosmogonic myths, the Supreme Being does not generally belong to the world of mythology. Instead his place is occupied by the culture hero, often regarded as a trickster, and by the divine twins. In other respects the function of the high god is not primarily that of a creator, nor is he primarily lord of the dead. It is indeed remarkable how often other beings appear as the originators of creation. In some cases where the high god is manifest as creator he is assisted by a secondary creator or "transformer" but in other cases he is just one of a number of creators.

This is, of course, a quite general portrayal of the nature of the high god. A true understanding of the essence of the various high gods may be attained only by analyzing them in their historical contexts.

19. Zerries is of the same opinion: Zerries 1961, p. 301.

3

The World Picture and the Deities of Cosmogonic Myths

The world in which the Supreme Being manifests his power is often carefully outlined in American Indian thought, though less so among the hunting peoples, whose mythology usually lacks the precision which ritual enactment gives to the myths of the horticultural peoples. The hunting tribes recognize a heaven and a world of man on earth; ideas of an underground world are very vague (and occasionally centered on speculations concerning the cosmic tree). Among cultivating tribes, on the other hand, a three-layered world picture predominates. Sometimes there are even more levels, all developed from the basic pattern heaven–earth–underworld.[1] In the horizontal dimension the world of man is restricted to an area—round or square—limited by mountains, a sea, or abysses. The tribal home is supposed to be situated in the middle of this area. The heaven is more nearly boundless, conceived of as a bowl or as a land above (this is, of course, a very generalized picture).

---

1. This threefold pattern is common to most archaic societies affected by the so-called Neolithic Revolution (about 10,000 B.C. in the Near East), and may have even a higher age, as Siberian and American data suggest.

In North America the Beaver Indians (Athabascan hunters of the Boreal forests) imagined that the world had been formed by the creator as a cross, with three stories on top of one another: heaven, earth, and underworld.[2] The cross, a symbol of the four winds and world corners, was also identified with the universe in most of North America. In the form of a cross within a circle, the symbol first appears in the Mississippian culture (700–1700 A.D.), a culture that was inspired from Mesoamerica and brought many new features in religion, ritual, and symbolism to the southeastern, prairie, and plains provinces of North America.[3] Indeed, the whole of this vast area shows the sacred circle design in the most diverse functions, as camp circles, sacred lodges, arrangements of buffalo skulls, stone enclosures on mountain tops ("medicine wheels"), emblems on rock drawings and dresses, and cultic implements (the Arapaho sacred wheel.)[4] As we shall see, the Sun Dance lodge of the plains was thought to be a replica of the sacred universe, with the middle post as the _axis mundi_.[5] The cross symbolism was enacted in such procedures as sacred smoking or the ritual movements of the Oglala Dakota youth when in quest of supernatural visions.[6]

This well-thought-out world picture, realized in cultic drama, occurred also in other places influenced by Mexican high culture (whether through idea diffusion, stimulus diffusion, or ethnic migrations will not be discussed here). Thus, as Alfonso Ortiz has shown, the Tewa of New Mexico also had advanced cosmological ideas.[7]

The Campa of the western tropical forest will serve as an illustration for South American Indians. The Campa presume that there is a series of worlds on top of one another. The heavens are divided into several strata, and through them flows an invisible river which, says the field recorder, was perhaps originally the Milky Way. Many stars are spirits—for

2. Ridington and Ridington 1970, pp. 51, 55, 56.
3. See, for example, Meggers 1973, p. 120.   4. Cf. Coe 1976, pp. 18f.
5. Hultkrantz 1973b, pp. 8f.   6. Brown 1953, pp. 56ff.
7. However, there is little concern with the above in Tewa cosmology: Ortiz 1969, p. 23.

instance, the Pleiades who flew to heaven on a raft at the dawn of time. The sun and the moon figure respectively as the Supreme Being and his father. Like the heavens, the world of clouds immediately over the human beings, the mountain ridges, and the outer periphery of this earth are populated by friendly spirits. The earth is held up by a deity with the qualities of a tree (perhaps an expression of the world-tree symbol). The underworld closest to the human beings has good spirits, but further down the spirits are of evil disposition.[8]

The idea of the cosmos encompasses a strange mixture of natural and supernatural thoughts. "Beliefs" constitute a set of assumptions that are sometimes religious, sometimes purely secular.[9] American Indians have secular beliefs about, for instance, the organism of man, medical remedies, and the world picture.[10] However, these secular beliefs have religious counterparts: soul beliefs, shamanic healing ideas, and notions of supernatural beings in different world strata. American Indian cosmology is anchored in supernatural causality, even though parts of their world picture make a rational impression.

The world picture is mostly a premise of expressed beliefs on religion and ritual, but it sometimes figures in myths as well. Cosmogony, or the origin of the world, is a sacred theme entirely taken care of by mythology. Thereby we enter a domain of religious thought that has a character of its own.

Just as a line may be drawn between the natural and the supernatural worlds, a boundary mark may be placed between religion and mythology. Even though practical religion, i.e., faith and ritual, often tends to coalesce with a more fabulous mythology (as in the great cultic dramas), the former is oriented toward the present moment whereas the latter points back toward events of a dim and distant past. The

8. Weiss 1972, 1975. Cf. also Grebe, Pacheco, and Segura 1972 (Araucanians).

9. Hahn 1973; Jones 1972, pp. 79f.

10. Cf. articles on folk biology in the special issue of *American Ethnologist*, 3 (3), 1976.

Indian myth always refers to a distant past when animals were still human and spoke with human tongue, to use the words of the North American myth-tellers. This was the time when the world was created and all the institutions were established in the realms of nature and culture, institutions that since then have governed human existence.

We have seen that the Supreme Being is at times regarded as a creator. Although he is discernible in mythology and his appearance there is one of individual substance and dramatic action to a greater extent than in religion proper, he is not a typical mythological personage. On the contrary, in mythology he withdraws in favor of other beings who are more closely connected than he to the very beginning of existence: the culture hero, the twin gods, the tribal ancestor. These beings are grouped together in the most diverse combinations in accordance with their historical context.

In North America there is a profusion of tales regarding the origin of the world, whereas the creation of man is a rarer topic. In South America it is the other way around. The North American creation myths are of numerous types, which have been thoroughly mapped.[11] One of these traditions, which is prevalent in North America and well known in North Asia and Europe, tells how the creator sent an animal down to the bottom of the sea to bring up sand or mud from which the earth was subsequently made. Note that this myth presupposes the notion of an original world ocean, a well-known idea from the higher civilizations of the Old World. The myth of the primal sea should be kept separate from the legend (or myth) of the great flood, which is recorded in America from the Eskimos and Hare Indians in the north to the Araucanians in the south. The myth of the primal sea is a creation myth, whereas the tale of the flood is a legend (although dating to archaic times) of how all men except for a couple of individuals were drowned in a great deluge which covered all the land. The two who escaped took refuge on a raft or an oak log (common in North American versions) or on top of a mountain or a palm tree (frequent in the South American

11. Rooth 1957.

legends). The primal sea represents primordial chaos, while the great flood is chaos of a later date, caused, for example, by the wrath of a god or the transgression of a taboo. It is certainly the case that the two versions share certain features. In the flood myth of some Guyana Indians and among the Assiniboin in North America the animals are set the task of finding land just as in the biblical story. As a rule, however, the two closely related traditions exist separately in America.

No other creation myth in North America is as extensive as the one about the Earth Diver who brings up land from the primal water.[12] Some other regional myths should also be mentioned. In scattered parts of western North America the Supreme Being or another deity occurs as a spider whose web constitutes the foundation of the earth (the Arapaho Indians use a name for the Supreme Being which may be translated "spider"). It appears that the belief in the creator as a spider is an expression of the idea of creation out of nothing discussed in the previous chapter: the spider weaves his web out of himself. In the southern California myth of the cosmic parents, which incidentally bears considerable resemblance to Polynesian creation myths, the spirits, human beings, and all of nature emanate from the union of the sky father with Mother Earth. A third type of myth suggests what I have called in another context an "emanatistic" speculation: from himself a primal being provides material for the whole universe. The earth, the forests, the seas, and so forth are created from the parts of his body. Thus everything created is here represented as parts of the god. Finally, we have the well-

---

12. As we shall soon see, there are some not altogether incontestable reasons for supposing that this myth of the "Earth Diver" is connected with the mythical twin gods. The adaptation of the myth to the beliefs in a Supreme Being has, it seems, sometimes resulted in the latter taking over the role of the culture hero, although it follows that he himself has to dive to the bottom of the sea (as in the Arapaho myth). A completely opposite interpretation of the chain of events as hypothetically reconstructed here has been given by M. Eliade (Eliade 1961–62, pp. 207f.; 1962). In my opinion it is even possible to regard the diluvial myth, and the role of the "transformer" attached to it, as a relic of a more ancient myth dealing with the primeval sea. (This has been partly argued by W. Anderson in a study of diluvian traditions in northern Asia.) See also Köngäs 1960 and Count 1952.

known "emergence myth." Strictly speaking, this is less a creation myth than a tale of how human beings ascended from the interior of the earth through a cave (identified by the Pueblo Indians as the *sipapu*, the underground cult room's symbolic opening to the nether world) and how they conquered the world in which they now live.[13] The myth is widespread in southern North America and northern South America and pertains to the religious thought pattern of the agrarian cultures.

The latter type of myth is well represented among South American Indians, whereas true cosmogonic myths are largely absent. In other words, interest is focused on the origin of particular components of the world, such as sun and moon, animals and humans. The creation of man is frequently described in a manner reminiscent of the biblical creation story. He is shaped from clay or wood, not by the Supreme Being, however, but by the culture hero; it is unlikely that we need take into account any form of missionary influence.

A closer examination of the American creation myths in their entirety would reveal to us that, surprisingly enough, the Supreme Being plays only an obscure part in many of them. In some he is a relatively passive figure and in others he does not appear at all. In all likelihood the high god, as mentioned earlier, does not belong to the realm of myth at all. The stuff of cosmogonic and etiological tales preferably involves beings who may be more easily handled by the fabricating and often irreverent storyteller.

The culture hero is such a being. He belongs almost exclusively to mythology, but he is not therefore a mere expression of literary fantasy, as Radin has suggested (and others with him).[14] Rather, to my way of thinking, we are here confronted with a being of fate from a dim grey past, a deity who has

13. Wheeler-Voegelin and Moore 1957.

14. Radin 1956. Radin describes the culture hero—or rather the trickster, since he assumes its trickster character to be the original feature—as a mirror of a man devoid of his moral obligations. Ricketts (1966) takes a similar stand ("the personification of all the traits of man raised to the highest degree," p. 347), thus anchoring this figure in a pre-religious past.

been reduced to a literarily reworked ridiculous and obscene figure in both North and South America, a degenerate symbol of the evil and distorted in existence. Mythology does, however, retain certain individual features of his original significance. He is the one who bestowed on mankind in its infancy its cultural institutions, its material and spiritual heritage. Still earlier he is, it seems to me, the one who transformed the world after its creation or assisted the high god in the act of creation. He has at times totally replaced the Supreme Being as creator in mythology.

It is not unlikely that this rivalry with the often ethically sublime Supreme Being is the cause for the change in character of the culture hero. In his futile competition with the Supreme Being as a creator he displays a ludicrous weakness which paves the way for his development as a trickster. And through his great deficiencies and clumsiness—compared to the Supreme Being—in the process of creation he inflicts much misfortune on humans, sometimes, it appears, intentionally. More than any other mythological figure he has thus come to represent the somewhat capricious, dangerous, often malevolent aspect of the supernatural. This course of development, however, must not obscure the fact that the culture hero is apt to show more ideal characteristics upon occasion, when he has entirely usurped the place of the Supreme Being (as among the Klamath and Modoc in Oregon–California).

Many attempts have been made to interpret the American culture hero as an astral god (for example, the moon) or as the primordial man. He may occur as one or the other but is best understood as a creator figure belonging to mythology. Through his functions he has come into more or less open conflict with the creator in religious belief, the Supreme Being, and is consequently designated as a secondary creator, "transformer," or merely a culture creator. It should be emphasized that he adheres principally to mythology and not to religion as such.[15] He is rarely the object of any cult and is

15. In some parts of America, for instance, among Great Basin and Plains Shoshoni, practical religion and mythology fall into more or less distinct categories. See Hultkrantz 1956, 1972a.

present only occasionally in the conceptual world of active religion. The activity of the culture hero is accordingly placed in the primeval time of myth and the explanation often given by the Indians for his passivity in the present time is that having completed his tasks, he has withdrawn, but he will return at some future time. A. van Deursen suggests that the notion of the return of the culture hero expresses the hope that the golden age of the past, in which he was engaged, will be restored, but ideas of that kind have certainly been absent in America outside the high culture before the time of the messianic movements. Ancient concepts of the return of the moon or the day are more likely to have been influential here. As was suggested above, the culture hero is frequently identified with the sun or the moon, especially in South America. In North as well as in South America the culture hero is seen at times, after his withdrawal, as ruler in the land of the dead, a circumstance which should probably be viewed in the same light of astral mythology.

We do not need to concern ourselves further here with the problem of the ultimate origin of the culture hero concept. There is much to indicate twofold roots, on the one hand in a mythology based on migratory motifs, on the other in the concept of a master of animals; the latter might explain his frequently theriomorphic appearance.[16] It must be remembered that the culture hero is only in part an American phenomenon. He occurs in Africa as ancestral father, creator, and founder of institutions, as well as trickster and animal being.[17] If, as I presume, there is evidence for a connection across the continents, he is obviously a most ancient god.

It is interesting to note that most Indian myths are centered around the figure of the culture hero. Certainly the development of his character together with the intentions of talented narrators have occasioned his decline into a fairy-tale figure, a merrymaker, who stimulates feelings of relief and malicious joy in his audience because of his many deviances from the

16. Cf. Pettazzoni 1954, pp. 21ff., 35, and Kock 1956.
17. Cf. Tegnaeus 1950.

norms of social behavior.[18] His popularity rests on this aspect of pure entertainment. In both North and South America there are stories of how he seduces his own daughter and abandons himself to sexual excesses or how he cheats and is cheated in return. Simultaneously in these narration cycles there is a nucleus of true origin myths with a more serious intention. The gap between the frivolous and the sacred may become so difficult to span that the culture hero and the trickster are reduced to two separate individuals. Thus the Navajo distinguish between the Coyote as a supernatural, sacred being and the Coyote as an obscene jester. There can be no doubt, however, that this distinction is secondary. The double function of the culture hero as ethical lawmaker and frivolous prankster should be compared to the "pattern of upside-down behavior," practiced among the plains and southwest Indians of North America.[19] This behavioral pattern includes buffoonery during sacred ceremonies, presumably to ease the pressure brought on by the tense and solemn atmosphere.

In his serious function the culture hero is primarily originator of the present conditions in nature and culture and of human fate. He is, as has been mentioned, an assistant creator or transformer of the world (for example, following the great flood). He is spoken of as the wandering magician who changes the shape of the landscape and divides living beings into animals and humans. The period previous to this is often specified as the age when animals acted as people and could speak. (The motif of the wandering culture hero, which may have sources in astral mythology, recurs in the tales of the continuously roving trickster.) Numerous myths, most of them from the West Coast of North America and scattered parts of South America, describe how the culture hero steals fire, daylight (or the sun), and water from the "other" world, how he releases the water (compare the dragon-slaying myths of the Old World!) and sets free the game which has

18. To Makarius, the trickster is a mythical projection of a taboo transgressor (Makarius 1969, 1973).

19. See Steward 1931, Parsons and Beals 1934, Makarius 1970.

been enclosed in some place like a cave inaccessible to humans. In several myths the culture hero is the great monster
slayer, who helps rid the people of giant cannibals and other
gruesome monstrosities of nature. Then there are a great
number of instances concerning the culture hero as inventor
of arts and crafts and as founder of laws and ceremonies. As
for the ceremonies, the cult sometimes is directed to the Supreme Being, but only the culture hero and other mythological beings appear in the institution myth. Finally, the culture
hero is responsible for human fate. According to a myth
found throughout western North America, the culture hero
and another being, generally the Supreme Being, dispute or
discuss the future of mankind. The culture hero is for death,
the other for life, either continued or renewed. The culture
hero wins either because of his aggressiveness in getting the
last word or through divination.[20] Here is clearly detectable
the same opposition between the culture hero and the Supreme Being as that so often expressed in creation myths.

Several North American culture heroes are familiar to re-
searchers in mythology and history of religions.[21] The Raven
who is a culture hero of the peoples on the Northwest Coast
directly corresponds to the Raven on the opposite side of the
Bering Strait who is the culture hero of the eastern Siberians.
In both regions he is a transformer, a bringer of light and
culture, and a trickster.[22] In the semi-deserts of western
North America and in California the Coyote is the predominant culture hero, with conspicuous trickster features. In
northeastern North America we find the Great Hare of the Algonkin (note the name typical of a master of animals), who is
at times represented as a white deity. Moreover, the Algonkin
have an anthropomorphic culture hero, Glooskap or Wisakä.
The former, who has much in common with a shaman, is
largely a productive, benevolent being like the Great Hare,
whereas the prevailing features of Wisakä ("Whiskey-Jack")
are those of the trickster. Anthropomorphic culture heroes are
less common elsewhere in North America, apart from the

20. Boas 1917.   21. See in particular Deursen 1931.
22. Bogoras 1902.

animal-shaped culture hero's occasional occurrences as a manlike being. For the Algonkin Yurok in northwest California, who are widely disparate from other Algonkin, the culture hero is of human form and, similar to Glooskap, has a more serious disposition. Finally, an analogous anthropomorphic culture hero "Montezuma" exists among the Apache and Pima groups in southwest North America.

It is far more difficult to gain a general overview of the various culture hero types in South America. Surely many of these tribes have a theriomorphic culture hero. The Pioye around the sources of the Amazon River imagine him as a tapir, and the two Mato Grosso tribes, the Paressí (Arawakan) and the Bacaïri (Carib), picture him as a bat and a spider, respectively. At the same time and independently, these theriomorphic culture heroes are thought to embody the stars or their constellations. Is it by chance that in particular the culture heroes and masters of animals in South America find their places in the stars? It should be pointed out, however, that anthropomorphic culture heroes, and there are plenty of them, are also identified with the stars. In South America they are more prevalent than in North America. The culture hero of human form is often presented as the son of the high god or as primeval man. In fact, his person coalesces not infrequently with that of the high god, so that renowned ethnologists such as Ehrenreich and Métraux have found it difficult to distinguish between them. Among the Mundurucú on the Tapajós River, for example, mention is made of a higher being by the name of Karusakaibö. He totally dominates the mythology of these Indians and is so elevated above other beings that Strömer, an Austrian scholar, has identified him as a high god. A closer analysis of this deity leads rather to the conclusion that he should be designated a culture hero: he is believed to have been a Mundurucú, he had a wife, son, and sisters, and the assumed location of his village can be pointed out. Besides, it is of interest that the Mundurucú have had quite a number of culture heroes as originators of various institutions: one accomplished the rock paintings in the area, another introduced gardening, a third was transformed to the tree which furnishes wood for bows, and so on.[23] Also in North American mythology, for example among the Winnebago, we meet with several culture heroes.[24] Usually, however, the specific culture hero and trickster mythology has developed around only one culture hero. According to some scholars (Brinton, Loewenthal, Söderblom) a distinction between the Supreme Being and culture hero is impossible to make. The concept of the "generator," coined by Söderblom, aims at precisely such an undifferentiated deity. Since both the Supreme Being and the culture hero may be creators they have in many instances coalesced not only in South America but in North America as well (for example, the Caddoan tribes).

The fusion of the high god and the culture hero as well as the coexistence of several culture heroes indicate how vacillating the borderlines may be between the higher divinities in the Indian religions. As we shall see, the Supreme Being is at times identified with such deities of heaven and atmosphere as the sun god and the thunder god. The inadequate distinction between the Supreme Being and the culture hero may result from a conflict of interest between mythology and religion, which often may represent two separate ideological systems.[25] The unity between the Supreme Being and the culture hero is then secondary.

It was suggested above that the culture hero must to some extent be regarded as a figure associated with various wandering myths. Belonging to these myths are the stories about the divine brothers or twins. Sometimes the culture hero is the father of the twins; sometimes his characteristics are detectable in at least one of them. Yet again, the twins may be perceived as representatives of a cleft in the composite nature of the cultural hero, as personifications of his two tendencies, one productive and the other destructive.[26] We also note that

23. Murphy 1958, pp. 12f.   24. Cf. Radin 1948.
25. Cf. Hultkrantz 1972a.
26. The Janus-like character of the culture hero has been closely studied by W. Müller (Müller 1956, pp. 90ff.). Notice that among the Saulteaux and Cree the name of the culture hero, Wisakä or Wesakachak, means "with a double face."

the relationship between the high god and the culture hero is distinctly reminiscent of the twin relationship. It seems likely that the twin myth is an elaboration of the mythological pattern which is apparent in the relationship between the high god and the culture hero, and that it has had a secondary influence on this original pattern, perhaps intensifying its tendency toward dualism.

Radin has called the twin myth in North America "the basic myth" of the Indians on that continent, and there is no doubt some justification for this.[27] The myth is, however, just as basic in South America, where it occurs with the usual astral associations concentrated (of course!) in the sun and moon. In some cases the twins have nothing in common with the culture hero or with mythological concepts, but in most cases, whether separately or together, they do perform heroic deeds and other exploits generally attributed to a culture hero.

Radin's survey and analysis of the twin myths in the New World establishes the twin theme in three distinct yet closely related sources.[28] Type A relates how the twins' mother is killed at their birth by a mysterious stranger who subsequently throws one of the twins into a well or a hole in the ground (notice the similarity of the fate of the placenta in childbirth). The rejected twin, who is described as aggressive and of a negative disposition, later returns to his brother and together they perform a number of more or less mischievous deeds. In another version of type A, well known from the Iroquois and Huron, one twin is born painlessly whereas the other, of an evil nature, kills his mother at his birth. Type B is the myth of the "children of the Sun," twins conceived by the sun. They are diminutive in size but correspond to the twins of the previous type in their diametrically opposed characters. Their foremost task is to slay the man who has killed a person closely associated with them. Having accomplished this deed, they journey to their father, the sun god. Type C

27. Under these circumstances it is strange that Radin considers this tradition a tale of entertainment that was secondarily transformed, in some places, into a myth.

28. Radin 1950.

combines the two previous types into one myth. It may be added that type A is indigenous to northern North America, including the plains, whereas type B pertains primarily to southwestern North America and type C to South America exclusively. Radin considers type A to be the oldest.

Now it is undoubtedly true that the twin tales in many cases occur as ordinary heroic tales without any reference whatever to religion or mythology in the strict sense, but they have most certainly originated in a religious source, for there is no other way to comprehend the remarkable parallels which exist between the twin myths of the Old World and the New. A couple of examples will illustrate these similarities.

In northeastern North America the twin theme corresponds to type A, as was mentioned. Among the Algonkin the agents are the culture hero and his brother the Wolf. The latter is finally killed, the act being committed either by his brother or by other beings, among the central Algonkin, for example, by the water spirits.[29] On the whole, the contrast between the brothers is insignificant. Among the Iroquois, however, it has intensified into a complete dualism reminiscent of that found in ancient Iran. The Tuscarora, one of the Iroquois tribes, relate the following. In the beginning of time it happened that a woman who was pregnant with twins fell through a hole from the upper world and landed in our own world, which was still dark and deserted at that time. One of the twins, whose nature was evil, forced himself out of his mother's body, thereby causing her death. The good twin devoted himself to creating plants and animals. The evil one tried to imitate him but succeeded only in producing barren ground and reptiles. The evil one created human bodies, the good one gave them souls. Finally the evil one challenged his

29. It is a remarkable fact that possibly dates from a distant prehistoric age that the wolf, brother or twin of the culture hero, does not only occur among the Algonkin but also among the Shoshoni and their neighbors (among whom Wolf faces the mischievous Coyote, "little wolf") and among the Yuma. In the sacred moiety system of the Tlingit the wolf, alternating with the eagle, acts as a counterpart to the raven. It is interesting to recall in this connection that among the Koryak of eastern Siberia the wolf and the raven are accepted as shamans and culture heroes (Czaplicka 1914, p. 263).

brother to single combat for world supremacy. He lost, and has ever since been condemned to rule the dead and to remain an evil spirit. As Count has remarked, this myth bears an amazing resemblance to the Iranian myth of Ormazd and Ahriman.[30] It should be noted that for the Indians the notion of the evil spirit pertains to the world of mythology and not to that of practical religion. This explains why the evil being is so often disregarded in some sources but accentuated in others, as is the case, for example, with the evil spirit of the Algonkin Indians.

In South America, where type C is predominant, one of the brothers, the Sun, is consistently portrayed as strong and successful, whereas the other brother, the Moon, is weak, stupid, and pursued by bad luck. The rule is that they cooperate and that the Sun saves the Moon from danger. Both of them are well-disposed toward their fellow men and they act as creators and culture heroes. Furthermore, in the Amazon region as well as other areas it is said that the mother of the twins, who was the wife of the culture hero or high god, was killed by the jaguar who tore out the twin embryos from her body after the deed. They were adopted and raised by a female jaguar. Having reached mature age, they killed their mother's slayer, then climbed up to heaven where they were transformed into the sun and moon.[31] There are striking resemblances to the Greco-Roman myth of Romulus and Remus (although the episode of Remus's death brings to mind the North American type A).

Other myths in North and South America reveal unquestionable affinities with the mythological patterns of the Old World, not least those of the Mediterranean and ancient Near Eastern high cultures. Consequently there is considerable justification for agreeing with Krappe's theory of the ancient historical connections of the twin myth with the Old World.[32] Count maintains that the twin myth and the dualism associ-

30. Count 1952. Cf. also Dähnhardt 1907, pp. 10f., 79.
31. Métraux 1946. Cf. Gusinde 1930.
32. Krappe 1930, ch. 4; Count 1952, p. 61. Bianchi holds a divergent opinion (Bianchi 1958).

ated with it came to America together with the flood myth.[33] This is quite possibly true, for the research of Walk and Count has confirmed that the evil brother frequently occurs as the Earth Diver in Asia as well as in North America. The primary import of the twin myth has been felt among agricultural peoples, having there become incorporated with the dual cult systems.

It is not unlikely that the myth of the twins in America as elsewhere has inspired the superstitions which surround the birth of twins.[34] Twins are regarded as manifesting supernatural powers, and they may prefigure either good fortune or bad. In societies where the latter is believed to be the case, the twin who is thought to embody the evil is killed or is adopted by another family. It sometimes happens that both twins are killed.[35]

Just as the culture hero frequently represents one of the twins, he may at times, especially in South America, coincide with the dim figure of the mythical tribal father. There is, however, little reason unreservedly to declare the culture hero to be the ancestral father of mankind. In many myths he is certainly portrayed as the creator of the first human beings, not as their progenitor, but this distinction is occasionally erased. Among the Guarayú, for example, the ancestral father, the culture hero, and the high god appear to have coalesced into one person. However, among the Ona with their distinct high god belief the tribal father is a culture hero but not identical to the Supreme Being. The ancestral father often shares one single feature with that one of the twin gods who falls victim to death, namely, that he becomes ruler in the land of the dead. He is the first one to have been initiated into this realm and is, consequently, the prototype of the dead.

In North America the mythical primal man seems to have

33. On the other hand, the idea of the primeval waters may be older than dualism, as Harva, Hatt, Count, and Eliade presume—at least we can speculate in that direction.

34. Harris has made the contrary supposition: he thinks that the myths were created as a consequence of the general observances in regard to twins (Harris 1906).

35. See, for example, Karsten 1926, p. 148.

come in direct contact with the practical-cultic aspect of the tribe's religious life more openly than the types of culture heroes discussed above. In a previous context we mentioned the manhood initiation among the north-central Californians (Pomo, Wappo, Maidu, and others), which is named Kuksu after the tribal ancestor. This deity is personified in the dances and is also the instructor of the novices. Among the Pomo, Kuksu is a creator next to the high god; among the Wappo he is identified with the moon (there are numerous associations with the moon in California mythology).

Just as in California, the primeval man of the Mandan in North Dakota participates actively in the cult, as is evident, for example, in the portrayals and descriptions of these Indians by the painter George Catlin.[36] According to the cult myth, Numank, the first human being, persuaded his fellow men to build a kind of ark before the arrival of the great flood and in this fashion saved mankind from annihilation.[37] In remembrance of this the *okeepa* festival is held (an annual festival related to the Sun Dance). As the festival begins, a white-painted man, representing the primeval man, arrives in the Mandan village. He comes from the western horizon, where he retired after the great flood.

Some of the mythological figures portrayed in the foregoing are scarcely traditional deities, but sheer creations of an imaginative mind. Others, like the culture hero, may be termed gods, but enjoy little cult. The world of American Indian mythology is indeed, like all mythology, complex and bewildering. The trend toward fiction tales, and absorption of migratory tale motifs, contributes to this situation.

36. Catlin 1967; Catlin 1841 (1), pp. 155ff. See also Chapter 5.
37. According to other information supplied by Maximilian Prince of Wied-Neuwied, gentleman explorer, contemporary of Catlin, the "arch" of the flood myth was a fixed refuge.

4

Gods and Spirits of Nature

In contrast to the colorful figures of mythology whose religious functions are primarily etiological (that is, they sanction cults and other institutions through foundational acts) are the more vaguely outlined divinities of practical religion. These are firmly grounded in the personal religious faith of the Indians: they answer to man's religious needs and are therefore objects of cult and worship. Consequently, these gods and spirits are generally well integrated into social, cultural, and ecological environments. In appearance they are almost invariably nature beings.

The Supreme Being belongs primarily to the world of practical religion. It is true that his cultic role is in many places limited and that prayers are often addressed to him without any display of outward ceremony, but he does at times take on a more realistic appearance, such as his manifestations in bursts of thunder and in flashes of lightning or in the benign or ruinous blaze of the sun. At first glance the relationship of the Supreme Being to the powers of nature often appears incongruous. We learn, for example, that among the Surara in northern Brazil the high god is considered identical to the moon (the sun is here of no account), but that the moon is moreover believed to be the dwelling-place of the dead and their chief, an old fellow with a long beard. H. Becher, who has submitted this information, assures us that the Indians in no way regard these statements as contradictory.[1] As a matter of fact, we are probably confronted here with two distinct conceptualizations: on one hand, ideas pertaining to the high god and his worldly connections; on the other, ideas referring to the phases of the moon and their relationship to human life (compare the correlation between the moon and the dying or withdrawing culture hero).

Such inconsistencies in religious concepts are often encountered when prominent phenomena of nature or the universe form the focus of the tendencies of religious conceptualization. The sun, the moon, heaven, and thunder may be separate divinities, personifications of natural phenomena, but independently of this they may also be manifestations of a Supreme Being, as among the Eskimos and the Assiniboin.[2] Shamanic speculation (that is, the esoteric speculation which occurs wherever shamans or medicine men keep together or are organized in secret societies) is aware of the inconsistency and attempts to overcome it. Shamanic speculation among the Oglala Dakota exemplifies this point. The various gods (for example, sun, moon, heaven, and thunder) have distinct personalities and functions, but together they constitute a unity, Wakan Tanka, "the great mystery," "the great holy."[3] The same name occurs to designate the high god perceived as an individual being among the Eastern Dakota. Several records from the Oglala seem to indicate that the latter also, at least outside of shamanic speculation, regard Wakan Tanka as a personal, delimited Supreme Being.

In the preceding we discussed the solar characteristics of the high god and the lunar characteristics of the culture hero. In earlier research, primarily represented by Ehrenreich, such astral associations were considered essential to these beings.[4]

---

1. Cf. Haekel 1959a, p. 40.
2. Cf. Hultkrantz 1962, pp. 374ff., and Denig 1930, pp. 486ff.
3. Walker 1917, pp. 79ff., Hultkrantz 1971, Powers 1975, pp. 45ff. Cf. also Chapter 1.
4. Ehrenreich 1905.

The matter is not that simple, however. In South America, to be sure, there may be observed a pervasive tendency to regard divinities and spirits as astral beings, but this is a mythological pattern without much significance for the central religious content of these concepts. Sun, moon, and stars are symbols of the gods rather than tangible incarnations. The schematic outline of some astral divinities in mythology is without a counterpart in the more profound religious faith.

The concept of a sun god unassociated with the mythical twins but instead expressly representing the religious idea of a Supreme God, a god of light or a god of life, is found in many places in North America. It is especially prevalent in the southern areas of the United States; among the representatives of the so-called Gulf tradition (from around the time of the birth of Christ) and the Mississippian culture (900–1700) in the southeastern states and among sedentary as well as nomadic peoples in the southwestern states.[5] For the Pueblo Indians in New Mexico and Arizona the sun is a powerful divinity even though divinities like the corn goddess are more significant. It is a noteworthy case in point that the sun is regarded as creator in only one Pueblo group, the Hopi.[6] The Hopi Indians perform special ceremonies at the summer solstice to delay the sun's journey toward winter, and at the winter solstice to hasten its progress toward spring.

The Gulf and Mississippian traditions are probably best represented by the Natchez on the lower Mississippi, excellently portrayed in French sources from the beginning of the eighteenth century.[7] Among them we find a total theocracy in which the priest chieftain, head of the sun clan, is also a representative of and a divine substitute for the Supreme Being, the sun. Eternal fire, symbol of the sun, burns in the chieftain's temple. This sun cult is no doubt a projection of

5. The Gulf tradition has probably been part of the circum-Caribbean civilization.

6. Stirling 1946, p. 396.

7. Cf. authors like Le Page du Pratz, Charlevoix, and Le Petit. The Natchez are also well known from Chateaubriand's novel *Atala*. For a thorough description of Natchez religion according to the old sources, see Swanton 1911, pp. 158ff.

that same religion which formed the basis for the higher religious development in Mexico among the Maya, the Aztecs, and others.

Examples of sun gods who play a prominent part in religion may be found among the plains Indians too, especially among the Sioux tribes. The Crow Indians in Montana, for example, regard the Sun as the Supreme Being in the religious cult (in the mythology he is replaced by Old Man Coyote), and oaths are sworn to him. He does not dominate the religion, however; this prominent position is held by the vision spirits here as in other plains tribes, with the possible exception of the Caddo peoples.[8] Everywhere in North America, except among the Eskimos and some eastern tribes (the Algonkin, Cherokee, Yuchi, and Seminole), the sun is perceived as a male being.

In South America the sun god is rare outside of the high culture, where he is well known as a leading figure. We do not here include the numerous examples of gods and heroes who have secondary or mythological associations with the sun. However, some tribes in eastern Brazil (for example the Canella) and in southernmost Brazil and Paraguay (the Guaraní) have maintained a sun cult and the concept of an anthropomorphic sun. Among the Waiwai in British Guyana the sun god is the one divinity to be worshipped with sacrifice and prayer. He is invoked to make an end to the continuous rains which are detrimental to hunting.[9] The Araucanians in Chile place their Supreme Being in the sun.

Compared to the sun the moon plays an insignificant part outside of mythology. Many divinities have lunar traits, for example, the ancestral father, Mother Earth, and the withdrawing culture hero. Even a female creator such as the great goddess of the Shawnee is associated with the moon. A true moon cult, however, is rarely found outside the high culture. Even an investigator as oriented to astral mythology as Ehrenreich admits that the moon is seldom mentioned as a divine being in South America.[10] In North America a god of

8. Lowie 1922, pp. 318ff.   9. Fock 1963, p. 34.
10. Ehrenreich 1905, p. 35.

the moon is found among the Eskimos, among a number of Pueblo tribes in New Mexico (however, the Zuni have a goddess, "the moon mother"), and among the Navajo Indians in the same area, whereas the moon divinity of the Apache seems to be a goddess. The moon goddess is also found in other areas of North America: the Fox Indians regard her as far more amiable than the sun god, who causes desiccation and sunstroke.[11]

Just as in other places around the world, a solar or lunar eclipse causes great alarm among American Indians. It is a common notion that the heavenly body has been devoured by a monster, for example, the coyote in North America or the jaguar in South America. By howling and screaming, beating on drums, boards, or canoes, and shooting arrows up in the air, attempts are made to scare off the beast. The Bakaïri in Brazil link the regular phases of the moon to the notion that a supernatural being in the form of an animal bites and eventually devours the lunar body.

As was mentioned earlier, the stars are also generally symbols of the gods and an actual star cult is rarely found. It is primarily in mythology that stars and constellations appear as active divine or heroic beings. They are often perceived as the hunter and his hunted prey, a clear indication that the astral world drew the attention of even primitive hunters. In South America it is common for supernatural beings to be considered to be present on earth with important functions to fill and at the same time to be identified with various stars. This is the case with some masters of animals, particularly among the Arawak in Guyana.[12] The double perspective confronting us here seems to result from a merging of the myth about the ancestors of animals with a religious belief in the masters of animals. In North America such associations are not as frequent, although they are by no means absent. The Coyote of the Shoshoni appears both as a lord of animals of sorts and as a constellation. Among the Caddo peoples we do indeed find a genuine star cult. In this connection only the Morning Star

11. Jones 1939, pp. 18ff.   12. Goeje 1943, pp. 17f. Cf. Zerries 1952.

of the Pawnee will be suggested, which renders "life, strength, and fertility," according to a Pawnee priest. The Morning Star represents the male and the Evening Star the female principle of existence.

Heaven as such is seldom perceived as a divinity except in shamanic speculation. General belief sometimes understands heaven as an expression for the being of the highest god. For example, the Haida on the Northwest Coast call the Supreme Being the "power of the shining heavens." All across America heaven is regarded as the abode of the Supreme Being.

Numerous myths, as well as much speculative belief, are centered around the Milky Way, generally represented as a huge pathway across the sky, "the ash road" for some tribes in the southwestern part of North America and in central Brazil, generally the path of souls to the land of the dead in North America and among the Bolivian Indians. Some mission Indians in California regard the Milky Way as a mystical world soul, a Supreme Being, of which the breath soul of each human individual forms a part. This world soul is at the same time perceived as the dwelling place of the dead. There are other symbolic references to the Milky Way which will be discussed further.

We find, not unexpectedly, that the phenomena of meteorology and the atmosphere too are regarded as manifestations of divine power. It is true that Ehrenreich remarks on the scarcity of atmospheric divine beings in South America.[13] In any case they are certainly less frequent there than in North America. This circumstance is not easily explained: one factor seems to be that the abundant tropical rain forest excludes man, as it were, from the activities of atmospheric powers. Moreover, historical traditions have certainly contributed to the focus of attention on divinities of a totally different kind: high gods, fertility goddesses, masters of animals, forest spirits.

High gods are, however, sometimes represented among the atmospheric phenomena. The Supreme Being is at times

13. Ehrenreich 1905, p. 29; and cf. p. 15.

manifest in the flash of lighting and in thunder, the latter being his voice; this belief exists among some Yuki Indians in California. Furthermore, they imagine the rainbow to be the multicolored clothes of this god. According to the same Indians, the bull-roarer is the instrument by which the god's voice, "the breath of thunder," is represented in the cult.[14] Thunder gods more or less identical with the Supreme Being are also reported from some places in South America. The Tupi have a thunder god named Tupan who was recognized at least by the missionaries as a high god equivalent to the Christian God. Pillán, the thunder god of the Araucanians and presumably an ancient Supreme Being, resides appropriately inside a volcano, the habitat of this people being the volcanic West Coast of Chile.[15]

North American Indians most commonly believe thunder to be caused by supernatural beings in bird guise, the thunderbirds.[16] By flapping their wings they produce thunder, by opening and closing their eyes they produce lightning. Many Indians are of the opinion that the thunderbirds are eagles or at least have the shape of eagles. Numerous depictions of eagle-shaped thunderbirds on blankets and solid rocks provide further evidence for such a belief. In eastern North America the thunderbirds are often four in number, one from each of the world quarters. The mystique of the number four and the sacred significance of the four cardinal directions in these parts of North America are clearly present here. In the same areas the thunderbirds are thought to be irreconcilably and bitterly struggling against evil water spirits, panthers, or horned serpents. This antagonism is possibly founded in the same dualism between heaven and earth which finds its cultic expression in the division into sacred moieties among the cultivating tribes. This dualism may also be related to the mythological opposition in the Old World between the thunder god and the water monster (compare India, for example)

14. Schmidt 1936.
15. The concept of *pillán* means literally "supernatural" and each spirit is therefore *pillán*. See Böning 1974.
16. Michelson 1930, pp. 51ff.

or between the eagle and dragon in the world-tree myth of Nordic mythology. The thunderbird motif is reported from all of northern Siberia, and among the Buryats around Lake Baikal the struggle recurs between the ruler of the birds, a gigantic eagle, and the many-headed water snake.[17] Concurrent traditions in America and Asia seem to be present here.

Ehrenreich maintained that the thunderbird was totally absent in South America. This is erroneous. The concept of the thunderbird exists in Gran Chaco, in Ecuador, and among the Caribbeans on the northern coast of the continent. Its range indicates a more extensive presence in earlier times than is now the case. Among the Arawak, Uitoto, and some other tribes in various parts of South America, it is said that a host of birds successfully killed the great water snake, also identified with the rainbow. Apparently this is an echo of the same dualism of which we have seen examples in North America.

In America as well as in the Old World there exists a close relationship among the various deities of the atmosphere. The thunder beings may share functions with or appear as gods of rain and wind. It is noteworthy, however, that they are less prevalent as rain and fertility deities within agrarian cultures in the New than in the Old World.[18] New World inhabitants rely on a number of specialized rain masters, such as mountain spirits (the Aymara), rain mothers (the Mundurucú), cloud spirits in bird guise (the Chamaco) or in human guise (Pueblo Indians in North America). Each one of the Mundurucú rain mothers answers to a certain kind of rain, the most violent one among them to thunder and lightning. In earlier times these mothers appeared to powerful shamans in the shape of black deer, a sure sign of approaching rain and the futility of hunting.[19] A similar specification of rain deities is found in the belief of the Pueblo Indians that

17. Baumann 1955, pp. 313f.
18. Another spirit of rain and fertility in the Old World, the serpent, occurs widely in America but is less concerned with fertility here: see Mundkur 1976. Cf. also the discussion in Chapter 11.
19. Murphy 1958, pp. 21f.

some cloud spirits cause thunder and others rain. Most of
these cloud spirits seem to have been recruited from the ranks
of dead ancestors.[20]

It is of some interest that the rain spirit among the Yaqui in
northwestern Mexico is characterized as an evil one-eyed
god.[21] One-eyed divine beings are present elsewhere in
North America, as the culture heroes among the coast Salish
and some eastern Algonkin peoples. Apparently we are here
confronted with a vast cultural relationship that links
America with the South Pacific, China, and northwestern
Europe.[22] The one-eyed god may originally have been a sky
god with sun and moon for eyes (a concept which occurs in
the Old World but is not clearly evidenced in the New). In
that case the Yaqui rain god is a specialized sky god, a symbol
of the eagerly expected but much too infrequent rains.

Some scholars are of the opinion that thunder beings in
bird form originate from the close association of thunder and
wind. At times the winds assume bird shape, at least in North
America. The giant bird of the eastern Algonkin is typical in
this respect: his wings create the winds. However, in the
Pueblo region the various wind beings—the wind old
woman, the wind old man, or the feather man—are perceived as anthropomorphic. In the Pawnee pantheon the
wind gods occupy a prominent place next to the star gods.
They are intermediaries between the Supreme Being, whose
status is imperial, and man. Across large areas of North
America the abodes of the winds are assigned to the four
quarters of the world. Consequently they are associated with
the sacred number four (compare the thunderbirds) and with
the color symbolism of the sand paintings in southwestern
North America. The wind gods are more scarce in South
America. The best known of them is probably the storm god
Uragan of the Taino, immortalized in the word "hurricane."
Among the Tucuna on the upper Amazon River the storm
demon at the girls' puberty rite is depicted as a spirit
equipped with a huge penis.[23] The Tacana tribes in northern

20. Hultkrantz 1953, pp. 185ff.   21. Giddings 1959, p. 12.
22. Gjessing 1948.   23. Nimuendajú 1952, pp. 82f.

Bolivia make wooden images of the wind god decorated with feather mosaics. Occasionally the whirlwind represents a deity in North America, especially in the Southwest. Elsewhere in the western United States it appears as an apparition of the spirits of the dead.

The cosmic dualism of agrarian tribes places the powers of heaven and atmosphere in more or less clear opposition to the chthonic powers, especially to the deities of earth and water. We have just seen how this confrontation is expressed in a power struggle between the thunderbird and the water snake. It is also expressed, perhaps more fundamentally, in the sexual distance between the celestial male and the chthonic female elements. Attention is then focused on the sky god and the earth goddess. According to the myth, the universe and mankind arose from the union of the heavenly father with Mother Earth.

The earth goddess or mother goddess is accordingly the foremost representative of the chthonic powers. In cultures where cultivation of the soil is among the foremost of societal concerns her cult is of paramount importance. In many such communities she is the all-powerful divinity. In daily existence her role corresponds to that of the woman-mother, the cultivator and keeper of domestic plants and the bearer of children to the world, just as the earth is the producer of plants and verdure. In South America outside the Andean high culture the great goddess is not always clearly represented as an earth goddess, but her functions leave no doubt about the original connection. The Cágabá of northernmost Colombia describe her in the following manner: "Woman is the most elementary expression of fertility and the most exalted deity of culture; she is the Mother, the creator. From her are born mankind, the good black earth, the edible plants, the animals, and all of nature. All these elements are 'Children of the Mother' and are subject to her 'law.'"[24] In like manner the Paressí in Mato Grosso believe all living things to have sprung from the earth goddess Maisö. Even the rivers poured forth from her womb. In North America the Fox In-

24. Reichel-Dolmatoff 1951, p. 81.

dians assert that "the earth on which we live is a woman. . . .
She provides us with all the food we eat and lets us live
and dwell upon her."[25] The Lenape maintain that the earth as
such is a goddess or that the earth contains a goddess. At
the annual festivals the blessings she bestows are gratefully
acknowledged.[26]

It is an indisputable fact that the concept of the earth goddess has grown strongest among the cultivating peoples. This
is especially the case in the Andean and Mexican high cultures, where her cult pertains to the more prominent characteristics in religion. Her origins may have been in the old
hunting culture which ranged all through America until
about 2000 B.C. and was maintained by many tribes until the
last decades of the nineteenth century. Far away from agricultural peoples lived, in the state of Washington, those Shahap-
tin Indians whose chief in the 1880s was the dreamer
Smohalla. Smohalla addressed the agent who was commis-
sioned by the military authorities to persuade the Indians to
cultivate the land:

> "You ask me to plow the ground. Shall I take a knife and
> tear my mother's bosom? Then when I die she will not
> take me to her bosom to rest. You ask me to dig for
> stone. Shall I dig under her skin for her bones? Then
> when I die I cannot enter her body to be born again. You
> ask me to cut grass and make hay and sell it, and be rich
> like white men. But how dare I cut off my mother's
> hair?"[27]

As elsewhere, the earth deity is here represented as animatistic, at one with her substratum and yet an intimately experienced personal being. Many hunting tribes in North America
manifest the same primitive belief in "our mother," "Mother

---

25. Jones 1939, p. 20.

26. This earth goddess is identical with the mythical woman who married a
star (cf. Chapter 3 and below). For instance, the goddess of earth and vegetation among the Navajo, Changing Woman, was married to the sun and bore
him the divine twins (Reichard 1950 (2), pp. 406ff., 481f.). Her anthropomorphism is strong in myth but less pronounced in practical religion,
where she is more or less identical with the earth.

27. Mooney 1896, p. 721.

Earth." The more recent peyote religion has accommodated Mother Earth to some extent under the influence of the Catholic cult of the Virgin Mary.

From a mythological point of view it is true that the agrarian peoples see the mother goddess as only one of the two primordial procreative beings. This idea of the emanation of life and the world through a sacred union seems to fade in practical faith, where the performance of the goddess is often enough emphasized at the expense of the sky god. She is mentioned, as we have seen, as the one who alone brings forth the earth and the plants, giving birth to them from herself. In some areas this belief has stimulated the thought that the world was created from the dead body of the goddess (compare the emanatistic creation myth in Chapter 2). As we shall soon see, this notion has deep roots in the complex of ideas about the vegetation goddess. For some peoples the procreative characteristics of the mother goddess have been transferred to the male god who has thus fully assumed her role as agrarian deity. Here we will mention only the Supreme Being of the Uitoto, who according to the myth produced plants and animals from his own body.

Undoubtedly through missionary influence, the mother goddess has been suppressed or replaced by a male divinity among some agricultural Indians. This is an established fact among the Cuna on the isthmus of Panama.[28] The opposite process, the displacement of a male high god by a female creator, is also known, namely among the Shawnee in eastern North America. Under the influence of the great goddess of the Iroquois and Huron religions a goddess who is identified with the moon came to replace the male Supreme Being of the Shawnee Indians in the course of the nineteenth century. This latter deity is in other respects common to all Algonkin tribes in the woodlands.[29]

Like the sky god, the earth goddess combines several of the powers of nature which in other contexts are readily endowed with independence and personal traits. As the god-

28. Wassén 1960.   29. Voegelin and Voegelin 1944.

dess of birth she may stand behind all the generative powers of existence. Among the Jívaro in northern Peru she appears both as earth goddess and as vegetation demon, in that all "female" plants come under her protection. Among the Pueblo Indians in New Mexico and Arizona there is, however, a distinction between Mother Earth and the corn mother or corn mothers. The latter may be numerous, representing as they do the various cultivated types of maize, whereas Mother Earth in her capacity as goddess of the soil is perceived as one and indivisible.

The vegetation goddess (or the mother goddess in her role as vegetation goddess) appears to have her strongest foothold in the agrarian areas of North and Central America. She is here a corn goddess, corn being the predominant grain. The corn goddess may also rule over grass and herbs, bushes and trees, as in a story told by the Arikara on the Missouri River. Among the Hopi in Arizona and the central Algonkin, the latter being hunters rather than cultivators, the corn mother is replaced by a male corn spirit—undoubtedly a secondary notion adapted to the interests of the patrilinear hunters. As was just pointed out, the functions of the corn goddess may be shared by a number of corn goddesses, as among the Pueblo Indians. Among the Iroquois three sisters are mentioned: the Corn Sister, the Bean Sister, and the Squash Sister, each one embodying the prolific power of the cultivated domestic plants.

The relationship between the vegetation goddess and corn tends everywhere toward identity, a circumstance which is apparent in both myth and ritual. In the eastern United States the Indians believe that the corn mother produces corn from her own body. It is told in a Creek myth how at her own request the corn mother is dragged across a newly burned field. When her son returns three months later, corn and beans are growing there. This is the so-called immolation myth (a term coined by G. Hatt), which in the southwest and among the Iroquois is replaced by the myth about the escape and return of the goddess.[30] It goes without saying that the

30. Cf. Hatt 1951.

Creek myth should be regarded as a ritual myth. The ritual corresponding to that myth is probably related to the ritual procedure reported in the middle of the last century by Schoolcraft from the Ojibway at Lake Superior: to ensure a good harvest an Ojibway woman would go out nude on a dark night and drag her best garment around her cornfield.[31] The Huron myth about the vegetation goddess may be ranked among the more conventional myths about the creation of the world from the body of a primal being. The goddess Ataentsic was hurled down by her husband, the chieftain of heaven, through a hole in the sky caused by her having torn up the tree of heaven (the world tree) by the roots. She landed softly in the lower regions that now make up our own world and gave birth to the divine twins. In so doing, however, she was killed by her evil son. Her good son formed the sun from her face and the moon and stars from her breasts, and out of her body sprouted corn, beans, and pumpkins.[32] There may be a direct link between the motif of the goddess's fall through the hole in the sky and the life rhythm of the crops: the genesis of the world is likened to the growing of crops from the earth, the goddess being the seed or the plant from which the world emanates. A reverberation of the same motif is found in one of the most famous Indian narratives, that of the Star Husband.[33]

The corn goddess may occasionally appear in the myth as a corncob, among the Seminole in Florida and the Cochiti in New Mexico, for instance. It is therefore interesting to observe that in the cult she is represented by a corncob among the Indians in Central America, Mexico, the southwestern United States, and on the plains. The Cochiti generally plant a superb specimen of a corncob, evidently symbolizing the power of vegetation or the goddess herself. Other rites involving the corncob include the flesh sacrifices by the Arikara at certain festivals, during which the "mother" is called upon to yield an abundant harvest.[34]

31. Beauchamp 1898, p. 198; Williams 1956, pp. 58ff.
32. Hale 1888, pp. 180ff.
33. The latter has been discussed in Thompson 1953.
34. Hatt 1951, pp. 854ff.

The concept of the corncob as the symbol of the vegetation goddess recurs in Peru, where it plays a significant part in the harvest ritual; the corncob is then wrapped in clothes. Elsewhere in South America, outside the Andes, there is naturally little evidence of corn goddesses. From the tropical forest areas, however, we have some information about a corn spirit who is sometimes appeased with dances, as among the Cashinawa on the Purus River. Along with the corn spirit the cassava spirit is present in these areas. This spirit is also cherished in the cult, since the cassava or manioc plant is used for breadmaking. Thus the Mundurucú hold an annual celebration during which the mothers of corn and manioc are honored and reconciled. We have seen earlier that the earth goddess of the Jívaro is also the guardian of vegetation. When the Jívaro plant manioc, they call upon this goddess, Nungui, the soul of the manioc, who is represented by a stone of remarkable shape. The women who plant the manioc are themselves seated on manioc roots and one of them caresses a red-painted manioc in her lap. A typical fertility rite![35]

Not only edible or domestic plants are represented by spirits. The South American Indians east of the Andes recognize an abundance of tree and plant spirits, a conceptual complex that is perhaps more than any other religious feature characteristic of the primitive inhabitants of this continent.

The so-called bush spirits in South America are partly wood spirits, partly tree spirits.[36] Ranked among the wood spirits, for example, is Corupira of the eastern Tupi, master of all the forest animals as well as guardian spirit of the forests. It is said of him that he keeps the secrets of the forest and punishes by leading astray anyone who fells or harms trees unnecessarily. As a result of these functions the wood spirit is subservient to the moon goddess, the mother of plants. His

35. See the commentaries on this rite in Zerries 1961, pp. 327f. Such religious rites could sometimes have, beside their religious import, most practical aims. For instance, the Warrau of the tropical forest have a palm-starching rite in which dancing and eating is performed in honor of the Supreme Being. By accumulating food for these festivals the Indians save it for a time of the year when they would otherwise starve. See Heinen and Ruddle 1974.
36. Zerries 1954, pp. 207ff.

close association with trees is emphasized in the belief that he dwells in hollow trunks. According to the Carib each tree has its own spirit which must be appeased when the tree is felled.

These examples from an exceedingly rich corpus of conceptual material clearly show that bush spirits are closely related to the masters of animals (insofar as they do not function as masters of animals themselves). Apparently they have also been formed according to the pattern of the masters of animals. The master of animals rules over all animals or over one animal species. He sees to it that no animals are killed unnecessarily, that they are treated with care, and that after they are killed they are buried with appropriate rituals. Belief in these animal spirits is extensive in South America.[37] In North America it is also extremely common, unlike the belief in bush spirits.[38] This was already related by the Jesuit missionaries by the seventeenth century. One missionary described the Montagnais Indians' belief that the beavers are protected by a powerful beaver who is as big as a hut. Another missionary told that the Ottawa revered a remarkable animal which could only be seen in dreams and to which they sacrificed to ensure a good sturgeon catch. Similar concepts exist in our own time among the North and South American Indians. Their link with an ancient hunting culture is apparent. Despite the fact that these are concepts of primitive simplicity and almost monotonous uniformity, when viewed quantitatively they can be seen to belong to the more predominant forms of religious expression among the hunting peoples.

An abundantly multiform belief in spirits is characteristic of the religions of tropical South American Indians. According to the conceptualization of the Guyana Indians innumerable zoomorphic spirits inhabit strangely shaped trees and stones, waterfalls, and other conspicuous natural phenomena in the forest gloom.[39] These spirits are consequently locally situated beings, unlike the ones mentioned earlier. They constitute a potential danger for the lonely wanderer since they are for the

37. Zerries 1954, pp. 9ff.   38. Hultkrantz 1961.
39. Roth 1915; cf. Holmberg 1950, pp. 90f. (Siriono).

most part of evil disposition, although easily outwitted by cunning humans, but they may also show their gratitude when they are helped. A number of legends describe marriages between supernatural beings and humans. "Spirits in general," Métraux writes, "are visualized as having a human appearance with some monstrous characteristic; they may be hairy or they may have protruding eyebrows or two heads; they may have no articulation at the knees, or they may be linked together like Siamese twins. Sometimes spirits look like skeletons or skulls."[40] The last is particularly the case when the spirits are believed to be identical to the dead.

Essentially the same concepts recur in North America. Although they do not seem to dominate the religious situation to the same extent as in the tropical jungles of South America, there is some justification for speaking of local-bound spirits in North America. Bourke's description of a canoe trip on the Colorado River in 1886 is particularly illuminating in this respect. His boatman, a Mohave Indian, could point out the habitats of the spirits—even the home of the dead—in the natural surroundings.[41] East of the Rocky Mountains both woodland and plains Indians denote certain remarkable natural formations as the abodes of spirits. The Micmac in easternmost Canada shun places that are haunted by the spirits. The Dakota and the Cheyenne on the plains revere the Black Hills as the homeland of the spirits. The Shoshoni around the Wind River assume that the rock carvings in the mountains have been made by spirits who live high up in the crevices. Large parts of Yellowstone Park used to be a taboo area which no Indians from the surrounding plains tribes dared approach without special ceremonies, on account of the spirit powers residing in the hot springs.[42] The Pueblo Indians in the southwestern states venerate lakes and other apertures in the earth's surface from which their ancestors emerged at the beginning of time and through which the dead return.

Among sacred places in North and South America mountains and stones hold a unique position. In South

40. Métraux 1949, p. 568.   41. Bourke 1889.
42. Hultkrantz 1954.

America they occur especially within the Andean high culture. There such places (*huacas*) are frequently revered in connection with the cult of the earth goddess, who in Peru is called Pachamama. We have already mentioned that a thunder god in Chile is thought to reside in a volcanic mountain. Other volcanoes in South America are held in respect due to their hidden dynamic powers. The Puruhá, a tribe on La Montaña, formerly sacrificed humans to the deity of the volcanic mountain. It is told of a neighboring tribe, the Jívaro, that they pass by high mountains hushed and quietly so as not to arouse the anger of the mountain. According to Karsten, mountain spirits are deceased medicine men.[43] A corresponding fear of provoking the mountain spirits is found in many places in North America. The Shoshoni, for example, dare not point a finger at the Grand Tetons, the magnificent mountain peaks on the border of Idaho and Wyoming. A sacred mountain plays a significant part in the origin myth of the Cheyenne Sun Dance: its interior is ruled by Rolling Thunder, who once instructed a young medicine man and his female companion in the dance ritual.[44] The mountain is probably identical to Bear Butte in the Black Hills.

In the shamanic speculation of the Dakota, Inyan, as all rocks are called, constitutes the oldest of all divinities, the ancestral father of all things and all gods. Foremost here is the expression of stone as representing the least variable material; the stone cult belongs to the distant past. Large boulders are decorated with colored swan down and painted red and green. Prayers and dog sacrifices are addressed to them. The Crow Indians keep small animal-shaped stones as powerful "medicine." The Algonkin around Lake Mistassini sacrifice to a mighty granite block on the shore before they will attempt to cross the lake. The stone is believed to be inhabited by a spirit. Further south in the United States it is thought that even the higher, personal gods are incarnate in stone: for the Natchez on the lower Mississippi the culture hero is represented by a stone, the Kiowa in Texas keep as their tribal fetish a stone doll, *taime*, to which prayers are directed during

43. Karsten 1926, pp. 331f.   44. Dorsey 1905, pp. 46ff.

the Sun Dance, and at the foot of a sacred mountain the Taos in New Mexico worship the two war gods, "the stone men." Fetishes of strangely shaped stones are believed to promote good hunting throughout the Pueblo area. The religion of the Taino in the West Indies is entirely focused upon a cult of images, *zemi,* frequently stones of anthropomorphic shape kept in caves. The stone cult is exceedingly prevalent in South America among the Andean Indians, but also in the tropical area east of the Andes may be found examples of gods incarnate in stone. We saw earlier that the mother goddess of the Jívaro is represented by a stone. The Warrau on the Orinoco keep in a temple a stone image portraying their Supreme Being. It is often said that the stones in the medicine men's rattles are representative of the Supreme Being or other high gods.

Just as the earth and all that it contains is thought to be the dwelling of supernatural power or supernatural beings, so also is water in its multitude of forms—seas, lakes, springs, or rivers. Water may in itself be supernatural. In 1513 the Spanish conquistador Ponce de León set out on an expedition to Florida firmly convinced that he would find the fountain of youth and rejuvenation of which he had heard the Mexican Indians speak. The fountain of youth certainly did exist, but only in the mythology of the Californian Maidu and Wintun Indians. According to this myth, which refers to the time before death entered the world, humans could regain their youth by diving into the water of life. The belief in the life-giving power of water is evident throughout the Americas in the numerous magic rituals aimed at rejuvenation of men's vitality or the return to life of the dead.

Vaguely animatistic conceptions seem to underlie the idea of the sea goddess of ancient Peru, Mamacocha, "mother of all waters" (the springs were called her "daughters") and "the great water" of the Mississippi, also called the "father of waters." In most cases, however, the waters are associated with animistic beings, mostly malevolent ones. Sedna, the Eskimo mistress of sea animals, belongs here, as well as the sea goddesses resembling her who exist along the Northwest Coast (and in northeast Siberia). The masters of whales and larger fish also rule the sea depths along this coast and the drowned dead are their slaves.

Especially well known in the same area is the double-headed sea monster of the Kwakiutl, Sisiutl, a gigantic snake with a head at each end and a human head in the middle.[45] The shamans maintain that they own parts of his body as powerful medicine. This water being may be related to the horned water snake in the eastern and southern parts of the United States.[46] Both of them are thus perceived as representatives of the chthonic powers in their battle with the divinities of the upper world, as was mentioned in connection with the thunderbirds. Among the Comox on the Northwest Coast the double-headed monster devours the chieftain of heaven. The Dakota in Minnesota tell how the thunderbirds, *wakinyan,* occasionally perish in the struggle against the water spirits, *unktehi.* The latter are described as gigantic buffalo with horns and tails that stretch toward heaven. Among other habitats they live under the St. Anthony Falls in Minnesota. There the Indians formerly hung up buffalo hides as offerings. The Algonkin around the western Great Lakes associate the cosmic battle with the origin myth of the medicine lodge. According to this myth horned water snakes drowned Little Wolf, brother of the culture hero. To appease the latter the water snakes were forced to present him with their medicine secret, the great medicine lodge.[47] These Algonkin water spirits have beautiful daughters who, like European mermaids, tempt amorous men into the watery depths. Also

45. Locher 1932. One must not neglect the possibility that the appearance of this water sprite is an immediate expression of the conventional art of the northern Pacific Coast Indians. This art splits in half and extends the figures it portrays. Cf., for instance, the discussion and pictures in Radin 1944, pp. 333ff. According to another opinion, the double-headed snake has oriental prototypes (Coe 1976, p. 125). Whatever the explanation, water snakes with two heads are also found among the Hopi, Acoma, and Navajo of the southwest.

46. Similar notions have been discussed in Barbeau 1952. Among the Kato of California the horned monster is a symbol of the earth.

47. This is thus the initiation myth of the great medicine lodge whose ritual will be discussed in Chapter 8.

among the Pueblo peoples in the arid southwestern states there exists a belief in a horned water snake, or horned water snakes—they are sometimes perceived as a whole collective. From his home in a spring the water snake controls floods and earthquakes. He is sometimes feathered and occurs in this fashion in two California tribes as well, the Pomo and the Kato (for the latter he is both horned and feathered). Undoubtedly the concept of the feathered snake belongs to the same image complex as the Aztec Quetzalcoatl ("feathered serpent") and the Mayan Kukulcan.[48]

The concept of the water serpent appears to be quite extensive, recurring in South America among the Indians in the Amazon region. Here the water spirit is identified with the dangerous anaconda, and canoe accidents on the river are attributed to the activities of this dreaded "water mother." The Chorotí in Gran Chaco told Nordenskiöld about a lake serpent as thick as two outstretched arms. Once it swallowed an Indian, but he stabbed the beast in its heart and managed to dig himself out. The tale is not only an adventure story but also an illustration—typical enough for South America—of how the moon is devoured by a mysterious animal at a lunar eclipse.

The Chorotí tell of one more water spirit, a little black dwarf who abducts children. Such diminutive water beings exist in other places as well, with special prevalence in the Great Basin of North America ("water babies"). There is above all, in both North and South America, a widespread belief in dwarfs on the land, at times associated with the concept of a more or less extinct "prehistoric" race, at times linked to the concept of spirit beings in nature. The latter belief generally pertains to a collective of small, often invisible, spirits, but we also hear of solitary beings. To the Amazon tribe Ipuriná the echo is a little arrow-shooting dwarf who resides in the trees. Among the Shoshoni in the semideserts of western North America there is likewise a belief in an arrow-shooting dwarf whose missiles cause disease and misfortune.

48. The plumed serpent was part of the Mississippian culture and clearly emanated from Mexico. See, for example, Hudson 1976, pp. 86ff.

Just as there are dwarfs so also are there giants, although their role in the popular imagination seems less prominent. Legends and tales deal with monstrous supernatural beings: the pursuing rolling head, also depicted as a rolling stone (and in South America at times identified with the moon); the woman with teeth in her vagina, and so on. It is, however, difficult to establish to what extent these motifs do indeed represent true religious belief. More credence is probably given to the stories among Californian Indians, the Kwakiutl and the prairie tribes, and their neighbors, of mighty beings under the earth who produce earthquakes. Among the prairie tribes the giant turtle upon whom the earth is supposed to rest shakes his shell.[49] The *windigo* of the Canadian Algonkin is a man-eating monster who arouses much fear. Anyone who eats human meat during a famine is transformed into a *windigo*.[50] Another dangerous category of supernatural being may be exemplified by the *yurupari* of the Mundurucú, who are invisible spirits who fly through the air with a whistling sound when accompanying the sorcerer's soul on his destructive expeditions. It is said that the sorcerer himself has created them just as in times past the European wizard constructed his *spiritus familiaris*.

49. This turtle is apparently represented in the stone images which are found on the northern plains and adjacent areas of the eastern woodlands. Cf., for example, Kehoe and Kehoe 1959.

50. Teicher 1960.

5

Totemism and Belief in Guardian Spirits

Toward the end of the eighteenth century the Canadian merchant J. Long lived among the Ojibwa Indians, an Algonkian tribe around Lake Superior and beyond. Relating his experiences among these Indians, he wrote: "One part of the religious superstition of the Savages, consists in each of them having his *totam*, or favourite spirit, which he believes watches over him. This *totam* they conceive assumes the shape of some beast or other, and therefore they never kill, hunt, or eat the animal whose form they think this *totam* bears." Having described how an Indian may lose his hunting luck if he transgresses these taboos, the author defines "this concept of destiny" as "totamism."[1] With this a term was introduced which in the form "totemism" has become one of the most common as well as one of the most obscure terms in the debate on the history of religions.

It must be made clear at the outset that the phenomenon which is related by Long and is well documented—especially

1. Long 1791, pp. 86f.

in North America—has not much in common with "totemism" as used by later theoreticians. This is partly due to the fact that Long misunderstood his informants. The word *totam*, usually rendered *ototeman* in the Ojibwa language, probably refers to a kinship group or lineage (the "gens") which is exogamous, that is, marriage between its members is prohibited. Since the emblem of the group is often that of an animal, the name totem has been transferred to it. Consequently the word totem is primarily linked to the group, not the individual, and the term totemism should above all refer to the beliefs and behavior of the group. There are almost as many definitions of totemism as there have been scholars dealing with this concept. The majority of these scholars have defined totemism as a mysterious relationship between on the one hand an animal species, a plant species, or some other class of natural phenomena, and on the other hand a more or less fictitious kinship group (a "clan" or "gens" depending on whether the lineage is matrilinear or patrilinear).[2] Totemism in this sense is common in large parts of the Old World and it exists both in North and South America. It is, however, exceedingly diverse both in form and content.

In South American totemism clans, men's societies and sometimes whole tribes are given animal names: the Guarina in northwest Brazil are known as the "howler Indians," and the Canella in eastern Brazil have two societies named after the wild duck and the agouti. As Lowie has pointed out, several of these cases involve a very incomplete form of totemism, a kinship of names. Given knowledge of the significance of names among the Indians—a name expresses an identity not only in form but also in essence—one may assume that the correspondence in names also denotes a more profound affinity in essence. A clear indication of a

2. Lévi-Strauss's concept of totemism and his interpretation of the North American Indian materials (Lévi-Strauss 1965), have been refuted in Hultkrantz 1972b. Although Lévi-Strauss's work still seems to convince structuralistic anthropologists it is more a philosopher's credo than an empirical investigation.

deeper connection is evident among the Arawak in Guyana, where each clan is thought to derive from the animal or plant whose name it bears. It is probably erroneous to interpret this as evidence of a belief in transmigration, as has been done by some scholars. The idea of descent from an animal is, rather, one of the expressions for the affinity between the clan and its eponym.

It must be recognized that the ethnographic information available to us at this point for South America offers few, scarcely illuminating, examples of totemism in the sense that the word is used here. Perhaps continued research will shed light on its occurrence in this area.

More reliable and detailed data are available from the North American Indians, whose totemism has become the subject of much discussion. Among the Yuchi in the southeastern United States we meet with an elaborate clan totemism in which clan members regard themselves as descendants of "certain pre-existing animals" whose names and identities they have assumed. The living animals are likewise offspring of these mythic animals and for that reason humans are kindred to the animals whose totems they represent. The people of the bear clan, for example, may not kill bears but they may use the meat and hide if someone from another clan shoots one. Totem animals are held in reverence, are called upon privately in critical situations of various kinds, and are "worshipped" officially in dances during the New Year ceremony. Finally, it should be mentioned that each clan member obtains protection from the clan totem at his puberty ceremony.[3]

This portrayal of totemism is by no means typical for North America. A certain feeling of affinity between the clan and its totem no doubt characterizes most cases of North American totemism (even if a merely zoomorphic clan name is notable in some groups, primarily those of the Iroquois in the northeast and the Zuni in the southwest). But the belief that the clan members are descendants of the totem is by no means widespread. In northwestern North America, for example,

3. Speck 1909, pp. 70f.

the totem is perceived primarily as the guardian spirit who was at one time the helper of the clan's ancestral father. It was stated earlier that the totem poles of the Northwest Coast are. a kind of heraldic poles-of-arms (and by no means images of gods) on which are depicted the tribal father and the guardian spirit, and possibly other figures as well from the natural world or the world of the supernatural. The taboo against killing the clan animal is fairly common in North America, although not as common as in Africa, where it constitutes the most dominant feature of totemism.

It has long been a matter of controversy among students of religion whether the totem spirit is truly the object of a cult. From a thorough analysis of the North American material Goldenweiser reached the conclusion that the totem was not worshipped. Consequently he maintained that the most essential part of totemism consisted in its interlacing of the totemistic conceptualizations and rites with the social system of the group.[4] The question is, however, whether Goldenweiser, as well as many other ethnologists, has confused two different topics, the supernatural prototype of the animal and plant species and the ordinary animals and plants. Toward the latter the clan member feels friendliness and respect; toward the prototype his attitude is not infrequently of a more religious nature. The strength of his religious conviction is naturally commensurate with how strongly he perceives the reality and significance of the totem spirit. In cases where the totem is scarcely more than a name denoting the identity and uniqueness of a clan, even the common eponymous animals are given little special attention. In other cases the totem spirit is a reality, a protector of the clan, in which capacity he may become the center for a religious or at least religio-magical activity. The clan chief on the West Coast of Canada strengthens the affinity with the totem by dressing in its attire and dramatically imitating its movements. On certain occasions he also relates the origin legend linked to the totem. The Yuchi, whom we discussed earlier, dance to honor the masters of animals and the totem spirits at the New

4. Goldenweiser 1910, Goldenweiser 1937, pp. 321ff., 325f.

Year or New Fire ceremony, impersonating these spirits to the best of their ability. The expected result is their continued blessings. It is of course questionable whether this behavior may be called worship. For my own part, I would define it as a cult of the type generally attributed to lower spiritual beings.

It was mentioned that during the puberty rites the young man of the Yuchi was given personal protection by his clan totem, which thereafter became his guardian spirit. Similarly we learn from the Northwest Coast that after fasting, bathing, and strict asceticism the individual may acquire a guardian spirit who constitutes one of the spirits belonging to the clan. The concepts of the clan totem and the guardian spirit are here remarkably fused. Some scholars have also maintained that clan totemism is derived from guardian spiritism which is more nearly universal in North America and has besides a more clearly religious character (the "American" theory of the origin of totemism). Before discussing this possibility we will examine the guardian spirit complex—that belief of which the explorer Long collected partial details among the Ojibwa and which he called "totamism."

The belief in a personal guardian spirit which can be inherited or attained through vision and in some cases taken over through purchase or transference occurs in both South and North America and in the latter continent belongs to the fundamental religious phenomena. Disregarding for now the assisting spirits of the shaman, there is very little information on personal guardian spirits among the South American Indians. It is true that the concept of a subservient *spiritus familiaris*, a spirit which its owner may send out at his pleasure, does occur here and there. The spirit in question here is hardly a guardian spirit in the conventional sense of the word, however, and is apparently not obtained through visionary experiences as is usually the case in North America. A couple of obvious examples of beliefs in guardian spirits may be mentioned, one of which brings to mind the vision spirits of the plains Indians. Among the Charrua in Uruguay, men who wish to obtain guardian spirits seek a secluded hill with a stone mound. Here the Charrua man subjects himself to various forms of self-torture such as fasting and gory self-mutilations, until he envisions the supernatural being who is to become his guardian spirit and upon whom he calls in moments of danger.[5] There has been much speculation as to whether this implies a last remnant of an old cultural link with North America. There is, however, among the Sherente, a primitive east Brazilian tribe, a similar attainment of the guardian spirit but in collective form. During an extended period of drought the men of the village try to find a cure for the crop failure by jointly striving for visions in which rain is promised. For three weeks two groups of men take turns in strict fasting. At the end of the period the men receive visions in which the guardian spirit appears. He recites one or several songs to his suppliant and gives directions about clothing and about the object which will become his fetish.[6] In this case we are reminded also of the visions of the North American Indians.

A concept of a guardian spirit of a unique type is found in the high cultures of South America and Mesoamerica and in the surrounding tribal cultures. It is sometimes called the "alter ego" concept, due to the intense identification of the individual with his guardian spirit, so much so that in certain situations it can become the exponent of his own ego.[7] Another term for the same concept is the Aztec *nahualli*, generally written "nagual"; the conceptual type itself has often been referred to as "nagualism." Since *nahualli* means "disguised, masked," the American scholar George Foster has maintained that the term originally referred to the sorcerer in his transformation as his guardian animal, whereas the guardian animal itself was designated by the word *tonalli* or *tonal*.[8] However, "nagual" has so often been used to mean the guardian spirit, intimately related to his protégé, that it is to our advantage to keep it as an appropriate technical term.

In nagualism are found in condensed form all those charac-

5. Serrano 1946, p. 196, Métraux 1949, p. 568.
6. Nimuendajú 1942.   7. Haekel 1952, Zerries 1962.
8. Foster 1944.

teristics in a guardian spirit by which it is linked to man: if the nagual is strong and powerful, so is its protégé; if one of them is wounded, so is the other, and in the same part of the body; if one of them dies, the other dies too. The Indian may change into his guardian spirit, at least if he is a shaman, and in that form travel far, for example, to the land of the dead. The nagual is at times the generalized spiritual representative of an entire animal species, at other times a single actual animal. It is told of the Tzeltal Maya, for example, that "a man who has a quarrel with another man deliberately shoots animals of the species to which his opponent's nagual belongs, hoping to hit that very animal which is associated with him."[9] The close and intimate link between the human and his nagual is also expressed in the fact that the human is usually perceived as having been mystically joined with the nagual ever since birth. It is mentioned, for example, that the first animal to appear after the birth of a child is its nagual. One is here reminded of the usual custom among Indians elsewhere to name the child after the first animal seen or dreamt about by the mother (or other relative or the medicine man) following the child's birth—a practice which not improbably springs from vague nagualistic conceptual tendencies. However, it may also occur, although not too frequently, that the nagual is acquired in the same way as in the individual totemism of North America (see below).

As was mentioned, nagualism in its extreme forms is centered in the American high culture and its extensions. Thus it is found among the Pueblo Indians. In the Pueblo Santa Ana each individual possesses from birth a guardian spirit who may even prevent his protégé from committing a wrong action and who receives food sacrifices before each meal. Also among the Pawnee in Nebraska, humans are protected from birth by a guardian spirit. More remarkable is the fact that we find guardian spirits of a nagualistic type among very primitive tribes such as the Ona in Tierra del Fuego and the Algonkin in the northeastern United States. Among the Ona shamans fight each other through their guardian spirits: if the

9. Blom and La Farge 1926–27 (2), p. 369.

guardian spirit is wounded, so is the shaman; if it is severely wounded, the shaman will die. Among the Penobscot, an Algonkin group in Maine, the shaman can change into his guardian spirit. The latter is in animal form, and if this animal is killed the shaman will also die.

Apparently the tendency toward an intense association with the guardian spirit occurs in cases where the human partner is a shaman or a medicine man. Haekel has pointed out that the concept of the nagual as common property in Mesoamerica possibly represents a secondary religious development. Originally the nagual may have been restricted to medicine men and socially prominent individuals.[10] Outside of Mesoamerica and the Andean high culture nagualism seems not to occur as a consistently formed complex of perceptions. Occasional incidents of nagualistic conceptions should be viewed as the result of intensified religious experiences in individual medicine men.

Guardian-spirit beliefs among the North American Indians have been organized chiefly according to another pattern, well known through the research of J. G. Frazer, R. Benedict, and R. H. Lowie: the "guardian spirit complex" is a term which refers to the conceptions and rituals pertaining to the personal guardian spirits which are acquired through visions.[11] Consequently they are not given at the birth of the individual but must (at least in the majority of cases) be sought in secluded places, where they appear in visions to the fasting suppliant. They appear in animal guise but are seldom if ever identical to the animal whose shape they have assumed. They endow their protégé with a capacity of one kind or another and as a visible, concrete token of this "medicine" provide him with a fetish, a "medicine bundle."[12] They

10. Haekel 1952, pp. 172f., 188.

11. Frazer 1910 (3), pp. 370ff., Benedict 1923, Lowie 1922. It is a moot question if occasional spirit patrons in the pueblo area should be seen as "guardian spirits," as Hartmann thinks they should (Hartmann 1976b), or as naguals. Functionally there is no major difference.

12. The spirit gives the instruction, and the client assembles the objects required and puts them in a skin pouch. The Crow had more medicine bags than other plains Indians, for they could both buy them and acquire them through visions. See Wildschutz 1960, p. 13.

are less closely linked to the individual than in nagualism and may leave him if he transgresses any taboo assigned by them. Common to the nagual as well as the North American guardian spirit, however, is the fact that they may be regarded as the result of a process by which the helping spirit of the shaman has become the property of the common man.[13] It seems probable that this change is associated with the Indian's well-known propensity for individualism.

The complex of guardian-spirit beliefs is widespread in North America except for the southwest area. The Pueblo Indians, less aware of the experiences of the hunter in the supernatural world and largely devoting themselves to the sober, regulated rituals of the cultivator, generally lack a belief in guardian spirits. Among some tribes in California and southeastern North America, among the northeast Algonkin, and among the Eskimos, the possession of guardian spirits is restricted to the shaman, which, as mentioned earlier, is probably indicative of a more fundamental relationship.

Benedict maintains that belief in the significance of the vision in North America is more common than the notion of the guardian spirit and is consequently a more fundamental element in the religion of the North American Indians.[14] There is much to support the validity of her thesis with regard to the plains Indians.[15] They seek visions at times of disease, death, war expeditions, and childbirth (in order to name the child) without mentioning the presence of a guardian spirit. For the Crow the very search for visions is socially more significant than the attainment of the guardian spirit in a vision. The behavior of the Iroquois is to a high degree adapted to the content of their dreams, and in older times a tomahawk might be unearthed or feeble old men might lay claim to young beauties by the sanction of a dream.[16] Through dreaming, the Mohave in southern California become medicine men, that is,

---

13. Haekel 1947, pp. 113ff.   14. Benedict 1923, pp. 28, 40, 43.

15. On the plains Indian vision, cf. Benedict 1922, Blumensohn 1933, and Albers and Parker 1971. The last article demonstrates how the vision quest changed with ecological conditions and was transformed to suit social ends.

16. Cf. Wallace 1958.

the dream releases their expectations of acquiring medicine man status by giving them a certainty of their vocation. The information given by early white observers that the Indians of New France are entirely ruled by their dreams is probably applicable to Indians in almost all of North America. The vision is not likely, as Benedict maintains, to be genetically more fundamental here than the concept of the guardian spirit. Both of these phenomena ought to be regarded as expressions of a "democratized shamanism," to use Lowie's term.

From a psychological point of view the visionary experience is basic to the development of the guardian spirit complex in North America. Visions may be of two kinds, spontaneous or solicited. The spontaneous vision (with which we may, to a certain extent, equate the nocturnal dream) appears suddenly and unexpectedly. It is experienced only by people with a particular predisposition. Shamans and future shamans are most likely to receive this type of vision, just as is the case among Siberian peoples. The spontaneous vision seems to occur for historical reasons primarily in the areas west of the Rocky Mountains, among the Eskimos in Alaska, the California Indians, the Shoshoni groups in the Great Basin, and the Yuma Indians. The solicited vision, on the other hand, is predominant east of the Rocky Mountains and in parts of western North America. This is the type of vision which is experienced by the great masses of Indians outside the small group of shamans (although the distance between medicine men and other visionaries, as on the plains, may become exceedingly small). In most cases the vision appears after fasting, and among the plains Indians also after mortifications and self-torture. Narcotics may be used. Tobacco-smoking is a sacred act in the majority of rituals in North America, most certainly owing to its stimulating power; it is no wonder that tobacco is frequently used as a means of evoking visions. Here as in other situations the shaman's resources for inducing ecstasy have been taken over by the lay visionary.

In some smaller Indian groups in southern California

visions are evoked exclusively through narcotic poisoning: the one who wishes to establish communication with the spirits takes a drink prepared from the root sap of an herb, the jimsonweed (*datura meteloides*). Other narcotic drugs have been used in closed cult societies for the purpose of evoking visions. This was the case, for example, in the "medicine societies" along the Missouri river, for whom mescal provided entrance to the supernatural world. In Mexico and South America other narcotics or materials resembling narcotics are similarly consumed in order to provoke visions: in Mexico mushrooms (*basidiomycetes*), among the Taino in the Antilles, *caoba*.[17] (For the peyote cult see p. 153.)

In a number of Indian tribes along the West Coast of Canada the guardian spirit acquired by an individual is inherited, that is, taken from the group of guardian spirits which had previously protected his ancestors. In such circumstances the vision is merely affirmatory and consequently of minor importance. On the northern plains the guardian spirits—or, more accurately, the talismans or medicine bundles supplied by the guardian spirits—may be transferred from one person to another. Thus a Blackfoot Indian may purchase from a fellow tribesman a medicine bundle complete with songs, these too initially a gift from the guardian spirit. In many cases the purchase sum is probably an expression of gratitude for the valuable gift and not payment in a strict sense. It is conceivable, nevertheless, that the method of transfer has been stimulated by the white fur trade, as some scholars have suggested.[18]

The quest for the guardian spirit may proceed in several ways. In eastern North America and among the plateau peoples in the west the young boys (in rare cases also the girls) seek visions. Following instructions from their elders,

17. As has been pointed out by, for instance, La Barre (1970, p. 143), nowhere on earth are there as many narcotic plants as in America. The recent enormous research on this topic shows that the Indians were very conscious of their hallucinogenic properties. Indeed, the whole Jívaro religion has been characterized as hallucinogenic (Harner 1972).

18. Cf. Wissler 1912, pp. 272ff., Lewis 1942, pp. 44ff.

they are sent out into the wilderness to pray and fast until they obtain a guardian spirit. Some scholars have characterized this procedure as a puberty rite. This may well be a proper term, although its ranking among the observances and ceremonies pertaining to puberty must be regarded for historical reasons as secondary, as Benedict has rightly maintained. Just as already at an early age the shaman adept may experience harrowing confrontations with the supernatural powers which later will guide his destiny, so the future warrior who approaches manhood sets out to seek and envision those powers which will guarantee his future luck. On the plains it has been common for grown men to seek visions not only once but several times. This pattern probably represents yet another step away from the initial prototype of the shamanic calling vision.

Typically, the vision of the guardian spirit is individual, sought and obtained in solitude and isolation out in the wilderness—for example, on secluded mountains and hills. Having prepared himself with purifying baths, sacred smoking, nightly vigil, and meditation, the supplicant is visited by the spirit. This spirit often appears in animal form but in some visions his shape changes from animal to human. The spirit endows his protégé with that supernatural skill which is his special characteristic or one which it pleases him to communicate, perhaps because his client has asked for this particular "medicine." At the same time he gives instructions on how to cherish this supernatural gift, thereby emphasizing certain taboo regulations, for example, the prohibition against consuming animals of the shape in which the spirit appears, or against hunting these animals, or against using implements of steel in partaking of food. The spirit also imparts medicine songs which will summon him or establish contact with him, later perhaps to be sung by the visionary in the ceremonial dances (as on the plains) or when danger is imminent—we need only refer to the frequently mentioned "death song" of the Indian novels.[19] Last but not least, the spirit describes the

19. See, for example, Landes 1959, p. 47.

appearance of the medicine bundle. Its contents may vary (generally it includes animal parts, pipes and rattles, and among cultivating tribes like the Pawnee also corncobs); in most cases it refers to the visionary revelation and its central figure. The medicine bundle is the visible sign of the presence of the spirit and is opened during ritual forms whenever there is need for the assistance and protection of the spirit.

Collective visions of the guardian spirit are less typical. Even though the puberty initiations mentioned above may be collective in nature, the puberty visions themselves are generally experienced in solitude, or at most a couple of young men may seek them together. Truly collective visions we find on the one hand among some South California groups, where stimulation is from drinking a decoction of jimsonweed, and on the other hand in the Sun Dance, the annual ritual of the plains Indians. The former is a puberty rite, which may be the case with the latter as well, but here visions are often sought also by the elders.

The search for visions in the Sun Dance to some extent follows the same pattern as individually sought guardian-spirit visions. Exhausted by many days and nights of constant fasting, austerities, monotonous dancing, and sleepless vigils, some of the participants in the rite fall into a daze and experience visions of supernatural beings more or less closely linked to the mythology of the ceremonial lodge. It seems as if the annual ritual, too, has been drawn into the magical sphere of the visionary experience because of its tremendous impact on the plains Indians. The most striking connection between seasonal rites and the visionary complex is found among the Mandan Indians on the upper Missouri. We have earlier and in a different context discussed certain aspects of the annual ritual of these Indians, the *okeepa*. The famous Indian painter George Catlin, who visited them in the 1830s, has given a lively description in pictures and words of the painful tests undergone by youths who wished to be accepted into manhood. They were suspended from the roof of the ceremonial lodge with ropes fastened by one end to the roof of the lodge and by the other to needles stuck into their chests just below the skin. Other needles pierced their legs and from them hung ropes dragging heavy buffalo skulls. It is testified that the richest and most genuine of all experiences of supernatural powers took place in the dazed or unconscious state of mind produced by torture. It is obvious that here the self-torture and the visionary search of the plains Indians have united with the annually recurring puberty rites, a unification so strong that the visionary search appears as an integrated part of the manhood festival.[20]

The visionary search and the acquisition of the guardian spirit may largely be regarded as individual undertakings, with the exception of the cases mentioned above. It occurs not infrequently that visionaries, having successfully obtained their guardian spirits, form societies in which those who have the same guardian spirit join together. This is the case among the Kwakiutl on the Northwest Coast, who in the winter replace their social organization based on family relationships with secret societies founded on common experiences of a certain guardian spirit.[21] The Omaha on the prairies have numerous secret societies in which are united those who have received the same visions: bear, buffalo, thunder, and ghost societies, among others. The bear society, for example, which consists of those who have had the vision of a bear, has its own song and its own magic practices. It is often difficult to distinguish these societies from those of the shamans: in any case, they are formed according to the same pattern.

Several societies have been formed as the result of the supernatural experiences of a single visionary. A typical example is that of the tobacco society of the Crow Indians in Montana, founded long ago by a youth who in fasting obtained a vision in which the sun god appeared. As a ceremonial "father" the youth afterward adopted proselytes, who then in turn received similar visions—a pattern characteristic of the plains Indians.[22] Similarly, through the founder's personal visionary contact with the spirit world local ethnic units

20. Catlin 1967; Catlin 1841 (2), pp. 169ff.   21. Boas 1897, pp. 503f.
22. Lowie 1935, p. 274.

may form cult societies. Among the Skidi Pawnee in Nebraska each village is in possession of a sacred medicine, according to tradition presented by a star to the village founder,
the stars being the typical spirit beings of the Pawnee. The
medicine or fetish is owned by the village chief, cared for by
his wife, and sanctified by a ritual performed by a special
priest. Along with these collectively maintained fetishes there
are also individual ones which are buried together with their
owners.

Some of these medicines have become the property of the
whole tribe and are surrounded with elaborate rituals, often
inspired by the dreams of leading personalities. In earlier
times many of them were carried at the head of war expeditions to ensure victory. Famous tribal fetishes are found
among the plains Indians: apart from the stone figure of the
Kiowa discussed earlier, the sacred pole of the Omaha, the
sacred hat and four sacred arrows of the Cheyenne, and the
sacred wheel and the powerful flat pipe of the Arapaho
should be mentioned. The latter, which according to tribal
belief existed before the great flood and is representative of
the Supreme God himself, may not come close to the earth
and may not be looked upon. Therefore during the Sun
Dance, for example, the pipe is kept on a stand wrapped in
several blankets. In this context we may recall the importance
of pipes and the pipe ritual in all of North America. The pipe
has evolved from the shaman's sucking straw, through which
he extracted disease spirits from the patient's body as well as
inhaled tobacco smoke to produce ecstasy. This use of the
primitive pipe no doubt accounts for its later significance in
ceremonial connections.[23]

Whether owned individually or collectively, the sacred
medicine is a symbol for the bond between man and his
guardian spirit: it constitutes a token of the protective relationship between the spirit on one hand and the human partner on the other, who may be either the individual in posses-

23. See Fenton 1953 and Krickeberg 1954. The rich ritual evolved in the
Upper Missouri area around the elaborately decorated calumet stems has been
described in Fletcher 1904.

sion of the guardian spirit or the collective of humans who rely on the help of the guardian spirit. It is more difficult to determine if the fetish is the object of actual worship; at times this seems to be the case, but one is under the impression that such incidents form exceptions to the rule. Far more important, however, is the question of whether the guardian spirit is itself the recipient of a cult. Many scholars are skeptical about this. Some categorically reject the thought, but in my opinion this is unwarranted. The supplicant generally devotes himself to prayer and spiritual submission at the time of obtaining the spirit, and through his actions the plains Indian seeks to arouse the compassion and pity of the spirit.[24] The rituals related to the opening or producing of the medicine bundle are also likely to be accompanied by prayers. Moreover, we have already found that the personal guardian spirit of the Pueblo Santa Ana receives food sacrifices. In any case, it may be established that a cult of the guardian spirit in North America is more prevalent than has hitherto been suggested.

Along with this, the Indian's relationship with his guardian spirit implies an intimate affinity and a reciprocity which in an intensified form may be called nagualism, as was pointed out above. The Indian acquires the characteristics of his guardian spirit. He paints or tattoos himself to resemble the spirit, decorates clothes and weapons with the claws, feathers, or fur of the spirit animal, assumes its name, fabricates a medicine bundle of the parts of its body, and so on. On the plains a man may not kill or eat animals in the shape of his spirit. Among the plateau Indians, however, he hunts those animals before others, because in so doing he is given special luck in the chase by the guardian spirit. Both cases express the close affinity between the hunter and his guardian spirit, the so-called "individual totemism."

Let us now again center our discussion on totemism and

---

24. On the other hand, on the north Pacific Coast the Indian tries through fasting and purifications to make himself so clean and transparent that the spirit is willing to take up his abode in him. Concerning beliefs in possession, see Chapter 6.

the possiblity of its origin in individual totemism. We have seen that the latter conceptual complex occurs primarily in North America, here constituting a characteristic transformation of older, fundamental shamanic concepts and rituals. It is true that American totemism is by no means originally an Indian phenomenon—thus it is lacking among the very primitive peoples, a clear historical hint. On the other hand, totemism within this double continent is apparently more widespread than the guardian-spirit complex. Thus it is difficult to regard the latter complex as the sole origin of totemism. This much seems certain, that both guardian spiritism and totemism express a tendency to identify the human being or the human groups with definite animal species, a tendency which seems to be inspired by the powers revealing themselves in animal form in the world of the hunting societies. Consequently there is a fundamental religious aspect to totemism, as has been clearly indicated.

In North America a direct and apparently generic connection between collective totemism and individualistic guardian-spirit beliefs may be determined with greater accuracy. The latter occurs more extensively than the former, being prevalent among primitive hunting peoples like the Shoshoni and the Eskimos, among whom totemism has not always gained a foothold. In religious attitudes and religious cults totemism seems to constitute a faint reflection of guardian-spirit beliefs. The primary religious experience is here replaced by a cult legend and the direct cult of the spirit has given place to a ritual apparatus, where the submissive religious attitude is less perceptible and the object of the rites less clearly defined. In both complexes the same ritual behavior is discernible: there is in both a prohibition against eating the representative or image of the spirit in the animal world, and in both there are dances imitating the totem (the guardian spirit) to the extent that the dancers dress in its fur or feathers, copy its movements, reproduce its voice, and so on. Also, the symbolic representative of the totem (the spirit) is in principle the same: the personal medicine bundle in guardian-spirit beliefs is exchanged for the clan fetish in totemism (an example of this is the sacred white buffalo hide for the *honga* gens of the Omaha). We have already seen how individual medicine bundles by inheritance or some other form of transference have become collective fetishes for societies, villages, and tribes—a development which undoubtedly alludes to something reminiscent of true totemism. It should perhaps also be pointed out that the disparity between the individual and the collective is sometimes bridged by clan totemism. The Ojibwa and the Menominee on Lake Superior erect a gravestone over a chief after his death, on which in pictographic form are rendered all his praiseworthy deeds and other significant events in his life. There is no indication of his name. Instead, his clan animal is depicted at the top, upside down to denote his death. The individual and his totem are here completely intermingled.[25]

This kind of data seems to support the accuracy of the proposition of certain American scholars that totemism in North America may in many places have evolved from guardian-spirit beliefs and nagualism. Such a development has been postulated for the western Athabascan, the Kwakiutl, and the Omaha, and evidence of it is thought to be found also outside of America, in Africa, Indonesia, and Australia.[26]

25. See the reproductions in Schoolcraft 1851–60 (1), p. 356.
26. For an appreciation of the "American theory of totemism" see Hultkrantz 1972b, pp. 224ff.

6
Medicine Men and Shamans

The French Jesuits who in the seventeenth century were active missionaries among the Indians of New France found serious competition for the Indians' souls from their doctors, or "medicine men," as the Jesuits called them. They were here referring to certain prominent individuals who by virtue of their supposedly supernatural equipment cured the sick and in addition mastered a number of more or less incomprehensible tricks. Accordingly, they were often also called "conjurors" in the Jesuit records. Gradually the missionaries acquired a more balanced understanding of the medicine men's activities. They realized that in the Indian view medical skill was only one of the symptoms of the supernatural capacity of medicine men, and the concept of "medicine" was expanded to comprise every manifestation of supernatural power. Terms like "medicine bundle," "strong medicine," and so forth, are direct translations from certain Indian languages, in which the word "medicine" is used to cover concepts such as *wakan* or *puha*. Our word "medicine man" has in the Sioux language a direct equivalent: he is a *wakan* man.

However, if the medicine man is defined as a person in

Raising the sacred tree, Shoshoni. Photo by author.

Buffalo head hung up on the center pole, Shoshoni. Photo by author.

Offering the skin of a stag to the sun. From Stefan Lorant: *The New World*.

Hopi Natashka Kachina dancers. Photographed at Walpi by James Mooney in 1893. Courtesy of the Smithsonian Institution, Bureau of American Ethnology.

Right: Man with skewers in breast and ropes attached, prepared for the Sun Dance, Plains Indians. Courtesy of the Lowie Museum of Anthropology, University of California, Berkeley.

Medicine Mask Dance of Coast Salish Indians. Painting by Paul Kane, courtesy of the Royal Ontario Museum, Toronto, Canada.

Thunderbird, or eagle mask, Kwakiute. Courtesy of the Denver Art Museum.

(closed)

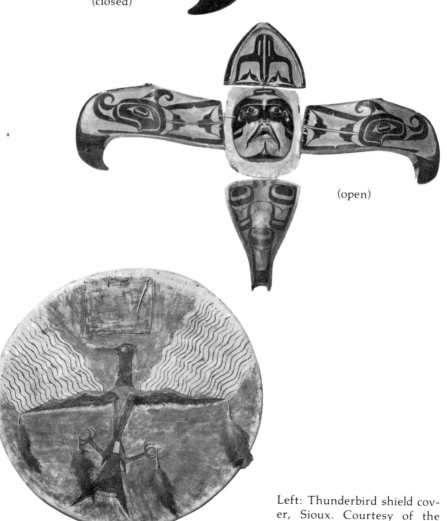

(open)

Left: Thunderbird shield cover, Sioux. Courtesy of the Denver Art Museum.

Left: Cornhusk mask, Seneca. Courtesy of the Lowie Museum of Anthropology, University of California, Berkeley.

Below: The corn dance. Drawing by George Catlin, courtesy of the New York Public Library.

Cornhusk mask, Seneca. Courtesy of the Denver Art Museum.

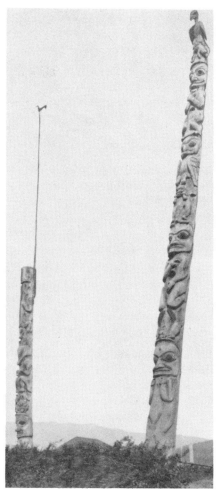

Totem poles, British Columbia. From R. B. Inverarity: *Art of the Northwest Coast Indians.*

Shaman healing, Tlingit. Courtesy of the Lowie Museum of Anthropology, University of California, Berkeley.

Right: Prayer to the sun by Hopi Snake Priest. From Ralph Andrews: *Curtis' Western Indians* (Seattle, Superior Publishing Co.); reproduced with permission.

Medicine bundle, Blackfoot. Courtesy of the Lowie Museum of Anthropology, University of California, Berkeley.

Mandan torture ceremony. Drawing by George Catlin, courtesy of the New York Public Library.

The Last Race, Mandan. Drawing by George Catlin, courtesy of the New York Public Library.

The interior of the sanctuary of the knightly orders at Malinalco, Aztec. Photo by Henri Stierlin.

The interior of the Whale House at Klukwan, Alaska. From Norman Feder: *American Indian Art* (New York, Harry H. Abrams, Inc.); reproduced with permission.

possession of supernatural power it is difficult to draw the line clearly between him and any other individual who has obtained the protection of the powers. I am thinking here especially of the many Indians in North America who have received supernatural gifts through visions. It is obvious that the medicine man is more religiously and mystically gifted than other vision seekers. The difference might be expressed by calling the medicine man an "archvisionary," to use R. Underhill's term.[1] He possesses a stronger supernatural power and generally has access to more helping spirits than other visionaries. Above all, he can cure the sick. This in itself indicates his control of extraordinary supernatural power, since healing often requires the highest mobilization of all physical and psychic resources, visionary insight (clair-voyance), ecstatic disposition, ventriloquism, dexterity, and gymnastic fitness. We may add one more characteristic of the medicine man: he uses his supernatural power for the benefit of society. Its consequences are not limited to himself and his family, as is the case with other acquired supernatural pow-ers.[2] It is his calling to sustain the community in its entirety and on this sustenance his social prestige and his political power are established.

It is not surprising, then, if in both North and South America medicine men have repeatedly come to dominate the religious life in such a manner that the whole religious pat-tern has taken its name from their activity: it is then, some-what inappropriately, called shamanism. I say "somewhat in-appropriately" since shamanism derives its name from the Siberian medicine man, the shaman who establishes contact through ecstasy with the world of the spirits. As we will presently find, by no means all American medicine men are shamans in this sense. Besides, the term shamanism ought to be used in a limited sense, denoting those conceptions and

1. Underhill 1957, p. 132.
2. This is the rule. However, where the community is identical with the family or a small group of interrelated families, the medicine man serves only the family or family compound. This is, for example, the case with the Carib-bean medicine man: cf. Kloos 1971, pp. 213ff.

rites which focus on the person and performance of the shaman, rather than being extended to mean an entire religious
pattern. In the following discussion I shall distinguish between the medicine man and the shaman, but I shall refer to
"shamanism" or "the shamanic complex" for the activities of
both, since that terminology has long been established.[3]

As for South America, a leading authority, Steward, has
characterized the religions of the marginal hunters and
gatherers as shamanism and magic. This estimation is somewhat one-sided, since many of these tribes have a dominant
belief in a high god, whereas others such as the Sirionó and
the Canella lack medicine men altogether. In case of sickness
the dead are here called upon directly without the mediation
of a medicine man: a relative of the sick person implores the
dead for help or manipulates their bones.[4] Among the technically more advanced groups in the tropical forest area
shamanism seems to have a stronger hold, and the guardian
spirits of the medicine men, seldom observed among the
marginal peoples, are here more distinctly outlined. The Tupi
chief is often a medicine man as well and in this function he
takes on an actual cult after his death. Within the Andean
high culture the shaman performs with healing methods inherited from more primitive times.

Similarly, shamanism lives on as a primitive undercurrent
in the Mexican and Mesoamerican high cultures. In North
America it is predominant within the primitive hunting cultures, in the east partly in communal forms (the shaman
societies), in the west with a more individualistic bent, for
here the influences from the collectivistic agrarian cultures are
less apparent. Ceremonial societies may replace the shaman
in his medicinal functions within the extreme agrarian cultures, especially among the Pueblo Indians. Among the Hopi
he is all but an outcast, and the borderline here between
medicine man and dreaded black magician is vague.

3. This is an accommodation to the use of the word among American
anthropologists. Furthermore, there is no convenient term to denote the
complex of beliefs and practices surrounding the medicine man. On the
concepts of shaman and shamanism, cf. Hultkrantz 1973a.
4. Steward 1949, p. 690.

This survey illustrates how common and fundamental the shamanic complex is in America. Its absence among some of the marginal peoples in South America is no doubt due to cultural loss, cultural depletion under ecologically unfavorable circumstances. It is noteworthy that the Fuegians, regarded by many as a "primordial" people, possess medicine men.

What we have here called the shamanic complex displays many nuances both with regard to the forms of vocation and activity of the medicine man and to the nature of his religious experiences. Focusing initially on the medicine man's central function as a doctor, we find that he is by no means always alone in this role. Next to this inspired magician appears the wise-man, who is not required to belong to the medicine men's guild. To cure the sick the wise-man makes use of his factual, empirically gained knowledge (whether self-experienced or assumed through folk tradition), but he does not always possess supernatural power. Curing by application of healing herbs or by surgical incision (such as trepanation) belongs to his methods. The inspired magician may also employ these methods, but on the whole he relies on his supernatural power, at times perceived as an inherent capacity, at times as a guardian spirit outside of himself. It is the use of his supernatural power for medical purposes which more than anything else characterizes the medicine man. The manner in which the power or the spirit approaches its client is reflected in his psychic structure of experience, so that we may distinguish, although quite schematically, two main types of medicine man: the visionary, whose trance is light and whose clairvoyance is distinctive, and the ecstatic, who may converse with the spirits or depart from his own body in deep trance (and then at times be possessed by his guardian spirits). Only the latter should really be called a shaman. Interestingly enough, these two types of medicine men correspond fairly closely to two separate ways of curing the sick and two separate means of diagnosis, both of which dominate Indian America.

Here we come to an interesting conceptual complex, the Indians' comprehension of the etiology of diseases and the therapeutic methods corresponding to these perceptions. As a rule the agent of diseases is a supernatural factor, and among the most widespread causes given for disease we may note enchantment, transgression of a taboo, intrusion of foreign objects or beings, and soul loss.[5] Within this series of causes of disease the two former make up a separate class, being less clearly accompanied by a certain type of therapy than the other two and merely constituting, as it were, the *ultima causa* for the presence of the other two designations for disease.[6] The notion that a human being may be struck by enchantment or sorcery is quite common in America. The conception that the disease is caused by transgression of a taboo is found among the Eskimo, Athabascan, Ge, and Tupi peoples, and within the high cultures, among others. The disease is often abolished after the patient's "confession" of the taboo offense to the medicine man.[7] In some tribes—the Yahgan, the Tzeltal in Mexico, and the Dakota—the disease is thought to be a consequence of ancestral sins.[8] In other words, the curse of the taboo transgression stretches over generations.

The medicine man is called to help in particular when the more direct cause of disease—intrusion and soul loss—are thought to be present. The first of these diagnoses implies that a spirit or an object has penetrated the patient. This disease object is often transmitted by a spirit or an evil-minded person, a sorcerer (in the latter case one may also speak of "black magic" or "witchcraft"). With a diagnosis of this type of disease the patient usually suffers from external injuries or internal pains, and no obvious changes in his consciousness are to be expected.[9] The task of the medicine man

5. Clements 1932.

6. Cf. Foster 1976, p. 778. The Papago of Arizona express their view of similar ulterior motives in making a differentiation between "staying sicknesses," due to crimes against the world order, and "wandering sicknesses," due to contagiousness. It is the shaman's task to diagnose the alternatives. See Bahr et al. 1974.

7. Cf. La Barre 1964, Pettazzoni 1931, and see the map of distribution in Clements 1932, p. 203.

8. Wallis and Wallis 1953.

9. The reader should be aware that this is a most generalizing systematiza-

is to remove the object which causes the disease. Through clairvoyance he determines its position and its nature and then he sets to work: with great technical skill he extracts the spirit or the object from the patient's body either by sucking it out (with a straw or with his mouth directly on the sick man's skin), or by blowing it away or, finally, by massaging it away. The extracted disease object is in some places displayed as an insect, a feather, or something of that sort.

In typical cases of the second diagnosis, disease through soul loss, the sick person is cured by a medicine man of extraordinary ability, a shaman. The diagnosis presupposes that the sick man's soul, generally the free soul (see pp. 131-132), of its own free will or by force has left the body. At times it may have wandered off into the natural surroundings; at other times it may have been carried away by malevolent spirits, especially the dead. In such cases it is up to the shaman to send his own soul or less often, one of his guardian spirits, to retrieve the runaway soul. It may happen that the soul which is carried away by the dead crosses the boundary to the land of the dead, and when this occurs the sick person dies. One who has "departed" under such circumstances, that is to say, appears to the living to be dead, may be recalled to life by a skillful shaman. Then the object for the shaman is to enter the land of the dead, where he is in danger of being caught, and bring back the soul in spite of opposition from the dead. Shamanic tales from various places describe how the shamans battle for life and death with the inhabitants of the other world, and how they are pursued by the dead on the return journey (the legendary motif of "the magic flight").

With this type of disease the patient's state of consciousness is generally anormal: he is delirious and more or less unconscious. To recover his soul the shaman must bring himself to an exceptional state of mind. Only in trance is his own soul able to release itself from his body, cross the threshold to the

---

tion. In many places the trend is to cure diseases affecting the patient's consciousness as if they were due to intruding agents. More will be said about this in a future work on shamanism by the author. Cf. what is said below about the age and distribution of the disease diagnoses.

invisible world, and thereby establish contact with the depart-
ing soul of the sick man. The American ecstatic shamanic
seance sometimes reaches the same dramatic effect as north
Siberian shamanism in its more extreme forms, particularly
perhaps among the Central Eskimos.

Several scholars have maintained that the intrusion diagnosis is older than the soul-loss diagnosis in America. Occurrences of the former are reported from almost the entire double continent. The latter has indeed been found here and
there but primarily in northwest America, from which the
conclusion has been drawn by Lowie and others that it
arrived relatively late from Siberia, where of course it is particularly dominant. More recent investigations, however, indicate that the soul-loss diagnosis actually has been prevalent
in both North and South America, although in accordance
with historical traditions and trends of various cultures it has
been less emphasized in parts of South America, for example,
and more pronounced in the parts of arctic and northwest
North America exposed to Asiatic cultural influences. It
seems that the two diagnoses complement each other: the
intrusion diagnosis is applied to bodily pains and injuries, the
soul-loss diagnosis to mental disorders and debilities. Since
the distinction is psychological rather than historical there is
nothing to negate the possibility that both diagnoses have
existed side by side from the beginning of the culture.[10]

A medicine man who is an able and skillful doctor owes his
success to his supernatural helpers, the guardian spirits. But
the power and helpfulness of the guardian spirit are at the
same time highly dependent on the individual qualifications
and spiritual experiences of his protégé. It is therefore appropriate for us to examine somewhat more closely the psychic
equipment of the medicine man, his vocation and training, as
well as the guardian spirits and his relationship to them.[11]

10. For a discussion of the relationship between the two diagnoses, see
Hultkrantz 1953, pp. 289, 448ff.

11. On these problems, see for North America Bouteiller 1950 and for South
America Métraux 1944 and 1949. For a survey of both continents, see Eliade
1964, pp. 288–336.

It has been pointed out many times that the Siberian shaman possesses a psychic constitution suitable to his ecstatic
activities. The same is to some extent applicable to the American medicine man, especially, of course, when he appears as
a shaman in the true sense of the word. We should note,
however, that American shamanism in general has a more
differentiated structure than the Siberian one and accordingly
demands less often the same intense psychic concentration
from its professional practitioners. To all appearances the
majority of American medicine men perform without subject-
ing themselves to any deeper ecstasy.[12] It is true that the
intrusion diagnosis may sometimes bring on a genuine
shamanic trance: this happens when, as in northern South
America, the medicine man sets out to the world of the spirits
to obtain advice as to how to proceed to cure his patient, or
when he summons his helping spirits to determine the diagnosis or expel the disease through their assistance. But such
measures are on the whole less common. As was pointed out
earlier, the soul-loss diagnosis should properly lead to a
genuine shamanic ecstasy, since the medicine man should
release his soul from his body. Modifications may be in order
here as well, partly because this diagnosis is made less often,
partly because the deep trance of the medicine man is frequently replaced by a consciously ritualistic procedure. Thus
among the Salish around Puget Sound the medicine men
perform a dramatic-mimic rite to restore a lost soul: equipped
with symbolic canoes and paddles they vivaciously enact the
voyage to the land of the dead, the battle with the dead, and
the recapture and restoration of the abducted soul.[13] This is
so-called imitative shamanism.[14] An intermediary form between imitative and genuine ecstatic shamanism is found in
demonstrative shamanism: the shaman proves his success in
curing the sick by holding up for all to see the disease object
that he has extracted or the soul he has restored.[15]

Among those tribes where true shamanic ecstasy is prac-

12. We find another point of view in Zerries 1961, p. 369.
13. Haeberlin 1918.   14. Ohlmarks 1939, pp. 122ff.
15. Hultkrantz 1957, pp. 255f.

ticed, it may show itself as an exercised skill, a result of intensive training rather than simply a natural disposition (we have interesting examples from the Kwakiutl in British Columbia), or as a skill acquired by exterior means. Thus it occurs that ecstasy is artificially induced: South American shamans swallow tobacco smoke and consume decoctions of narcotic plants to attain the proper rapture.[16]

The preceding has shown to some extent that the professional presuppositions of the medicine man vary according to his adjustments to the demands of milieu and tradition. As was once pointed out by Benedict, the most successful medicine man is the one whose psychic resources best answer to the expectations of the group. Consequently there is no reason for us to look for a general type of intellect, endowed with certain characteristics, nor are differences in sex of any particular significance. In this connection something should be said regarding female shamanism.

Male shamanism is predominant all through America, even though there is almost everywhere simultaneous mention of female "medicine men," usually women past menopause. The presence of medicine women is especially noticeable among Indian groups in Oregon and northern California and in Venezuela and Mato Grosso. Their capacity and social position vary from place to place. Among the Bear River Indians in northwestern California males are considered less powerful as medicine men, and therefore most of them are women. Conversely, the women of the Guaraní in Chaco are regarded as less efficient doctors than the men. Besides, only the male medicine men are here entitled to lead great ceremonies, for example, the harvest festivals. The ability to fall into a trance seems to distinguish both male and female doctors, although in this respect the former are credited with more efficiency and better results. The medicine woman among the Bear River Indians extracts the disease ("the pain") from the patient's body with her hands and falls into a cataleptic trance immediately afterward, an example of how the curing of an

16. In Central America the Mazatec shamans sank into a trance induced by the consumption of mushrooms (Wasson et al. 1975).

intrusion disease may be combined with ecstasy. Among the Eskimos some women occasionally perform as shamans, but it is testified that only with difficulty do they achieve the same magical effects as their male colleagues.

Among South American medicine men a unique position was held for a long time by the Araucanians of central Chile. During the nineteenth century they were women, but according to our older sources they once were transvestites, truly homosexual or effeminate men dressed as women.[17] Transvestitism is extremely prevalent in North America; the transvestite, the "berdache," here represents both male and female potency, thereby possessing special supernatural power. Transvestites occur as medicine men among the Netsilik Eskimos, the Sioux, and the northern Californians, among others. Dreams, myths about bisexual gods, and specific personal features (inherent sexual debility or enforced sexual exhaustion through masturbation) have each stimulated the development of the berdache complex.[18]

By their nervous psychic disposition, special bodily features, or other distinctive traits many youths are considered predisposed to becoming medicine men and therefore at an early age, sometimes as young as ten, they come to the attention of older medicine men and others who are interested. For the rest, the process of becoming a medicine man develops along separate lines. The three important ways of obtaining the rank of medicine man, as determined by Bouteiller for the North American Indians, are acquisition by heritage, by a "calling" from the spirits, and by voluntary pursuit of the powers.[19] These means often exist jointly in the same society, as is the case among the Paviotso in the Great Basin.[20] On the other hand, the cultural pattern tends specifically to promote one or the other.

In North America the notion of heritage is prevalent along the West Coast and to some extent in the southeast. A

17. Métraux 1942, pp. 309ff.
18. Cf. Angelino and Shedd 1955. See also Schaeffer 1965 on a female berdache.
19. Bouteiller 1950, pp. 57ff.   20. Park 1938, p. 22.

deceased medicine man is there succeeded by a descendant, to whom he sometimes appears in a dream. Among the Cherokee the magic formulae so typical of them are handed down but not, however, the supernatural powers themselves. The idea of nomination by the spirits is found within approximately the same area but with special concentration in northern and central California and the Great Basin. In many ways it coincides with the concept of the inherited capacity of the medicine man, both of these ideas possibly offshoots of a common form of Siberian shamanism: after the death of a shaman the spirits—that is to say, the guardian spirits of the shaman, as in America—call on a person belonging to the same family as their recently deceased protégé. We note, moreover, that functionally and with regard to geographic distribution the idea of nomination or vocation corresponds in North America to the spontaneous vision within "democratized" shamanism, that is to say, the belief in guardian spirits discussed earlier. In the same manner, the vision quest associated with the acquisition of guardian spirits corresponds to what I have here called the solicited pursuit of powers. This last-mentioned path to the rank of medicine man is common all over North America, from the Eskimos in the north to the Yuma tribes in the south. Indeed, the procedure resembles that of the average man's pursuit of a vision to such an extent that one receives the impression of a very close and mutual connection.

Since the South American ethnographical material is still disconnected and incomplete, particularly with regard to religious concepts and rites, undertaking a similar survey is more difficult. It is, however, possible to confirm that in many places the office of medicine man is hereditary in the sense that an already established doctor transfers his profession to one of his sons. Throughout the whole continent but with particular prominence in the southern parts and up to Gran Chaco, the potential medicine man is suddenly struck by a call from the spirits; in many places they handle him roughly and among the Araucanians he is forced to accept the office against his will. In other parts of South America, perhaps primarily in the forest region, it is usual for one who wants to become a medicine man to establish direct contact with the spirits through asceticism, various rites, and other preparations. To this end narcotic herbs and drugs are employed. Among the Jívaro, for example, one who wants to become a medicine man receives for payment oral instruction as well as the supernatural capacity itself from an older medicine man. The latter squirts tobacco juice from his mouth into the mouth of the novice, thereby also transferring to him his invisible magic arrow. In this manner the novice has received supernatural power, which after a year or so of maturing within him enables him to act as a medicine man. Every evening for a long time to come he also drinks a narcotic beverage, prepared from the poisonous liana (*banisteria caapi*), for the purpose of enabling him to see his helping spirits, foremost among them an anaconda and a water monster.[21]

In the above-mentioned case the charismatic view of the vocation of medicine man is totally disregarded: he is trained for his profession and his contact with the world of spirits is automatically established. Such an understanding of what it means to become a medicine man is found also in North America, primarily in the southeast. Among the Cherokee he becomes a medicine man who learns the magic songs and formulae necessary to cure diseases caused by animal spirits and who properly handles the medicinal herbs used for both internal and external treatment.[22] In this case the break is clearly visible between the spirit-inspired shamanism of the hunting society and the agrarian societies' concept of the medicine man based on rites and skills.

On the other hand, it should be pointed out that spiritual and physical training are essential for the medicine man to attain full working capacity, even if he has received his calling from the spirits. As has been rightly maintained by Métraux,

21. Karsten 1955.
22. Mooney 1891. The animals cause diseases when the postmortem rites due to their bodies have not been observed rigorously (pp. 319ff.). Similar data may be found among the Eskimo and several South American tribes: see Zerries 1955.

the medicine man must in his work make use of a technique
which follows a traditional pattern and which therefore
requires practice and learning. The training is at times so
elementary as to be drawn into the mystical experience: in
many places in South America the guardian spirit, often a
master of the animals or one deceased (for example, a dead
medicine man), is said to impart the right technique. Similarly, the Mohave medicine man learns in dreams how to act.
There is no doubt, however, that the dream here integrates
and sanctions already known observations and experiences.[23]
But as a rule in both North and South America the medicine
man receives his training from an older, experienced colleague or in a sort of school for medicine men. Such schools
exist among the Carib in Guyana, where the novices by asceticism and the drinking of tobacco juice evoke hallucinations of the supernatural powers. Among the Yahgan in
Tierra del Fuego the novice after receiving his supernatural
calling goes to a school, where he is trained for several
months in fasting, singing, and curing the sick, all of which
takes place in seclusion. Among the Dakota on the upper
Missouri the potential medicine man calls upon an older
medicine man and requests acceptance as a pupil before receiving his supernatural experience. Among the Patwin,
Pomo, and Nisenan in central California the novice is trained
by an older relative. Compared to these practices visions and
other supernatural experiences seem to play a relatively un-
important role.

   It should be added that the training of the medicine man
incorporates intellectual, ritual, and gymnastic elements,
with the practical purpose of developing a technique for curing the sick and, to that end, establishing the proper contact
with the supernatural powers. It is of special significance that
the medicine man learns to evoke and associate with his
guardian spirits—without them his every action on the level
of magic, including the curing of diseases, is usually mean-
ingless.[24]

23. Devereux 1957, pp. 1036ff.
24. The Mundurucú medicine man constitutes a remarkable exception to

The guardian or helping spirits may be diverse in nature and have many shapes. In South America they are often spirits of the dead, particularly spirits of dead medicine men, or animal spirits generally identical to the masters of the species. In North America, also, the majority of helping spirits appear in animal shape, but it is doubtful if these spirits are to be comprehended as masters of animals. In principle the guardian spirit is identical to the supernatural power owned by the medicine man, since at the time of the initial vision he took part in its nature and capacity. The medicine man's possession of supernatural power is symbolized by the medicine bundle. He is not infrequently thought to harbor in his body some mysterious substance which is related to the spirit, for example, a quartz crystal (as on the Northwest Coast and among the Carib), an arrow or a knife (among the Jívaro and the Yaguá), or an indescribable "pain" (in northern California). This substance may also assume a living and personal shape and may be sent out by its owner as a disease object. Consequently, a medicine man easily runs the risk of becoming accused of sorcery, especially in the southwestern United States: accusations against medicine men for witchcraft and destruction have assumed major proportions among the sedentary Pueblo Indians as well as among the more ambulatory Navajo and Paiute groups.[25]

The relationship between the medicine man and his guardian spirit or spirits—the number may vary considerably and generally corresponds to the medicine man's qualitative ability—may be described most simply as personal inspiration. Of course this does not rule out the possibility that possession, in its psychological sense, may occur. Several scholars regard it as rather common and refer to the fact that the spirit sometimes is thought to be manifest in objects or

the rule. He becomes a doctor because of an inherited capacity. In fact, all members of a doctor's family take up his profession. The medicine man has not been blessed with a supernatural vocation in a true sense, nor has he received instruction in the art of curing diseases (perhaps that is why the diagnosis of soul loss is missing here). See Murphy 1958, pp. 25ff., 29ff.

25. See in particular Kluckhohn 1944 and Whiting 1950. See also Parsons 1939 (1), pp. 62ff.

beings inside the body of the medicine man (we have just seen this exemplified) or even inhabiting the human being. The latter is the case with the Okanagon, Havasupai, Dakota, and other North American tribes.[26] Nevertheless, psychologically speaking there is rarely a question of true possession. One would be equally justified in declaring the presence of possession when a disease is traced back to the intrusion of an object or a spirit. True possession is only present when the man's own personality is totally suppressed by or in alternation with that of the spirit by whom he is occupied. Such a situation is not frequent even in Siberia, the homeland of shamanism, and there are few convincing cases in America. In North America we hear of such possession mainly among Eskimos and Indians of the Northwest Coast, that is to say, in ethnographic areas where ecstatic shamanism has its strongest foothold. The Eskimo shaman (*angakoq*) summons his guardian spirits by singing and drumming, and when his soul has vacated his body they occupy it. One of them speaks through the shaman, whose voice and behavior change entirely in accordance with that of the possessing being. Similar, although not always as clear-cut, possession phenomena are reported from the Kiliwa in Baja California and from South American tribes such as the Yaruro in Venezuela, the Bororo in Brazil, and the Yahgan in Tierra del Fuego. The entranced medicine man of the Bororo constitutes a medium through which the dead communicate with the living: the spirits possess the medicine man and speak through him, their presence causing convulsive spasms in his body.[27]

Indisputably, through its possession of the medicine man the guardian spirit is experienced as a reality, especially by the laymen, in a more ostentatious and convincing manner than

26. Among the southern Okanagon of the North American plateau the guardian spirit is supposed to reside in his client's breast or heart.

27. These examples have been supplied by K. M. Stewart (1946, 1956). Unfortunately, Stewart has uncritically accepted a number of testimonies which do not describe a real possession, but instead portray a dramatization by the shaman of a spirit entering into him; such a dramatization is not automatically equivalent to psychological possession.

during its appearance in states of inspiration. Possession works by suggestion, and not least in the curing of diseases. The spirit communicates the nature of the disease and how to remove it or, as among the Yahgan, he uses the body of the medicine man as his tool while working with the patient. Where the technique of possession is not put into practice, the same purpose is attained (although not the same psychological effect) through a vision or other inspiration in which the guardian spirit reveals the nature of the disease and advises the medicine man on the course of action. In many tribes the guardian spirit need not even appear, at least not noticeably; the medicine man acts, as it were, by virtue of his spiritual equipment. This is particularly the case if the disease is a result of intrusion. If the condition of the patient indicates that his soul is lost, the medicine man needs the assistance of the guardian spirits to be able to carry through his extra-bodily journey: on his expedition he is accompanied by them and as a consequence of the alter-ego belief he may at times transform himself into their shape. It may happen also that the shaman refrains from undertaking the journey to the other world and instead sends his guardian spirits after the runaway soul.

In summary, then, there are occurrences of possession, but they should in no way be considered typical of American shamanism. Not even the material from the Northwest Coast is fully convincing in all respects.[28] The essential relationship between the guardian spirit and the medicine man is based upon personal inspiration. The trance constitutes the means to a deeper contact, whether it be concerned with the summoning of the spirit (for information about the disease or for the healing of the sick) or the dispatching of the spirit (for the departed soul). The trance requires a capacity for habitual ecstasy and frequently makes great demands on the psychophysical capacities of the medicine man. The result is often

28. Franz Boas, who knew the Indians of the north Pacific Coast so remarkably well, is vague on this point. He vacillates between a possessional and a non-possessional interpretation. See the remark made on this subject by Lowie in Lowie 1937, pp. 152f.

catalepsy, convulsions, or violent personality changes, all of which are open to interpretation as possession.

A good example of a trance with strong inner tensions is offered in the shamanic rite denoted as the "shaking tent," "conjuring lodge," or "spirit lodge." This rite is performed among the northern Algonkin and certain neighboring plateau and prairie-plains tribes. It takes place at night in a darkened lodge. The shaman, bound fast hand and foot, calls on the spirits and falls into a trance. Soon the tent begins to shake, sparks are visible in the smoke hole, and strange animal sounds echo from various parts of the tent. When the worst of the storm has subsided there begins something like a spiritualist séance: the representatives present from the spirit world inform the medicine man through a control about various things on which he has sought knowledge, and they assist him with the curing of sick persons who are present. The spirit lodge of today is experiencing a remarkable renaissance; the author has himself attended a séance where the majority of those present were youths.[29]

In certain connections the shaman or the medicine man wears a mask; this too has been erroneously interpreted as possession. As a matter of fact, the mask indicates a desire for identification with the guardian spirit, an experience of unity with the spirit in no way, however, equated with possession. When the Tlingit shaman calls upon his guardian spirits he puts on a mask to represent each spirit that he summons. He may also put on the mask as he sees the spirit and then perform a wild dance around the fire with violent twists of his body.[30] The "false faces" of the Iroquois are famous: they are a society of medicine men named after the members' grotesque wooden face masks symbolizing various kinds of supernatural beings. Wearing these masks and equipped with tortoise-shell rattles, the medicine men move about the village accepting tobacco from the inhabitants and curing the

29. On the spirit lodge see Hultkrantz 1967, Schaeffer 1969. See also the articles by Collier, Cooper, and others in Primitive Man 17 (3–4), 1944, pp. 45ff., and Lambert 1956, pp. 113ff.

30. Krause 1956, pp. 194f., 199f.

sick.[31] In many places in California there are so-called bear doctors, medicine men whose guardian spirit is the bear and who are transformed into bears as soon as they wear its hide. From several places in Central and South America we hear of medicine men who are changed to jaguars in a similar way.

This tendency toward identity with the guardian spirit, found also in individual totemism, is expressed in other ways as well. The Tlingit shaman, like his Siberian colleague, dresses in a costume alluding to the guardian spirit: it includes a blanket, a hat, trousers, and a nose peg. While in a trance the medicine men in California speak a private language belonging to the guardian spirit and often consisting of archaic words—perhaps due to the fact that the spirit belongs to a time long since past (this is clearly the case, of course, if he is identical to some distant ancestor). The secret shamanic language found among the Eskimos also seems to be constructed of archaic words and phrases. Finally, in some areas, especially on the Northwest Coast, it happens that medicine men with the same guardian spirit unite to form a secret society.

Among the paraphernalia of the medicine men masks and other disguises have been mentioned here. An important aid for establishing contact with the other world is the drum (often of a tambourine shape), used primarily in North America, and the rattle, which occurs throughout the two continents. In South America the gourd rattle is a sacred instrument enclosing the stones in which the spirits hide; the sound of the rattle is accordingly interpreted as the voices of the spirits. The Indians are generally of the opinion that the drum and the rattle summon the helping spirits or frighten away evil spirits. We may add that both of them also serve as instruments of exaltation.

The influence medicine men exert in tribal Indian societies can hardly be overemphasized. The medicine man cures the sick, he reveals things hidden in time and space,[32] leads

31. Fenton 1941, Krusche 1975, Ritzenthaler 1969.
32. Castaneda's reports of his apprenticeship with the Yaqui medicine man Don Juan have not been taken into account in the present description (Cas-

ceremonies and rites, and is in many places the foremost authority on the traditions of the tribe. His supernatural equipment enables him to secure the success of the economy of the group through magic and other ritual activity. In many places he is a rainmaker and a frequent supervisor of New Year, hunting, and harvest ceremonies. Among the Shoshoni in the Great Basin he uses magic to attract the antelope and make them an easy prey for the hunters; among the Eskimos, the Mundurucú, and other groups he journeys in a trance to the masters of the game, requesting them to place their animals at the hunters' disposal. The medicine man also makes war medicine. We may here recall the famous medicine man of the Shawnee, Tenskwatawa, brother of the great chief Tecumseh: bedecked with talismans he stood on a hill behind the battle line singing his magic songs and pointing his feathered spear at the enemy. Besides, the medicine man may be employed in various tasks where there is need for his supernatural capacity. We hear of medicine men with the power to control the course and strength of the winds or to expose evil-minded magicians or to help make women fertile. This last ability is characteristic of the medicine men of the Shipaya in central Brazil, among others. The medicine man is often the preferred bearer of traditions, whether the tradition be exoteric, as is the case when the medicine men are not established as a separate guild, or esoteric, which can easily be the case with secret shamanistic societies.

Finally, it should be mentioned that in many places the mythology and religious legends are permeated by the concepts of shamanism.[33]

taneda 1968, 1971, 1972, 1974). I have given an appreciation of his writings in another connection (in a Swedish review). Don Juan's teachings communicate an interesting picture of a medicine man's world as seen from within, but are of limited use in the comparative study of formal categories of religious expression applied here. Cf. Noel 1976.

33. See Opler 1946 and Hultkrantz 1957.

7
The Great Tribal Ceremonies

We have already caught glimpses of the cults and ceremonies in discussion of their connections with the beliefs that motivate them. The cult apparatus, however, deserves an explication of its own, because few so-called primitive peoples have devoted themselves to religious ritualism with greater emphasis than the Indians, especially the North American Indians. It is certainly true that the most pronounced ritualism is found only connected to the high culture and that ceremonialism is nearly absent among the more "primitive" tropical Amazon tribes and the Shoshoni of the semidesert in North America; nevertheless, ceremonialism is on the whole quite prominent among the Indians. In large parts of North America—the Northwest Coast, the plains and prairies, the southeastern woodland area, the southwest—ritual dances have acquired an intrinsic value, at times obscuring their religious content. The North American ceremonies are often called dances due to the prominent part played by the traditionally fixed rhythmic movements in ritual drama.[1]

1. Cf. Lowie 1915.

Most Indian rites have as their background the great transitions in natural and in human life. Changes in nature are significant for the sustenance of the hunter, gatherer, or cultivator, and the seasonal rites—hunting rites, "first-fruits" (firstling) rites pertaining to the ripened fruit, sowing, planting, and harvest rites—accordingly aim at creating the necessary preconditions for a good yield and are often of concern for the whole society. Life crises, on the other hand, are confined to the individual and his family; hence the rites corresponding to them are generally of restricted following, except for the collectively arranged puberty rites.[2] However, with the strengthening of the chief's power or with the emergence of an upper class, the rites after the death of a prominent leader, for example, may become a matter of national consequence. In certain great tribal rites the phases of natural and human life are coordinated to a cosmic unity. These rites, the collectively organized annual festivals and the ritual systems associated with a binary social structure, no doubt constitute the most important cultic expressions of the Indians and will here be given paramount attention. Considering the succinct character of this presentation, only gleanings will be offered from an abundance of data.

Central among religious ceremonies for most Indians, hunters and gatherers as well as cultivators, are the annual rites denoting the beginning or the climax of the hunting season or the crop year. These may vary in nature from the simple rites performed around animal bones by hunting and fishing groups to the complex ceremonies which take place in the village communities of the cultivators. These ceremonies are often under the auspices of the Supreme Being. Their main purpose is to renew the world and life itself with the aid of the powers, in particular by replenishing the supply of food. In this respect they are reminiscent of some separate "economic rites" in tribal hunting communities, particularly the rites performed around the bones of slain animals.

Our ethnographic material affords no reliable clue to solv-

2. Among the Apache the girls' adolescence rites are the most spectacular ritual arrangements.

ing the question of historical sequence between these simple bone rites and the seasonal ceremonies which have sometimes included similar rituals around the bones of game animals or fish. In both cases the bones have been rearranged in skeletal order subsequent to the meal, thereby securing the rebirth of the animals, that is to say, a continued supply of edible game. In any case, it is obvious that in many places, such as on the plains, minor individual bone rites have occurred alongside seasonal rites within which the same type of bone ritual has been encased. There is a notable difference, however, in that the separate rites are sometimes repeated for each felled animal, regardless of when it is hunted (for example, for the bear and the whale), whereas the bone rites in the collective seasonal festivals are always initial rites linked to the beginning of the hunting season. It is also possible that certain bone rites (primarily the salmon rites on the Northwest Coast of North America) have undergone a secondary development into seasonal rites under the influence of "first-fruits" ceremonies with fruits and berries. The circumstances in northwestern California may well justify such a hypothesis, as we shall soon see.

The great annual festival, also called the New Year rite, is a ritual drama, a recreation of the world undertaken on the ritual level. In certain tribes, especially groups in an agrarian environment, it reiterates the act of creation as it was represented in the myth of primordial times. (In America the direct link between myth and rite is apparently better established among the cultivators than among the hunting peoples.) It is above all a rejuvenation festival which marks the transition from the old year to the new, from death to life, from sterility to fertility. This has found expression in the rites, which emphasize the importance of abundant food supplies, lasting health, and renewed blessings from the powers. Puberty ceremonies and tribal initiations are frequently linked to the annual ceremonies, giving further weight to their rebirth symbolism. All the rites mentioned above, which summarize the most significant phases of the annual festivals, may occur as independent ceremonies but are often organized around the basic theme of the annual festival—the concept of rebirth. This holds true for the "primitive" tribes, and it once was so for the peoples of the high culture. The Inca ceremonies, for example, served several purposes simultaneously: they included manhood rites for the princes, rain and fertility rites, and exorcism of diseases.[3]

Those rites which aim at securing the provision of food always play a prominent part in the seasonal festivals of the Indians. In the small fishing villages of northwestern California the annual festival is celebrated by constructing a sauna which functions simultaneously as a cult house and a men's clubhouse, an institution typical of California. The ceremonial sauna alone, however, is found all over North America except for the Pueblo area. The sweat bath, achieved by pouring water over heated stones, is believed to cleanse the individual of both inner and outer (ritual) impurity and is commonly used in preparation for cult festivals and visionary encounters with spiritual powers.[4] The northwest Californians, for example the Hupa Indians, regard the sauna as a microcosm; its construction and the simultaneous lighting of the new fire symbolize the cosmogony. The arrival of the salmon sets the time for these two activities. The first-caught salmon receives special homage and its capture and disposal are surrounded by rites.[5] The salmon ceremonies seem to be patterned after the first-fruit ceremonies with nuts and acorns, of which there are a multiplicity of examples all over California.[6] In any event, in the ritual complex of northwestern California we find a definite fusion between primitive hunting magic and a recreation ceremony of cosmic scope.

Concern with food is significant also in the Sun Dance of the plains Indians, which should be interpreted as an annual rite, as was clearly understood by W. Schmidt.[7] The Sun Dance, which is held at the outset of summer (nowadays also

3. Cf. Steward and Faron 1959, p. 130.

4. Cf. Krickeberg 1934 and Lopatin 1960. For a good description of a sweat bath see Walker 1966.

5. Kroeber and Gifford 1949. On the fishing rites cf. Chapter 10.

6. Cf. Schuster 1964.

7. Schmidt 1929, pp. 815ff. As was mentioned in the Preface, the Sun Dance has a close counterpart in Siberia. In western North America a near

later in the summer), was originally a thank-offering to the Supreme Being for the plants and animals—primarily of course, the buffalo—he had seen fit to provide for his people, and at the same time a prayer to him for ensured sustenance during the year which was now about to begin.[8] These motifs still hold their given place in the Sun Dance, although without their earlier prominence. The Mandan on the upper Missouri, dancing in a buffalo costume and imitating the sounds and movements of the buffalo, directly express the main act of prayer of the Sun Dance.

Among the gathering peoples and some cultivators who have taken over the ideology of the gatherers the ripening of fruits or crops determines the time of the annual festival. The Creek and Chickasaw of the southeastern United States celebrate the "busk" or *bosquito* ceremony in the month of July when the green corn is being harvested. After four days of purification of houses and people—the latter rid themselves of inner impurities by drinking "black tea" which causes vomiting—the new fire is kindled and the new corn, hitherto forbidden to be touched, may now be eaten.[9] The tribes around the Amazon River in South America observe a New Year festival, *yurupari,* focusing on the celebration of the newly ripened palm fruits. On the upper Orinoco the festival ceremonies are directed to the beneficial spirit who rules the seasons and lets the palm fruits ripen. During the festival sacred trumpets are blown under the palms to make them prolific in fruit, and specially consecrated men whip each other, presumably to stimulate fertility.[10]

Those to whom cultivation was especially important, such

---

parallel is the round dance: see, for example, Ridington and Ridington 1970, p. 60 (Beaver Indians).

8. The Sun Dance, most well-known of the cultic festivals in aboriginal North America, has been described at length in works by Goddard, Lowie, Skinner, Spier, and others, published by Wissler in Anthropological Papers of the American Museum of Natural History 16 (New York 1914–21).

9. See, for example, Witthoft 1949, Hudson 1976, pp. 365ff. Here should also be mentioned the midwinter ceremony of the Iroquois containing a new fire rite: Tooker 1970, pp. 83f. See also Lips 1959–60. For the southwest, cf. Haeberlin 1916. In this dry area the corn dance is primarily a dance for rain: see Hartmann 1976a, p. 17.

10. Koch-Grünberg 1909, p. 189 (quote from A. von Humboldt).

as the Pueblo Indians and the peoples of the great civilizations in Central America and Peru, scheduled their annual
feasts between harvest and sowing (compare the Aztec festival calendar in Chapter 14).

As was mentioned above, another ritual element of the
annual festivals is praying for good health and the cure of
disease. In certain parts these prayers have become increasingly important. Nowadays many take part in the Sun Dance,
for example, only to secure good health for themselves or for
their sick relatives. Under such circumstances, of course,
medicine men and shamans have an important task to fulfill.
At the annual festival of the Uitoto in western Colombia the
medicine men of the tribe drive away all evil spirits that cause
disease.

A third ritual element, the puberty rites, have earlier been
touched upon in connection with the discussion of the vision
quest in North America. They are generally found in one
form or another throughout America. Whether their frequent
association with annual rites is due to practical or to ideological reasons is impossible to tell. It is also quite possible that
they have originated from the annual rites—questions of
such distant origin are always controversial. Of the previously mentioned festivals, the busk ceremony as well as the
Sun Dance are associated with puberty rites. Sometimes tribal initiations are common to both sexes; sometimes the initiations are divided into collective *rites de passage* for boys and
individual admissions for girls.[11] The manhood trial for boys
is generally characterized by fasting, ordeals, and a symbolic
transition to new life—that is to say, a rite of death and renewal totally in accordance with the spirit of the annual festival. On rare occasions the ceremonies for boys are combined
with visionary experiences; as we have seen before, these
were quite common beyond the framework of the annual
rites. With regard to the rites of death and revival there are
great similarities between the initiations in Tierra del Fuego
and California.[12] The initiation of girls is in most cases charac-

11. On the puberty rites of Apache girls see, for example, Basso 1970, pp.
55ff. Cf. also Opler 1972, pp. 1133f.
12. Loeb 1931.

terized by isolation in a special, remotely situated hut at the time of first menstruation. (The married woman must stay in the same hut when she delivers her child.) Because of their ritual impurity girls at first menstruation and women in childbirth must not come into contact with other people. They are dangerous even to themselves and must in many places scratch their hair with a special scratching stick. They are also subject to food and drink taboos.[13]

The prime objective of the puberty initiations is to make the boy or the girl suitable for marriage through a "rebirth"; that is their only function among the Canella, for example. They may also automatically serve as tribal initiations, which is often the case in California, or as admissions into closed men's societies or age groups (see pp. 116-117). In some cases the initiations of medicine men as well are done in connection with the annual festivals, which will be discussed later.

The annual rites are often under the direct guidance of the medicine men: they conduct the prayers, lead the dances, preside over the puberty ceremonies, and instruct those who are being prepared for their own vocation. At the same time they act as mediators between man and the powers. This finds a quite drastic expression in the so-called pole-climbing rite. We may here recall that many Indian tribes acknowledge the notion of a cosmic axis, and that this axis, the link between heaven and earth and often a symbol for the Supreme God, may be represented in the cult by a sacred pole. This pole is sometimes raised in the center of the ceremonial area, or sometimes forms the central post of the cult lodge in which the annual rite is celebrated. There are comparatively few examples of such poles in South America, but in North America they are numerous.[14] Our sources relate that the Indians gather around the sacred pole, perform ritual dances, and pray to the Supreme God or to the spirits and, in South America, often to the spirits of the dead as well. The medicine man tries to establish direct contact with the supernatural

13. See, for example, Driver 1941. Among the Yekuána of the Orinico the girls' puberty hut is situated inside the ordinary lodge: see Wilbert 1958, p. 56.
14. See Haekel 1955.

world by means of the pole. Among the Yaruro near the sources of the Orinoco heavenly spirits descend the pole, possess the medicine man, and through his mouth deliver their message to man. The Maidu in California also tell of spirits climbing down the pole. Among the Salish in the northwestern United States the medicine man falls into a trance in front of the sacred pole of the dance house during the winter dance, an annual rite akin to the Sun Dance of the plains Indians.[15] In other cases the medicine man climbs the pole to experience in a vision the spirits or the Supreme God (as among the Sherente and the Araucanians in South America), or to pray to the Supreme Being (as among the Kutenai and the Crow Indians in North America). The acrobatics of the medicine man on the pole in certain forms of the spirit lodge (he is suspended at the top of the conjuring lodge by one foot) indicate an historical connection with the ritual complex. Evidently the cultic pole has been considered an instrument of the Supreme God and has served simultaneously as a connecting link between this world and the one above. Either the spirits themselves in the visionary experience of the medicine man or he himself in public view has used this passageway between the two worlds.

The climbing of the pole by the medicine man recalls corresponding ritual behavior in north Asian shamanism.[16] Here we are probably confronted with a most archaic and constitutive feature of American Indian religions.

As we have seen, the annual ceremony occasionally takes place in a sacred lodge, at times specially built for the occasion, at times permanent and quite often identical to the men's lodge house (particularly in South America). As was apparent in the preceding, its central post represents the world axis. The ceremonial lodge itself is a cultic replica of the universe, a microcosm within the macrocosm, for only in this ideological framework does the "new creation" dramatized

15. Compare the more "democratized" trance in front of the Sun Dance pole: it is common to both medicine men and other participants in the ceremony.

16. See Harva 1922–23, pp. 133ff., and Paulson 1962, p. 132.

inside the lodge become meaningful. In North America, where we are most markedly confronted with this cosmic symbolism, it is connected, for example, with the New Year lodge of the California Yurok, the well-known "Big House" of the Lenape (the Delaware) and the Sun Dance lodge of the Cheyenne on the plains. As for the ritual house of the Lenape, Speck declares that: "Its floor [is] the earth; its four walls, the four quarters; its vault, the sky dome, atop which resides the Creator in his indefinable supremacy. To use Delaware expressions, the Big House being the universe, the center post is the staff of the Great Spirit with its foot upon the earth, its pinnacle reaching to the hand of the Supreme Deity."[17] It is true that the ceremonial house itself in construction and planning is not a particularly ancient element in the culture of these Indians, but its fundamental ideas probably constitute part of a primeval heritage.

This cosmic outlook is applied also in connections other than the New Year rite. In the Pueblo area, for example, the various cult societies assemble in an often half-underground cult room, the *kiva* (or *estufa*), which in some Pueblo groups contains a covered opening to the nether world, the *sipapu*. This opening is considered identical to that place from which the first humans once emerged from the earth's interior. It is also believed to lead down to the realm of the dead.

The ritual lodge may symbolize the universe and this is to some extent true as well of the open ceremonial area where the annual rites are celebrated. But sometimes the cosmic symbolism is extended to include the whole village or camp site. The camp circle of the plains Indians at the time of the Sun Dance and the arrangement of houses around an open plaza by the southeastern Indians are thus perceived by the inhabitants as miniature reproductions of the great cosmic room. It is above all when nomadic hunting tribes have turned to the more sedentary lifestyle of the cultivator that the whole habitat, at least momentarily, is brought into the sacred sphere. Society is then a reflection of those elementary

17. Speck 1931, p. 22.

powers that generate and sustain the crops, who are given mythological projection in the narrative of the sexual encounter between the sky father and the mother goddess in the act of creation.[18] In other words, in the agrarian societies of northern South America, Central America, and eastern and southwestern North America, we find a religio-ceremonial order with binary halves (moieties) which, alternating with each other or, in some cases, in hierarchical order, dramatically illustrate the creative forces through ritual representations. From its foothold in the agrarian cultures this dual system has spread to certain fishing peoples (the northwest Indians) and to the big game hunters of the plains (the plains tribes, of course, partly deriving their cultures from the agrarian culture east of the Mississippi). Most primitive hunting and gathering peoples both in North and South America lack this sacred dichotomy.

Many ethnologists have maintained that division into moieties is often combined with exogamy and that it may be a superstructure to or a transformation of the clan system. A closer examination of the moieties in America (a matter that cannot be reviewed here) indicates that although this view is frequently correct it is nevertheless nearly always a matter of a sacred dichotomy rendering mythological associations as well as maintaining ritual functions. The moieties are linked to or bear the names of beings or forces expressing the cosmic dichotomy. Most common are heaven and earth moieties, "above" and "below," or moieties named after birds and land animals (or aquatic animals), as is the case among the Winnebago and in the phratry system of the Northwest Coast Indians. Among the Iroquois and the Omaha, as among the Inca, the moieties have sexual associations: the earth half of the Omaha is regarded as female, the heaven half as male. Even when the halves are named after the upper and lower

18. The twin myth is also flourishing: among the South American Tereno Indians the two moieties are called "the good" and "the evil," a circumstance that seems to indicate, according to Lowie, a connection with the mythology of the divine twins. This dichotomy is only topical on the occasion of the yearly war dance. Cf. Lowie 1949, p. 332. See also above, Chapter 3, note 29, on the dualism between the wolf and the raven among the Tlingit.

parts of the country, as among the Apinayé, or are called east and west, as among the Canella and the Tucuna, or summer and winter, as among the eastern Pueblo Indians and the Pawnee, the same fundamental cosmic dualism is revealed behind the name-giving practice.[19]

The ritual functions of the halves depict the pattern that their names are supposed to symbolize. The Canella in the highlands south of the Amazon River outlets have matrilinear exogamous moieties, one of them including the inhabitants of the eastern, the other those of the western part of the village circle. During the rainy season a race is held between the children of the two halves, painted respectively with red and black colors. One half represents east, sun, day, earth, red, and the dry season, the other west, moon, night, water, black, and the rainy season.[20] It is apparent that these binary halves which divide existence between them, in the same manner as in the religions of ancient Iran and China, are thought to promote the life-giving rhythm of the universe and nature by means of their ritual activity.

In eastern North America the dynamics of dual forces are symbolized by the moieties' playing of *lacrosse,* precursor to modern ball-games. Each moiety forms a team which with rackets directs a ball—perhaps an astral symbol—back and forth across the ballcourt, that is, the central festival area of the village. The collaboration of the halves is also expressed in their assisting each other at initiations into secret societies, as among the Tlingit and the Bororó, or at burials, as among the Haida and in the Inca realm. At burials the half that is bereaved of a family member gives itself up to sorrow and lamentation while the other half conducts the ceremonies.

Characteristic of the dual system in southwestern and especially in eastern North America is the division into one moiety of war and one of peace, the former associated with the sky (primarily storm beings), the latter associated with the earth. The Creek in the southeast form an important excep-

19. Concerning the names and functions of the moieties, cf. Olson 1933, pp. 401f., and Zerries 1963–64. See also Haekel 1938, pp. 426ff.

20. Nimuendajú and Lowie 1937.

tion in that their red and white halves, that is, war and peace moieties, are associated with land animals and birds respectively. Among the Omaha bordering the plains the dual system moves into complete function in the summer when they raise their tents out on the rolling plains. Those gentes (clans, *huthuga*) who form the southern half of the camp circle look after the sacred tent in which the war medicine is kept and which is under the auspices of the thunderbird; the gentes in the northern part of the camp are entrusted with the functions of peace.[21] The general principle is that the war chief and the camp militia are selected from the war moiety, while the chief, who presides in times of peace, belongs to the peace moiety (compare the summer chief and the winter chief among the Iowa). This political system, formerly common in southeastern North America and later characteristic as well for many of the prairie tribes, thus clearly has a sacred background.

This sacred chiefdom reached its peak in that formative culture which on the foundation of the dually organized agrarian culture in pre-Columbian times stretched along the coasts of the Caribbean Sea all the way to Florida and adjacent parts of North America. Termed "circum-Caribbean" by Kirchhoff, and called the Gulf tradition at the mouth of the Mississippi and the Mississippian tradition farther to the north, this culture is distinguished by its temples with images and priests, its ceremonial ballcourts, and its sacrosanct rulers. The Natchez Indians on the southern Mississippi were representative of this civilization. Their monarch, the Great Sun, absolute at least in theory, was regarded as a descendant of the sun god (the Supreme Being), was carried about in a palanquin, and received the reverence due to a divinity. At the time of his death those close to him were killed, including his

21. The binary system of the Omaha is well known for its ramifications and logic construction. Cf. Fletcher and La Flesche 1911, pp. 137ff., 194f., and see the analyses in Müller 1956, pp. 152ff., and 1970, pp. 130ff. An important point is that the cooperation of the moieties visualizes the fulfillment of human wishes about harmony and balance in existence and thus takes the place of prayer: see, concerning the Pueblo Indians, Toelken 1976, p. 17.

wife, and his subjects sometimes voluntarily let themselves be executed in order to take part in the honor surrounding the king after death, honor which was to be accorded to him by his survivors in this existence as well as by the dead in the one to come.[22]

Thus the religious role of the chiefdom is most accentuated in the socially stratified beginning high culture where the hereditary peace chief of the agrarian village has risen to nearly divine proportions. Already in simpler cultures the chief seems to have attained a supernatural aura: the plains Shoshoni consider it self-evident that a successful chief possesses supernatural power, and the Botocudo elect the most skillful medicine man as their political leader.[23]

22. Swanton 1911, pp. 100ff., 138ff. See also Radin 1959, pp. 83ff.
23. Cf. Lowie 1960, pp. 285ff. See also Boglár 1971, p. 333 (Piaroa in Venezuela).

8

Cult Organizations

In addition to the great tribal rites, and partially in association with them, there are religious ceremonies which are managed by more or less closed cult corporations. These may have different structures. In South America the men have distinguished themselves from the women in specific men's societies, and in North America they have further separated themselves from each other by age group. Women's societies also occur sporadically. Earlier we observed how religious sodalities could develop from the visionary experiences of leading individuals; the secret societies of medicine men are closely related to these fellowships. Finally we note the priestly societies organized around sacred rites and cult objects.

Although the importance of the men's societies may be rather more sociological than religio-historical, they sometimes also function as cult organizations, not least in connection with the annual rites. It is typical of these clubs, which in America are found chiefly in California, around the Amazon, and in Tierra del Fuego, that women and children are excluded from the social and sacred community of the men. Among the Ona, for example, the men appear disguised as evil spirits and demand food from the frightened women. The behavior of the men's organization at the annual ceremonies is characterized by great secrecy. The Arawak south of the Amazon and other groups in adjacent territories celebrate the so-called *yurupari* festival at the ripening of the palm fruits. The ripe fruits are carried in open baskets into the village, and at the head of the procession are men blowing large sacred trumpets. These trumpets represent the vegetation spirits and are at other times kept in a hidden place outside the village known only to the members of the men's society. The function of the giant trumpet among these Indians recalls that of the bull-roarer at the tribal initiation rites of the California Indians: this instrument which is kept secret from women and children can, as we have seen earlier, represent the dead, the culture hero Kuksu, or the thunder god. (The age groups on the prairies and plains of North America are of interest in this connection inasmuch as they organize dances and ceremonies with varying religious content: for instance, they may be in charge of setting up the Sun Dance.)

The women's societies are less frequently encountered than the men's, but like them they are likely to have cultic functions. Thus among the village tribes on the upper Missouri the so-called goose women perform special ceremonies to promote a good corn harvest and to attract the buffalo herds. This task was also discharged by the "society of the white buffalo cow," a female order among the Mandan named after a legendary albino buffalo, presumably the mistress of the buffaloes.

Much more interesting than the above-mentioned forms of organization are the secret societies characteristic of certain types of religion in North America but scarce in South America. In North America they have three main centers; California, the Northwest Coast, and the territory around the Great Lakes.[1] The Californian *Kuksu* societies were discussed above and we will presently return to the rites of the North-

1. Cf. Kroeber 1932, fig. 6, p. 409.

west Coast and the central Algonkin. In South America the
societies occur sporadically on the outskirts of the high culture. Thus the Mojo in eastern Bolivia have a jaguar society
consisting of members who, having been bitten by jaguars,
have consequently become medicine men. They worship the
jaguar god in a special temple, the "drinking house," decorated with the skull and claws of the jaguar; they perform
magical rites to protect the village from jaguars; and they
purify hunters who have killed jaguars. Furthermore, the
jaguar men are supposed to be able to transform themselves
into jaguars.[2]

There are different opinions among scholars as to the origin
and fundamental character of the secret societies.[3] It is fairly
safe to view the North American societies within the wider
connection of puberty rites, men's societies, and the institution of the medicine man. Loeb's analyses of different ceremonial organizations show that the tribal initiation rites, the
men's societies, and the secret societies often follow the same
patterns, and that the rites of introduction to the tribe in one
place correspond to initiation rites to the secret society in
another. Data from the Northwest Coast and the Great Lakes
prove that members of the societies *de facto* had the capacity
and functions of medicine men.[4] The historical constellations
may differ, but in general it may be suggested that the puberty rites have provided a pattern for forms of initiation, the
men's societies (wherever they have existed) have encouraged
tendencies toward seclusion and secrecy, and the institution
of the medicine man has contributed by rendering purpose
and force to the societies.

2. Métraux 1943, pp. 12ff.

3. As Lowie has shown, the well-known thesis proposed by Schurtz that
secret societies were born from the antagonism between the sexes is widely
exaggerated. All such developmental theories must be taken with caution.
When in Chapter 10 a sketch is presented of the probable lines of evolution
this is done with the definite reservation that the final result was not necessarily reached in America—it may very well have preceded the first immigra-
tion waves to this continent. Analogies with the Old World are not lacking—
far from it. However, we find numerous links in the chain of evolution in the
New World itself.

4. Cf. also Eliade 1964, pp. 313ff. Cf. Lindig's discussion of the Omaha and
Iroquois medicine societies: Lindig 1970.

Secret societies seem largely to be collective transforma-
tions of the institution of the medicine man, with an accompanying weakening of the visionary and a strengthening of
the dramatic elements. In principle, of course, "medicine-
manhood" and shamanism constitute an individually oriented conceptual and behavioral complex without immediate relation to belief in a god, for example, or to collective
rites. Consequently, it reveals its genetic connection with the
hunter's world view and his almost atomistic society. But
we have seen that medicine men receive instruction from
older colleagues, being in some places trained collectively so
that there is reason to speak of actual "medicine-man
schools." This collective training is partly intended to help
them obtain visions (unless they have already had them) and
partly to introduce to them the professional knowledge and
secret traditions of the medicine man. The training is completed with an initiation rite marking the transformation of
the candidate from an ordinary being to an inspired bearer of
specific supernatural gifts. In Oregon and northern California
the newly-appointed medicine men tread the "doctor's
dance," in which their teacher acts as fore-dancer; among the
Toba in Gran Chaco the novices are lined up, whereupon they
are whipped by the instructing medicine man. In other parts
of South America the medicine man pretends to shoot powerful objects—stones, arrows, and so on—into the body of the
initiate.[5] This ritual initiation undoubtedly breaks with the
fundamental idea in shamanism according to which a vocation (a "calling") and the resulting extraordinary experiences
form a natural introduction to the profession of medicine
man. Only in those cases where the supernatural experience
is artificially brought about at the time of the initiation, as in
the Mandan *okeepa* ceremony, may we speak of a meaningful
initiation. In other cases the initiation becomes either a ritual
repetition of that mystical moment when the novice, in a

5. These mysterious objects that are thereafter enshrined in the medicine
man's body fill a double function: on one hand they embody his supernatural
faculties, his "power"; on the other hand they are identical with projectiles.
The medicine man can send out the latter against an enemy to make him sick;
cf., for example, the Indians of northern California (see Chapter 6).

trance, receives the power of the spirits, or else a substitution for that supernatural experience. We have seen above how even in the shamanizing act a genuine ecstatic experience may be replaced by a dramatic pantomime.

There is therefore much that points toward the medicine man's ritual initiation as being something secondary, an analogous representation of the tribal puberty ceremony.[6] The genuine, unsought shamanic inspiration is seldom to be reined in to such an extent that the "calling" and the ritual initiation coincide. The latter seems to me to be essentially an extension of the puberty rite. (Contrary to this the puberty vision, as we have seen, is likely to have derived from the shamanic visions.) Among the plains Sioux, for instance, initiates are divided into those who will be appropriated as full-fledged members of the tribe and those who will be incorporated among the medicine men.[7] The symbolic death-and-rebirth rite, often enacted through torture or self-torture as in the Sun Dance of the plains Indians, may have a shamanistic background, but it is also part of the cyclical conception of life displayed in the collective puberty ceremony and connected with the annual festival that marks the transition from the old year to the new, from death to new life.[8] Consequently many medicine-man initiations take place within the framework of the annual feast. Usually, however, they tend to be free of this setting. The exclusive experiences of medicine men and mutual interests in their profession lead to new forms of organized coexistence, and initiation rites are probably transferred to them, as well as other significant parts of the ceremonial for New Year rites.

6. This is an hypothesis. I am not unaware that in Siberia the vocation and learning period of the shaman-to-be is finished with a formal initiation ceremony, the one among the Tungus taking place at the annual rite. Similar initiations among the southern Siberians, such as the Buryat, have been interpreted by Harva, and after him Findeisen, as the result of influences from the religions of Far Eastern civilizations. Cf. Harva 1938, pp. 485ff., 496ff., and Findeisen 1957, pp. 66ff.

7. Walker 1917, pp. 60ff.

8. For the rest, A. van Gennep seems to be quite right when in the ninth chapter of his famous work *Rites de passage* (Paris 1909) he declares that the theme of death and rebirth naturally reappears in numerous rites expressing transformation and renewal.

Against such a background the development of secret societies in North America becomes fully intelligible. In its most pronounced form the secret society is an assembly of ritually initiated medicine men who proceed with the celebration of the annual rites in an exclusive and esoteric setting.[9] In its secondary, derived form the secret society is an association of individuals who obtain certain distinct privileges in this life or the next through the initiation rites and who are entrusted with medical or cultic functions. In both cases the medicine men have directed the development, and their ideas and objectives are basic to the aspirations of the societies. This becomes obvious when we take a closer look at the ritual of the secret societies on the Northwest Coast and among the central Algonkin on the Great Lakes.

The Kwakiutl on Vancouver Island and on the mainland to the north celebrate their great annual rites in winter under the guidance of the remarkable *hamatsa* or cannibal society, foremost in rank among the secret societies of the tribe. Its supernatural protector is "the cannibal of the North," a mysterious being partly connected with the cosmic pole (with a cultic impersonation in the dance house), partly figuring as an apparent representative of the dead. Initiation into this society, which recruits exclusively from the higher aristocracy of the complicated Kwakiutl social system, proceeds in the following manner. At an opening ceremony attended both by the old *hamatsas* and by the novice, the sudden call of the cannibal god's pipe is heard from the woods. The novice then rushes up and disappears from the ceremonial house. He retires to some isolated, remote part of the deep forest and here, it seems, he hears from an older *hamatsa* his clan's origin narratives, which tell how his ancestor once met a member of the spirit world who since then has been the guardian patron of the clan. The novice now spends some time in seclusion and fasting, and at last he beholds in a trance the spirit who appeared to his ancestor. In a state of excitement he returns to the ceremonial lodge and disappears behind a screen that represents the dwelling of the cannibal god. Next morning he

9. The shamanic origin of the secret societies has been particularly underlined by Loeb. Cf. Loeb 1929, pp. 266ff.

appears again and together with the senior initiates he tears to pieces and consumes parts of a corpse. The novice also bites those who approach him, for he embodies the cannibal god who has "seized" him in his chamber. Gradually he is healed from his sacred madness.[10]

The shamanic background seems clear. The first part of the initiation, the visionary experience in the forest, follows to a moderate degree the same pattern as that of the shaman at the moment of vocation, even though the shaman falls ill and experiences spontaneous visions. The second part of the ritual recalls the dance of the shaman in his father's house after the return from the forest. It is, however, expanded by a substantiating rite, the devouring of and identification with the society's patron by the novice—in other words, a rite of death and rebirth.[11]

A rite of the last-mentioned type forms the main element of the initiation ceremony in "the great medicine lodge" among the central Algonkin around the Great Lakes and among their closest Sioux neighbors. The ceremonial lodge here, as among the Kwakiutl, is a replica of the universe, a fact that plainly indicates its origin in the sacred structure of the annual rites.[12] The founders of the society were probably to be found among the Ojibwa (or Chippewa) Indians. For them the society, called _midêwiwin_, consists only to a small degree of real medicine men.[13] The members (_midê_) are generally recruited from men and women interested in occult procedures, who can pay the necessary entrance fees and who

10. Boas 1897, pp. 500ff. See also Müller's scrutiny of the documents and his interpretation of the rites: Müller 1955, pp. 65ff. For a modern appreciation of Kwakiutl religion see Goldman 1975.

11. On the shamanic origin of the rite see also Drucker 1940, pp. 229f.

12. For a closer examination see Müller 1954. Müller makes a distinction between two lodges: an older lodge in Minnesota that is centered on the Supreme Being, and a more recent lodge in Wisconsin that is centered on the culture hero. In the latter lodge the candidate represents the culture hero during the adoption ceremony. Some American ethnologists, notably Harold Hickerson, consider the medicine lodge to be a post-contact rite: see Hickerson 1962. If that was the case, which is far from proven, the invention was probably made on the pattern of an annual New Year ceremony.

13. Recently a specialist suggested that the grand medicine society originated as a protest against individual medicine men (Dewdney 1975).

wish to belong to the society for social, religious, or medical reasons; they are frequently sick people in search of healing power in the mysteries. All initiates are regarded more or less as medicine men, especially those who have reached one of the two highest of the society's four levels. Nobody is accepted into the society who has not first been instructed by an older, respected member for a considerable period of time. He gives information about various things, such as the manner of invocation and exorcism, medicinal plants and their use, and so on. At the same time he instructs the candidate in the sacred primordial myth.[14]

After these thorough preparations the initiation can take place. Essentially it has the characteristics of a rite of death and rebirth, its mystical power enhanced by the assertion that the novices receive visions at the same time. The initiate-to-be is brought to the medicine lodge, *midêwigan,* where all *midê* have gathered. The foremost among them "shoot" *mîgis* (white clam shells) into his body, by touching him with their medicine bundles. The initiate now falls down "dead" but comes to life again, having once more been touched with the same sacred objects. As a sign of his new distinction as a *midê* he then receives a sacred song and a medicine bag for his *mîgis* symbolizing the supernatural powers that he is now supposed to possess.[15] It is evident that the ritual depicts the course of events related to the acquisition of a supernatural helper by a medicine man or other visionary. It is also evident that it resembles the shooting ceremonies that we just reported from the medicine-man schools in South America. In still other places in North America we find the shooting ceremony as an initiatory rite, namely among the California Luiseño.

Among the central Algonkin the purpose of the medicine dance is to strengthen the vital force of the initiates and to

14. The most renowned among these etiological myths derives from the Menominee who represent the Wisconsin lodge (cf. note 12 above). According to this myth the culture hero received the medicine lodge as a token of the reconciliation between himself and the lake spirits which had killed his brother the wolf.

15. Hoffman 1891, pp. 143ff.

prolong their lives. The Menoninee of Wisconsin, moreover, pledge that the initiates will after death be guaranteed a good reception in the realm of the dead. The Winnebago, a Sioux tribe on Green Bay, believe that a whole series of reincarnations are secured by participating in the medicine society.[16] Consequently, we see how the New Year rite's conception of reincarnation has been given an eschatological emphasis within an esoteric framework, exactly as was the case in the Eleusian mysteries.

The secret societies and assemblies of medicine men have had an important religious function in stimulating theological speculations on the divinity and the fate of man. Much of what seems to be advanced in Indian belief has its origin here. Furthermore, by their very character these societies have created the presuppositions for an esoteric shamanic tradition. Among the Menominee, for instance, there exists in popular belief an irreconcilable conflict between the water beings and the culture hero, whereas the traditions of the medicine society tell of their final reconciliation.[17] In this connection it is of interest to share Walker's records of the training of medicine men among the Oglala Dakota, a branch of the great Sioux family. In a secret ceremonial language each candidate is informed of Wakan Tanka, "the great mystery," "the great supernatural being" who constitutes the sum and substance of all gods and spirits in the universe. He is one, and yet he can be experienced in numerous shapes such as thunder, sun, buffalo, rock, and so on. These beings are found in groups of four and four, subordinated to each other in hierarchical order and along superficially classifying principles. To all appearances the system is an attempt to combine the experiences of a number of spirits and gods in nature and the atmosphere together with the experience of one Supreme Being which, due to its character, must manifest itself in all areas. Walker's informant willingly admitted that this whole speculation was a mystery known to the medicine men but not to the people.[18] With these and similar data from other

16. Radin 1945, p. 25. 17. Cf. note 14 above. See also Chapter 4.
18. Walker 1917, pp. 78ff. Unpublished field notes by Ella Deloria, herself a

peoples as his point of departure, Radin has formulated, although much too generally, his thesis on the distance between the medicine man or "the religious formulator" and the "man of action."[19] It can be said against Radin's thesis that where secret societies are lacking, the medicine men are by no means always the outstanding thinkers or the best protectors of tradition.

According to Loeb, priest societies should also be counted among secret societies. It is true that the borderline between the shamanic medicine man and the priest at times appears slight; for example, both may indeed receive training for their mission and to a high degree the training creates the priest. It is also true that the priest societies are clandestine in nature and often keepers of secret traditions, but since their objective is totally different from that of the secret societies described above they will not be designated as such. Priests and priest societies belong to technically more advanced cultures with permanent cult sites and collectively preserved cult objects, where their role is that of the cult servant, not of the inspired magician. In America, therefore, we find them above all within and in the vicinity of the high culture. Only in North America do they seem to have crossed this borderline (probably resulting from a process of deculturation, since formerly the impact of the high culture was felt rather far to the north).

We have already been able to establish that in some places in South America the medicine men officiate at annual festivals and other ceremonial proceedings. Their priestly functions are most conspicuous on the periphery of the Andean high culture. Among the Diaguita in northernmost Chile the medicine men form a special class, which is made apparent in various ways, for example by their living at a distance from other members of the tribe. Like other medicine men they

---

Dakota, seem to give a more popular version of the world of the gods. To a certain extent the oscillation between unity and plurality in the concept of god was also a popular heritage, as several sources seem to imply. Cf. Hultkrantz 1971, pp. 72ff., Hartmann 1973, pp. 186ff., Powers 1975, pp. 53f., Brown 1976, p. 30. The sophistication of Dakota philosophical and religious thought has been demonstrated and emphasized by Brown (1970).

19. Radin 1957.

cure the sick, but in addition, they direct the religious rites performed for the benefit of the field crops; on these occasions they sacrifice to the powers deer heads penetrated by arrows. A neighboring tribe in eastern Bolivia, the Mojo of the Arawak family, appoint special medicine men to priestly functions, while others serve as village oracles. The same classification occurs among their neighbors, the Manasí, but here the difference between the two groups is intensified, although they are subjected to the same training. In the Cuna tribe on the isthmus of Panama there were at the arrival of the Spaniards holy men who were at once priests, prophets, and medicine men; nowadays there are only medicine men, one testimony among many others to the decline of the circum-Caribbean civilization from a rising high culture to a primitive peasant culture.[20]

Also in North America there is a gradual transition from medicine man to priest. In the eastern woodlands and on the plains the priestly office is above all associated with the fetish complex, here developed to great intensity, as was earlier observed. Individual medicine bundles or fetishes connected with the supernatural experiences of a definite person have here to a certain extent changed to collective fetishes common to societies of visionaries, as among the Crow and the Dakota, or to clans, as among the Sauk and the Fox in Wisconsin, or to villages, as among the Pawnee in Nebraska. The keepers of these holy fetishes preside over them with such ritual formality that in this function they must be characterized as priests. Sometimes the original visionary or his descendant is the keeper of the sacred treasure, as for example the hereditary warden of Arapaho's famous flat pipe; sometimes the task is entrusted to someone else, for instance, to a person who has beheld in a vision the spirit connected with a tribal fetish used through many generations. Among the Pawnee the priests (who are also medicine men) carry out

20. The Cuna medicine men use a mnemotechnical pictography to remember magical chants belonging to certain shamanic procedures, for instance at childbirth. Cf. Holmer and Wassén 1953.

special rites around the village fetish when the first thunder is heard at the beginning of the planting season.[21]

A firmer priestly organization is found in the Pueblo culture, this northern offshoot of the old Central American civilization. As cases in point we may choose the Zuni in New Mexico and the Hopi in Arizona, the two "classical" Pueblo groups. In the Zuni pueblo there is found alongside a widely known men's society, which in its dances represents the ancestors (*koko*), a great number of fraternities with predominantly priestly functions. Unlike the men's society, they perform their ceremonies in hidden cult rooms, and their ritual is for this reason partly unknown. Among the more significant of these corporations are the twelve medicine societies, each one specializing in a certain disease. These societies, which perform in the winter season, have much in common with the shamanic secret associations discussed above, such as initiation rites with death-and-rebirth symbolism and cures of disease (extraction of alien objects) under ecstasy. More decidedly priestly in character are the fifteen *ashiwanni* who—in similarity to the men's society, by the way—are obliged to dance and sing to bring about rain. Taking place in summer, their dances are addressed to the rain gods. They may confine themselves up to eight days in their cult room (*kiva*), where they have an altar as well as fetishes. The role of the priestly corporations in the Zuni society is stressed by their appointment of the high priest (*pekwin*) as well as the political officials.[22]

The Hopi Indians have two well-known organizations of priests, the antelope and the snake societies, and their ritual performances are popular tourist attractions in the American southwest. These societies, possibly originating from the horn and snake clans, perform their dances in winter and

21. Such rituals surrounded all bundles. For example, the Plains Potawatomi (Mascouten) opened their tribal bundles so that these could distribute health, happiness, and blessings: see Howard 1960, p. 222. A good description of an Arikara medicine fraternity, the Buffalo Society, has been given in Howard 1974.

22. Stevenson 1904, pp. 62ff., 163ff., 409ff.; Bunzel 1932, pp. 512ff., 528ff.

give each other mutual assistance. The antelope society performs a dance with vegetation symbolism in which an ear of corn plays a central part, while the snake society executes a rain dance, the "snake dance," during which the dancers have venomous snakes in their mouths. The dances are inserted into a nine-day cycle typical of the Pueblo Indians: the first seven days are devoted to secret preparations in the subterranean cult room, with purification ceremonies, singing of liturgical hymns, and dramatic representations of the cultic legends. On the following two days public dances are held on the village plaza: the dance of the antelope priests on the eighth day, and the snake dance on the ninth.[23]

The priest, the master of ceremonies, the cult servant, plays a much greater part among the Pueblo peoples than the medicine man, who is here held in contempt, as among the Hopi, or feared as a wizard, as among the Cochiti. The priest is undoubtedly better adapted to meet the demands set by the cultivator and his sober view of life. Although he has taken over from the medicine man the practice of preparing for his sacred mission through isolation and fasting, dancing in fantastic costumes, and much else, it is through this knowledge of rites and traditions and not through his own mystical experiences that he maintains his position. The medicine man is often a distinct personality, violent and dramatic. The priest, on the other hand, is generally a more restrained and harmonious individual. In the Pueblo community the priest becomes the ideal manifestation of the balanced mentality, said by Benedict and others to be fairly typical of the Pueblo Indians.[24]

23. Fewkes 1897, pp. 275ff.

24. It should nevertheless be pointed out that Benedict's interpretation (Benedict 1935, pp. 56ff.) is too generalizing. Certain Pueblo rites are of an orgiastic, far from "Apollonian" character: see Dozier 1970, pp. 78ff.

9

The Soul and Life Hereafter

For the American Indians as well as for most other "primitive" peoples religion primarily serves the present life: it protects livelihood, health, and success. The thought of life's termination is pushed aside even though the wealth of legends concerning meetings with apparitions and travels to the land of the dead display a greater interest in the next world than would seem likely from the explicit evidence of the creeds themselves.

Death is an anomaly, a disturbing and frightening element of existence. It disrupts the group, spreading sorrow and bereavement among family members and threatening the individual with bodily annihilation. The inner and outer attitudes toward death vary in accordance with the cultural milieu and cultural pattern. The plains Indian awaits his own death stoically, almost indifferently, but he fears the ghosts that haunt the burial grounds and the darkness outside the camp. When someone dies, the Athabascans burn the hut of the deceased and flee the site of death. On the whole, their fear of death is less than their fear of the deceased. Similarly, the spirit of a dead Ijca Indian is chased out of the village nine days after death. The Finnish scholar Karsten has tried to show with numerous examples from South America that this fear is actually concerned with the spirit of disease which, having penetrated the sick person, emerges after his death both as a surviving soul and a death demon.[1] But this explanation is too specific and may, if at all, be referred to only if death is brought on by the "intrusion" of a foreign spirit. Fear of the dead, of the substance of death, and of the frightening circumstances of death are surely of much greater significance here.

Mythology provides an account of why death came into existence. In many areas of North America west of the Mississippi it is told, as was mentioned earlier, that two divine persons, generally the Supreme Being and the culture hero, at one time determined the fate of man. The Supreme Being wanted man to live forever, but his colleague called for man's death lest the earth become overcrowded. And through the persistence of the culture hero or by divination this conclusion was reached: Man must die after a short life span.[2] The establishment of death in primeval time is in many instances indicated in myths of the culture hero, one of the twins, or the primeval man being the first to die and thereby becoming ruler in the realm of death. Thus the brother of the Menominee culture hero, Wolf, who was drowned by the water sprites, became lord of the dead.

The belief in a life hereafter was in earlier times firmly established in primitive Indian tribes and statements to the contrary should be considered with reservation. An integral view of the world and of life, the weight of inherited traditions, and the repeated evidence of visionaries who have looked beyond death have strengthened this belief. Special significance should be accorded the visionaries, some of them ordinary individuals who in feverish dreams or through dreamlike sensations in a coma imagine themselves reaching the land of the dead. However, most are medicine men who in intense ecstatic visions experience a journey to the land of

1. Karsten 1926, pp. 183, 477f.   2. Boas 1917.

the dead to hold council with the dead or to bring back a captive soul.

In this connection some attention must be given to the conception of the soul, which is at once the result of and the basis for these remarkable experiences. In all of North America except the southwest the belief recurs in one form or another that man is equipped with two kinds of soul, one or more bodily souls that grant life, movement, and consciousness to the body, and one dream or free soul identical to man himself as he is manifested outside of his body in various psychic twilight zones. When the body lies passive and immobile in sleep or unconsciousness this latter soul sets out to visit faraway places, even the land of the dead. The free soul of the ordinary individual finds its way at random. The medicine man may intentionally direct his free soul there and, contrary to the layman, he generally may then return to the world of the living. Death comes when man's free soul is definitely caught in the world of the dead; then also the body soul, often conceived as breath, slips its moorings.[3]

This ideology of the soul, which has counterparts in Europe, Asia, and Africa, is prevalent also in South America, even though a systematic investigation of pertinent concepts is still lacking and consequently the exact circumstances cannot be determined. Several tribes that have been thoroughly investigated, for example, the Mundurucú, display an obvious dichotomy in their conception of the soul. However, there are in South America many instances of soul-representations of a different structure. Such is the case among the Waica on the upper Orinoco, who appear to lack a true concept of a free soul, and among the Jívaro, who seem to have merged the concepts of a free soul and a guardian spirit.[4] Such irregularities occur to some extent in North America as well, where, for example, the Yuchi and the Sioux tribes display an interesting four-soul system (four being of course the sacred number) based on an original dualism of the soul. Another remarkable development in North

3. Hultkrantz 1953, in particular pp. 52f., 272f.
4. Harner 1962, pp. 258ff.

America, particularly observable among the Naskapi of Labrador, is the progression of the free soul to a "guardian soul" when liberated from its dependence upon the body.[5] However, among the Ona in the southernmost part of South America the guardian spirit has become the free soul of the medicine man, having incorporated at least some of the most important functions of the free soul in the process of shamanization.[6] The high cultures and their fringe areas in both North and South America present a monistic conception of the soul. It is not unlikely that a weakening of shamanism here has led to a corresponding weakening of the dualistic conception of the soul.

The belief in dual souls and in a soul that can be released from the body seems to have been stimulated primarily by the experiences of the shaman. As was mentioned earlier, one of his most important tasks is to send his free soul to the land of the dead in order to save and restore the free soul of a sick person—the latter having either blundered over to the other world on its own initiative or having been lured there by deceased relatives in need of company or envying the living his good fortune in being alive. This technique of curing the sick stands or falls with shamanism. In the sober atmosphere of the high culture both the experiences of trance and of the shaman lose their significance, thereby somewhat reducing the strength of the belief in the releasable soul.

The journeys of the shaman and to a lesser degree those of the dreamer and the febrile sick have also provided material for the numerous folkloristic tales about the journey to the land of the dead. The difficulties the shaman encounters in reaching the realm of the dead—difficulties that the sick person is not always subjected to since his soul is magnetically drawn there—constitute the basis for many legends of nightmarish obstacles along the way. In North America there are descriptions of water and sheets of fire blocking the road, rocks threatening to crush the traveller, monsters threatening to devour him; by the gates to the land of death a human-like

5. Speck 1935, pp. 41ff.; cf. Hultkrantz 1953, pp. 374ff.
6. Gusinde 1931–37 (1) pp. 744ff.

Cerberos is waiting to snatch his brain, thereby erasing his memory of the glory of life. Whoever happens to eat the tempting giant strawberries on the way has forever deprived himself of the possibility of returning to life. In eastern parts of North America, for example among the Ojibwa in the north and the Choctaw in the south, there is a tale about the slippery pinewood log leading over a rapid stream, across which the soul must pass; at times the log changes to a writhing snake. Balancing on the log, evil humans slip and fall into the whirling waters and are transformed into fishes and toads.[7]

Similar tales circulate among the Indians in South America. In some of these the medicine man is also described as a psychopomp or a "guide of souls." The Manacica believe that immediately following the funeral ceremonies the dead person sets out on his journey to the land of death with the medicine man as his guide. The two of them have a long way to go. The road leads through jungles, across mountains, seas, rivers, swamps, and up to the large borderline river that separates the land of the living from that of the dead. Here they must pass across a bridge guarded by a divinity.[8]

In both North and South America the Milky Way is regarded as the path of souls. This must be considered in the light of the belief among certain tribes, for example the Kwakiutl on Vancouver Island, that the Milky Way is identical to the cosmic pole. (At times the rainbow serves the same function.) The Thompson Indians in British Columbia picture the path of souls with a diagram of a cosmic tree. The cosmic pole is, as we recall, a connecting link between heaven and earth frequently utilized by the medicine man. Once again we are reminded that shamanic experiences underlie the conceptions of the road to the realm of the dead.

The path of souls is not always one and undivided. In the northern hemisphere the Milky Way splits into two streaks. Not unexpectedly, the Indians have associated this phenomenon with concepts of different passageways to the other world and of dissimilar fates after death. Tradition has it that

7. Hultkrantz 1957, pp. 69ff.   8. Koch-Grünberg 1900, pp. 129ff.

one road leads to heaven, the other to the underworld, or that one path leads to the blessed land of the dead and the other brings downfall and annihilation. We will presently return to the ideas that have motivated this differentiation.

To most Indians the realm of the dead constitutes the natural goal for the wandering of the dead beyond the grave. It is indeed true that the concepts of this realm are at times vaguely defined, as is the case with the Athabascans in Canada. But in general, belief in the realm of the dead is there, although unformulated and without fixed outlines. In many instances, however, the formulation of mythology and legend provides quite a vivacious picture of conditions on the other side, one which, supported as it is by the insights of visionaries, has become incorporated into the expectations of the faithful and their anticipations of life after death.

A pervading characteristic in the descriptions of the land of the dead is its representation as a true copy of the world of the living. The classic representation of the other world in North America is that of the "happy hunting grounds." This idea was originally attributed by the whites to the tribes east of the Mississippi, but it does, in fact, more appropriately characterize the nomadic tribes west and north of this river. Accordingly, many plains Indian tribes picture the dead as existing on a rolling prairie, successfully hunting buffalo, living in *tipis* (tents of buffalo hide), feasting and dancing. East of the Mississippi expectations of postmortem existence are closely connected with maize cultivation and agrarian festivals, as is natural among more or less agricultural peoples. Similar details are to be found in descriptions of the other world in the northeastern part of South America. Disregarding certain peculiarities soon to be mentioned, a more detailed presentation of the various other worlds in different parts of America would merely give a picture of life on earth made better or worse.[9]

Where life after death is conceived as something unreal or at least less factual, the concept of the death world loses

9. One may find relevant examples among plains and woodland Indians in North America in Moon Conard 1900. Concerning South American Indians, see Tentori 1955, pp. 199ff.

its severity and its firm contours. It either becomes less attractive—shadowy, pale, gloomy—or else it is replaced by the notion of *das ganz andere* defying any idea of form and content. The peculiar character of the other world is also expressed by describing everything there in reverse, as among the Indians at Puget Sound: During the day the dead are skeletons, but at night they look like humans, alive and energetic; they walk upside down, they do not hear loud speech but listen to yawnings, and so forth.

The location of the land of the dead may vary. Sometimes it is not precisely determined, at other times it is considered quite close to the land of the living. It is the belief of the Cubeo, a Tukano tribe in the northwestern part of the Amazon territory, that the ancestral grounds are situated in the immediate vicinity of villages of the living. The Blackfoot in Montana and Alberta place their other world, "the sand hills," out on the plains a day's journey away from the camp of the living. It is, however, more common to imagine the dwelling place of the dead as situated at a great distance from this world and preferably on a different level: westward out in the sea (tribes along the Pacific Coast), beyond the sunset (Amazon tribes), in heaven (numerous hunting-and-gathering peoples) and underground (some agricultural groups, for example, the Pueblo Indians). Although the opposite can be exemplified, it is generally true that the "other worlds" above ground seem more propitious and cheerful than the one below.

Expectations or anxieties concerning the next life may also depend upon the spirit pervading a culture, the cultural pattern in a socio-psychological sense. Sometimes the joy of life is so strong that existence beyond death must appear empty and frightening under all circumstances. However, an individual's attitude toward the transition to the other world is above all determined by the conceptions he entertains about his own destiny. Many Indian tribes expect humans to be allotted different dwelling-places after death depending on their social status or on various external circumstances.[10]

10. In rare cases the differentiation of destinies after death is reflected in a curious fractionalization of the destinies of the several souls. Thus, among

Such a differentiation is realized when "the evil" are separated from "the good." It is doubtful that Christian impulses have stimulated the development of such a concept; rather it may be safely maintained that they have gradually come to strengthen an already established dualism. Elimination of socially inferior elements—thieves, adulterers, murderers, and others, according to the prevailing system of moral values—is required of the living by the moral code of the tribe, and is also reproduced in the other world. This agrees with the circumstance mentioned above that whatever characterizes present existence is by analogy reflected in the next life. "Sinners" are excluded from participation in the other world. They must rove about as ghosts on earth or else they perish on the journey to the next world or are restricted to a land different from that of the ordinary dead. It is worth noting that the Indians lack a concept of a last judgment beyond the grave, as well as the concept of an actual retribution. If at times the destiny of the morally deficient is described in gloomy colors it is meant as a warning against antisocial tendencies.

Other evaluations may also contribute to differentiation beyond the grave, such as reactions to the circumstances surrounding death. In many American religions a separate realm of the dead is assigned to women who have died in childbirth, to people struck by lightning, to suicides, drowning victims, and others whose death is unexpected or violent. Because of the extraordinary circumstances of their deaths these categories of individuals have been enclosed in a tabooed region and consequently they arrive in a place beyond the reach of the ordinary dead. Those who are left unburied and those who have not received the proper funeral rites are also dissociated from the mass of the dead. Whereas

---

the Bella Coola of the north Pacific Coast and the Kiowa of the southern plains one of the souls goes to heaven, while another goes to the underworld. Usually, however, the free soul departs for the realm of the dead and the body soul dies or (less often) reappears as a roving ghost. This is the case, for instance, among the Tewa of New Mexico and the Shipaya at the lower course of the Xingú.

the former groups, except for the suicides, at times are better off than other dead, those who are unburied generally lead a dismal ghost existence on earth. Spooks and apparitions appearing as rattling skeletons or ethereal translucent spirits frightening the wits out of people with their shrill whistling are recruited partly from the unburied bodies, partly from the putrefying corpses in the burial grounds.

Diverse occupations, and in more advanced cultures rankings in the social structure as well, automatically lead to a more or less clearly outlined differentiation after death. The Mundurucú, for example, believe that the men who blow the sacred trumpets travel to a land where the forests abound in game and the waters in fish and where people may play their instruments and live the good life. Men and women who can perform the ritual dances for the mistresses of animals, the "spirit-mothers," go to another land where they spend their time dancing together with the animals appearing there in human shape. Those who have been killed by the Yurupari spirits must go to their less idyllic realm.[11] Among the Mundurucú as well as among other tribes in both North and South America, whites have their own dwelling place.

The belief that the dead person wanders to the other world is paralleled partly by the concept that life continues in or near the grave, partly by a view of his existence as a new individual on earth in the shape of a man or an animal. Belief in reincarnation is widespread all over America, reaching a climax among the Eskimos, where it also takes on its most peculiar forms. The Eskimos link reincarnation to the naming ceremony of the child.[12] Some Algonkin tribes east of the Mississippi practice a remarkable adoption rite: an outsider, adopted by a family that has lost one of its members, takes over the name of the deceased and is then regarded as the dead person reincarnated.   ⅄

Burial customs are numerous. Inhumation is primarily observed in South America (furthest south and in the Amazon

11. Murphy 1958, pp. 23f.
12. Wachtmeister 1956. This author has published, in Swedish, a detailed work on belief in transmigration in North America.

area), alternating with burial in huts and in coffins placed above ground. In North America platform exposure is customary across vast areas of the continent east of the Rocky Mountains and in Canada. In addition, there are occurrences of burials in trees and in coffins and cairns above ground. The Pueblo Indians and scattered groups in other areas bury their dead in the ground. Cremation is mentioned here and there, on the West Coast, among other places. The Amazon peoples are known for their secondary burial, that is, when the flesh has decomposed the bones of the dead person are dug up from the grave and placed in an urn. In ancient times the Iroquois and Algonkin south of the Great Lakes practiced secondary burial: every tenth or twelfth year at the "feast of the dead" the remains of all those who had died since the previous feast were buried in a large communal grave.[13] Endocannibalism, that is, eating from family corpses or ashes, is reported from the western Amazon area and from the lower Mississippi (the Tonkawa), among other places.

Burial customs provide evidence that the dead occasion both fear and love but not worship. On the whole, ancestor worship has never been particularly strong among primitive Indians in America.[14] It occurs most distinctly in South America, especially among tribes situated closer to the northernmost part of the Andean high culture. The Cubeo hold their tribal meetings under the auspices of the ancestors, who appear when summoned and are then symbolized by giant trumpets. Among the Cágaba the ancestors no longer play any active role, but are held in reverence by virtue of being founders of all cultural institutions, including religious ceremonies. The Uitoto as well as other groups in the northwestern part of the Amazon region believe that the ancestors return during the initiation and funeral rites of the men's society. It is characteristic, however, that the dead here constitute a collective of nameless and forgotten figures, instead of

13. Hickerson 1960.
14. It is possible that the lack of linear kinship systems (so prevalent in Africa) has been an obstacle to the evolution of an ancestor cult: cf. Tatje and Hsu 1969.

identifiable individuals as in the high culture.[15] A near equivalent to the Uitoto cult can be found in the southwestern areas of North America, where the men's society of the Pueblo Indians attends to the cult of the *kachina* (among the Hopi) or *koko* (among the Zuni)—rain and fertility spirits largely recalled from deceased ancestors. Unlike the Uitoto spirits, however, these may be identified through the masks worn by the members of the men's society in the famous *kachina* dances.[16]

In some tribes the dead appear as guardian spirits for the medicine men. Not infrequently in South America, deceased medicine men become protectors of their living colleagues. It is exceptional in North America for ordinary visionaries to have the deceased as their guardian spirits. However, medicine men performing the conjuring rites of the spirit lodge have ghosts for their spirits.

15. Steward and Faron 1959, p. 304.
16. See, for example, Fewkes 1903 and Dockstader 1954. The feelings of identity with the *kachina* in the man wearing its mask have been well expressed in Sekaquaptewa 1976, pp. 36ff.

Historical Patterns of Development and Modern Forms of Religion

After this rapid phenomenological survey we shall now attempt to capture the main features in the development of the history of religions among the tribal Indians of America. Considering that we are dealing with peoples who have left no written documents—in any case none prior to the arrival of the Europeans—we must rely on reconstruction, and at that a reconstruction with many reservations. Finally, we shall note certain significant religious forms of modern times. Most of these may be illustrated by source material left by whites who had been in contact with the Indians. In some cases we have access to unique Indian autobiographies, collected by ethnographers and missionaries.

A correct history of Indian religions can hardly be written until a series of specific investigations in the fields of archaeology and ethnography have clarified many complicated problems, if such an enterprise is now at all possible. After all, America includes two continents with thousands of ethnic groups, each one with a long history in the areas of religious conceptualization, mythology, and cult forms. As is well known, many religions of the tribal jungle Indians are still unexplored today, and there are numerous disconcerting gaps in our knowledge of the religious life of the North American Indians. With only a few exceptions, our information of the religions of the Shoshoni, Athabascans, and coastal Algonkins is highly diffuse and incomplete. Unfortunately, many of the peoples we are dealing with here have disappeared without leaving noteworthy traces of their religions. Moreover, even in areas better known ethnographically, continuous development is only partially observable, and by pre-Columbian times reduced to mere traces.

Therefore our survey must be limited to the main patterns of historical development. With the aid of an ecological method enabling us to compare archaeological strata with later ethnographic cultures we may establish an historical sequence between various types of religious patterns that otherwise are found to a certain extent side by side. This means that we may identify the broad, fundamental stages of religion and characterize them with reference to an evolution definitely manifested throughout America from a tribal hunting culture (hunting, fishing, and plant-gathering) via a farming culture to an irrigation culture (cultivation aided by irrigation). The idiosyncratic changes within the large religious structures we do not reach.[1]

The oldest stratum of religion, then, is represented by the conceptualizations and rites of the hunters (and of the fishers and the gatherers). The interest of the hunter is focused on the luck of the chase, the health and prosperity of the individual, and the security provided through the continuity of the world and the life process. Through rites of a partly magical, partly religious nature the hunter seeks to assure himself of a good supply of food. The Winnebago Indians anticipate the results of the approaching hunt by shooting arrows into

1. For the religio-ecological approach to American Indian religions see Hultkrantz 1965b. For an historical-ecological approach to American Indian cultures see Meggers 1973, Steward 1955, pp. 78ff.

the tracks of the prey; the Mandan, dressed in buffalo masks, portray in a mimic dance how the buffaloes are wounded by their arrows and cut up by their knives. It is important that the felled prey be ritually buried with their bones arranged according to the structure of the living body, as only in this way may the return of the animal be assured.[2] This ritual procedure is sometimes applied to each individual animal. This is especially the case in the whale cult widely found among the fishing peoples around the Bering Sea[3] and in the bear cult present in the more northern parts of North America (and Eurasia).[4]

The bear cult displays great uniformity in rites as well as concepts over very large areas. One may mention, for example, how Lapps as well as Indians relate in legends how the bear sucks his paws in his lair. In both places there are attempts to rid oneself of the guilt incurred at the killing of the bear: he is either asked for forgiveness or the deed is blamed on strangers or on the bear's own negligence. When the skeleton is buried the bear is asked to report to his kin, the other bears, how well he has been treated and he is asked to urge them to present themselves to be caught.

When other animals are subjected to a ritual burial it is mostly in connection with the first kill during the hunting or fishing season. Such is the case with fish ceremonies in some tribes on the upper Orinoco, such as the Achagua and the Sáliva, and among the fishing Indians along the West Coast of North America down to northern California. Among the Hupa and the Karok in northwestern California the first-caught salmon denotes the beginning of a new year and a new fire is therefore kindled.[5]

This animal ceremonialism is at times addressed not to the spirit of the animal but to the master of animals or the animal species. This spirit, the owner and leader of the animals, must also be propitiated before or after the hunt. The concept

---

2. Cf. Paulson 1959. See also Chapter 7.
3. Hultkrantz 1962, pp. 386ff. Cf. also Lantis 1938.
4. Hallowell 1926, Paulson 1965.
5. Gunther 1926, 1928; Kroeber and Gifford 1949.

of the master of animals is perhaps not characterized by any special degree of differentiation, but its significance cannot be too highly emphasized. The master of animals appears to lie behind the development of the guardian spirit of the individual hunter, the one who primarily gives good luck in the chase, and he may have altered the concept of the culture hero in a theriomorphic direction.[6] Otherwise the majority of spirits in the religious world of the hunter are as a matter of course given animal shape. This is true also of many beings in mythology. The characteristic animal shapes of North American mythology constitute an archaic element in the world view of these Indians.

The medicine man or shaman, the miracle worker inspired by his guardian spirits, provides for the health and welfare of the hunter and his family. Those rites which aim at the preservation of health are as fundamental in significance as the hunting rites. (In modern Indian reservations they hold a prominent position, the rites associated with food production and wars having become less current.) In many places in South as well as North America the medicine man has established control over the hunt and its magic. A great number of supernatural beings—free souls, helping spirits, spiritual beings from the realm of the dead—owe their existence in man's mind primarily to the visions of the medicine man. We have already characterized as a "democratized shamanism" the custom, widespread in North America, of seeking guardian spirits through visions.

The Supreme Being provides the ultimate guarantee for the security of the hunter's existence. In many of these tribal cultures he appears as a leading figure, a power beyond the powers, and his direct contact with mankind is manifested chiefly in the yearly rites. The great annual festival may be said to confirm the tendencies to secure world stability and the continuity of years in a conservative culture deeply rooted in traditions. The annual rites are more characteristic of the American hunting cultures than has been generally maintained.

6. Hultkrantz 1961, pp. 61ff.

In each representation of a religious pattern it is the rites that are likely to become the focal points around which religious imagery is organized. One must not be misled by this into thinking that the structure of Indian hunting religions has a ritual fixation. As a matter of fact, the immediate experiences of the supernatural and hence individual conceptualizations are generally more highly valued among the hunting and gathering peoples than among the cultivators, for example. As we will find, this has to do with the cultural pattern itself.

The Indian hunting cultures, primarily located in the northern and western parts of North America, in southernmost South America and parts of eastern Brazil, are distinguished by their simple technology, their uncomplicated social structure (here we disregard the intricate accounts of kinship structure) and their tendency toward individualism. This tendency, sometimes turning into social atomism, but mostly contributing to social cohesion, as among the Kutchin (Loucheux) in Alaska, is clearly revealed on the religious level in the isolated world of experiences of the individual, his fasting visions, and his reliance on his own power or his guardian spirit. With the growing dominance of social segmentation, the hunting cultures, particularly the more complex ones, developed a certain collectivism, manifest in such religio-social phenomena as totemism, clan fetishism, and secret societies. Frequently, however, agrarian ideological traditions contributed here, as for example in Brazil and on the prairie.

The farming cultures of the New World are chiefly found in southern North America and northern and central South America, having superimposed themselves upon the old hunting cultures without completely obliterating them. Whereas correlations between the American hunting cultures and those of the Old World are evident—and in North America most directly so—such genetic connections between Indian agrarian cultures and Asiatic neolithic farming cultures are more dubious. It is obvious that the agrarian-ideological influence in many places in America has not been particularly penetrating. As Witthoft has pointed out, in the corn belt of eastern North America, agrarian religious rites are based upon the firstling rites of the hunters and collectors.[7] One single but expressive example: when gathering corncobs the Miami take special care not to harm them, for to do so risks receiving a bad harvest in the next year. Compare with this the rule of the hunters that harming the bones of the animal means loss of luck in the chase.[8]

From an ideological point of view, agrarian cultures focus on the powers that surround agriculture and its products, their religious symbolism being elicited from the ripening processes of the fruit and the seasonal life cycle of the crops and vegetation. At the same time this culture displays a clearly collectivist tendency, apparently connected with the sense of community in life and work.[9]

As a result of this collectivist attitude the conceptualizations resulting from the trance and dream experiences of the individual hunter are of less worth than the seasonal rites connected with labor, primarily the rituals of sowing and harvesting. It is an observable fact that rite on the whole becomes predominant over belief, that the medicine man relies more on initiation and achieved knowledge than on experiences of the supernatural, that he functions as a master of ceremonies and is often a member of a medical fraternity (for example, the "false face society" of the Iroquois). The individual miracle-worker is replaced by the priest, the protector of tradition and the curator of the cult, especially in communities where the permanency of settlement and, accordingly, the cult, have become well established. No priests are found among the migratory manioc cultivators who burn the woodlands of the tropical Amazon country, but there are priests among the sedentary Pueblo Indians cultivating corn in the southwestern United States.

Such predominance of rituals in these religions is illus-

---

7. Witthoft 1949, p. 84. In South America likewise the agrarian rites have partly recovered the hunting rites: cf. Zerries 1961, pp. 326f.
8. Schoolcraft 1851–60 (5), pp. 193ff. Cf. Hatt 1951, p. 874.
9. See Underhill 1948.

trated by the fact that each important conceptualization is captured in a myth or a legend constituting the text of an agrarian rite. Mythology here, more patently than among the hunting peoples, serves a double function. On one hand, as among the hunting peoples, it may provide a self-contained system of concepts. On the other hand, it makes current and gives sanction to matters of faith and cult, frequently in the form of an etiological narrative. The ritual myths are at times reminiscent of those in the Old World. The myth about the creative union between the sky father and the earth goddess, typical of many agrarian religions, is enacted by ritual intercourse or in ceremonial dualism involving moieties of heaven and earth. Frequent correspondences with decidedly agrarian rites are also found in the narratives of Mother Earth or the vegetation goddess, a central religious belief in this culture with its generally matrilinear social structure and female influence on economic life (the women sow and harvest). We have earlier been able to observe the myth of the corn goddess's fate as a mythological projection of the events and rites that are associated with sowing and harvesting. It is characteristic that in myth as well as rite the goddess is represented by an ear of corn.

The great agrarian festivals are linked to planting and harvesting, or in some cases to planting, ripening, and harvesting. Here the cultivators have in part been able to join with the traditions of their predecessors, the gatherers. It is not out of the question that the ritual trinity in agrarian ceremonies is based on rites at the decisive crises of human life (*rites de passage*), birth, puberty, and death.[10] In many cases the harvest festival seems to be a direct continuation of the annual ritual of the hunters and gatherers. The Cherokee, for example, place their green-corn festival in August at the harvesting of the corn. It is introduced by a new-fire rite and a ritual purification by water and medicine.[11] We have seen earlier

10. The observation was made by Underhill: see Underhill 1957, p. 134; cf. Witthoft 1949, pp. 4f.

11. Cf. the "busk" feast of the Creek (Chapter 7). Ritual purification is an important element in the preparations of all the ceremonies. It is usually performed through sweat baths but may also be attained through inhaling

among some Amazon tribes that the annual feast coincides with the ripening and harvesting of the palm fruit. The rain ceremonies, particularly common in very dry regions, are partly linked to the great agrarian rites, partly independent. Fertility and rain spirits are often impersonated in masked dances.[12]

In this type of religion with a chthonic orientation the origin of man and his fate are naturally likened to that of a plant sprouting from the earth and later decaying into it. Once in the dawn of time man arose from the nether world to which he must return; interred in the earth, man becomes a citizen in the realm of death.[13]

Primitive cultivators provided the foundation for the emergence of the early high cultures characterized by sedentary habitat, sometimes practicing irrigation construction — the result of an expanded cooperation, controlled from above, between large population groups — a pyramidal social structure, and a centralized chieftainship. From a religious and ritual point of view this culture offers a strict priestly organization, capped by a "sacred kingship," temple constructions (often on hills or specially built platforms) with images of deities, and splendid fertility and martial rites with cannibalism. We have earlier characterized a beginning phase of this culture as "circum-Caribbean," and it is of interest to know that the developed high cultures in the Andes and among the Maya and Aztecs in Mexico evolved from the same

---

the aroma of sweet sage (Shoshoni and other tribes of the high western plains), vomiting (Taino, Creek, Navajo), and confessions (Eskimo, Athabascan groups, Iroquois in the Handsome Lake religion—see below—Cágaba, and Inca).

12. The use of masks is not restricted to the fertility rites of the agriculturists. Men's societies have masks, and so have secret societies. At the initiation ceremonies into the men's societies among the tribes of Tierra del Fuego and into the secret Kuksu societies of the California Indians the masks worn symbolize the spirits, in particular those of the ancestors. In the South American forests all sorts of animal spirits are represented by masked men upon return from successful hunting or fishing.

13. Cf. the tale of the emergence of man from the underworld (Chapter 3), the diffusion of which coincides with the extension of Indian agriculture in southern North America.

preconditions. In the northern periphery an offshoot of the high culture was the Mississippian culture.[14]

The theocratic chiefdom of the Natchez has been discussed in a different context. For these Indians, typical representatives of the offshoots of the high culture in southern North America, the chief on earth corresponds to the sun in heaven, the god who is the creator of all, even of those spirits and gods who serve under him and who are links between himself and mankind. A similar kind of sun worship is found everywhere within the rising high cultures of North and South America. It seems to belong to the theocratic system. Other divine beings are significant according to their position in the cult system of the social hierarchy. An almost "feudal" ranking order within the spirit world is clearly illustrated in the Taino (Antilles) organization of their cult of guardian spirits. An individual was here the owner of one or several images of wood, bone, stone, clay, gold, etc., shaped to anthropomorphic or theriomorphic figures with prominent sexual organs. These images were called *zemi*. The *zemi* of the *cacique* or chief, which was kept in a special temple, had greater power than that of other individuals, and the *zemi* of the high chief was worshipped as the guardian spirit of the entire nation at the great harvest festivals.

The temples did not always house images. Thus for the Powhatan in Virginia and the Acolapissa at the estuary of the Mississippi the temple on the plaza served as a storage room for the bodies of the dead or their cleansed bones (concerning secondary burials, see p. 138). The Taensa and the Natchez on the lower Mississippi kept an eternal fire in their temples; one is here reminded of the sacred fire, guarded by vestals, of the Maya and the Incas.[15]

Another feature characteristic of these theocratic cultures was bloody fertility rites with human sacrifices. Wars were arranged with the single purpose of gaining prisoners to be offered to the life-giving powers. The Jirajara and the

14. On the ancient Mississippi culture and the so-called Southern Cult see Howard 1968.
15. On the sacred fire see Loeb 1962.

Caquetio in northwestern Venezuela, for example, sacrificed humans to the sun to get rain. Highly reminiscent of the sacrificial practices of the Incas and above all the Aztecs, these human sacrifices, in combination with ritual cannibalism, were especially common among the Tupi and the Caribbeans and widespread in the Amazon area. Cannibalism with religious motifs prevailed here, however, and the concept of sacrifice had to yield. Even as "primitive" a tribe as the Tupinambá in eastern Brazil has practiced cannibalism on its captured enemies.

Ritual human sacrifices are found in North America outside the peripheral areas of the high culture, but there is no doubt whatever that ultimately they emanated from it. They are best known from the Yuchi and the Pawnee.[16] To please the god of the Morning Star (the planet Mars) and obtain the renewal and rebirth of life on earth the Skidi Pawnee in certain years sacrificed a young girl whom they had stolen from some hostile neighboring tribe. The girl was placed on a platform, then killed with a shot from an arrow, whereupon the high priest stepped forward and opened her breast with a flint knife. He stuck his hand in the opening and then smeared his face with the warm blood. The sacrificial flesh was cut up and the pieces were carried out to the fields, where the blood from them was splattered on the corn plants recently put in the ground.[17] To all appearances the young girl was thought to represent the goddess of the Evening Star, who personified the power of vegetation. This gory rite was discontinued in the 1830s.

The spirit of collectivism and ritualism which permeated the farming cultures has to some degree also rubbed off on nomadic hunting groups who settled down in the vicinity of the cultivators' habitats. The Navajo in the southwestern United States offer the best example. These former hunters

16. The religion of the Pawnee reminds us in many ways of the high culture. The Pawnee know a ruling Supreme Being whose will is executed by a great number of star spirits who serve as intermediaries between him and mankind. They celebrate complicated rites of profound symbolism. They have a priesthood, and they make human sacrifices.

17. Dorsey 1907, Linton 1926. See also Frazer 1955, Part 5, vol. 1, pp. 238f.

and gatherers (and ultimately sheep-herding nomads) have taken over nine-night rites for rain and fertility from the sedentary Pueblo Indians and at the same time have transformed them to rites for the cure of diseases. In connection with this they also replaced the organization of healing priests with the medicine man and his crowd of helpers, invited persons who support the rite by directing their thoughts to good things. During the ceremony the task of the medicine man corresponds to that of the Pueblo priest: he recites parts from a rich mythology intertwined with Pueblo Indian myths.[18]

A process of an opposite nature took place among the plains Indians in post-Columbian times. Under pressure from the white invasion east of the Mississippi, Algonkin and Sioux Indians emigrated from the forests to the prairie and plains. Here the former corn cultivators were transformed to hunters for ecological reasons at the same time that they adjusted to the lifestyle already established within the area of older prairie tribes. Through this adaptation the old fertility rites—the Sun Dance in a more nearly original form—were changed to rites for the duration of game (the buffalo), and the importance of individual visions increased.

Consequently, plains religion in its later form owes its existence indirectly to the whites, although in its composition it betrays little European influence. It is a different matter with many other Indian religious structures that have originated in more recent centuries. Through missions, commercial connections, and colonial endeavors indigenous religions were gradually tainted by Christian propagation and, to some extent, by European values. Finally, the deterioration of the political and military power structure of the old Indian societies caused a rising of national opposition movements within a religious framework, sometimes in the form of syncretic revivals. In many places prophets proclaimed

18. Underhill 1956, pp. 50ff., Vogt 1960, pp. 26ff., Vogt 1961, pp. 306f., Lamphere 1969. The patient identifies himself with the sacred persons he impersonates and with the harmony of the universe. As Toelken says, "It is partly that orientation which cures one" (Toelken 1976, p. 22).

visions of clear-sightedness, in which the old culture and the ancestral religion were again restored in purified form. The perspective was clearly eschatological and what is called "nativistic": there was a desire for a renaissance of the more vigorous and significant spiritual values within the inherited culture and an elimination of foreign influence. Elements of messianism, a goal-oriented ethics, an eschatological message, all seem to bear witness to a Christian background for these movements.

It would not be entirely justified, however, to reduce these so-called "prophetic movements" or "messianic movements" to a paganism remolded to Christian ideas. Nor can they be viewed exclusively as one stage in the divergence between primitive and western cultures. Their roots go deeper than that. Wherever a tradition-bound culture has come into difficult straits, where there is open dissatisfaction with existing conditions, there seems to be seed for a messianic movement.[19] The ecstatic visions of shamans or other clairvoyant persons release cherished dreams for the oppressed multitudes. The situation may then be sharpened through contact with foreign cultures, especially if this contact leads to frictions. The pressure from a technically superior civilization may provoke national aggression and, if Christian impulses are in force, religious expectations and demands are strengthened and specified. That such a development is natural is illustrated by the history of the messianic movement among the Tupians in South America.

Already in pre-Columbian times the so-called "grandfather cult" evolved among the Tupí-Guaraní. Burdened by the trials of existence, many groups set out on expeditions to reach the blessed land where the sky and thunder god, "the grandfather," was believed to reside. These eschatological wanderings, as it were, inspired by shamans, grew in proportion after the Portugese conquest of the Tupí and the Spanish conquest of the Guaraní in Paraguay. The Indians were hoping for immortality, renewed youth, and an idle life in the

19. For an example of the rise of nativism in a crisis, see Riley and Hobgood 1959, pp. 356ff. (Tepehuano).

promised land. The whites, on the other hand, were to be expelled. Even Christian ideas of a savior were included in the conceptual staples. Most remarkable is the fact that these wanderings took place for centuries up to our times and actively contributed to the widespread expansion of these Indians.[20]

In North America since the seventeenth century a number of messianic movements have come into being, at times connected with acts of violence aginst the whites, as in the uprising of the Shawnee prophet (1805), sometimes characterized by peaceful coexistence, as in the reformed Iroquois religion of Handsome Lake (a vocational or "calling" vision, 1799). These movements included elements of Christian belief to varying degrees, above all in ethics, messianism, and eschatology. Forms of Christian liturgy were also appropriated, as in John Slocum's Shaker religion (a "calling" vision, 1881). Most famous and also the last among these revivalistic prophetic movements was the Ghost Dance, which swept across the Great Basin and the plains in 1889–1890. Its founder, the Paiute Indian Wovoka, had beheld God in a vision. He was then told that the dead would return and with them the old, happy wilderness life, provided that the Indians tirelessly devoted themselves to round dances (a typical dance form for the Indians of the Great Basin area). Soon the Indians assembled for dances that lasted four to five days, with some of the dancers fainting from exhaustion and receiving visions in which they believed they saw their deceased family members. The movement spread to the plains where it assumed anti-white dimensions among the warlike tribes; the Indians dreamed of the return of the buffalo and the expulsion of the whites into the sea. The culmination of this development was reached with the military action against the dancing Sioux Indians in Dakota: Chief Sitting Bull was murdered and an encampment of Sioux Indians was massacred at Wounded Knee (1890). The popularity of the Ghost Dance gradually ebbed since the prophecies were not fulfilled.[21]

20. Métraux 1927, 1928; cf. also Métraux 1957, pp. 108ff.
21. Mooney 1896; cf. also Lindig and Dauer 1961, pp. 41ff. For some modern

Mutual antagonism against the whites and close contact between the tribes following the establishment of reservations created the necessary climate for unanimity of Indians across tribal lines. This pan-Indianism found its chief ideological means of expression in the peyote cult which began its expansion at the same time that the Ghost Dance swept across the continent. The cult's origins were in Mexico, and from the beginning of the 1880s it took hold in large parts of Indian North America, especially in the plains. Peyote (the Aztec *peyotl*) is a cactus species (*Lophophora williamsii*) growing along the Rio Grande. It contains mescaline and when eaten causes lively color hallucinations. Fixed rites developed around this plant and its consumption, and these take a whole night to enact. The peyote cult has its own theology, concentrated around the marvelous plant and with obvious traits of Catholic Christianity. On the other hand, the peyote movement tries to replace Christianity: God has sent Christ to the whites, peyote to the red man. At the same time the peyote movement has acted against the inherited, indigenous tribal religion, causing friction on reservations wherever it has appeared. The popularity of peyote is partly due to the fact that visions are rendered easily accessible, and fasting, isolation, and self-torture are unnecessary. Partly it is due to the fact that the Indians, pushed aside and suppressed, are here provided with a clearly defined conception of life, acceptable to all. Since 1918 the peyotists have been organized as members of the Native American Church and in societies affiliated with it.[22]

In most recent times agnosticism and atheism have spread, especially in the younger Indian generations on the reservations in Canada and in the United States. Messianism and nativism are today likely to lead to development along more secularized paths, and profane nationalism and belief in social progress in many places supersede the religious and

---

appreciations of the Ghost Dance, see Aberle 1959, Walker 1969, and Overholt 1974.

22. La Barre 1938, Slotkin 1956. The motivations of converts have been analyzed in Hultkrantz 1975.

chiliastic expectations. But signs of a revival for the old tribal religions are simultaneously discernible, even among Indians who have materially and socially accepted the conditions of the whites.[23] The future will show if this indicates a last flaring up of the waning flame of paganism or a harbinger for a new religious era on indigenous grounds.

23. See, for example, Dusenberry 1962.

Religions of the
American High Culture

11

The History of Culture and Religion in Nuclear America

Not long ago it was considered natural that different Indian religions had existed side by side without markedly influencing one another and it was assumed that they had developed entirely from their inherent historical conditions. The more these religions were studied, the more obvious it became that they had been in contact with each other and had even been exposed to significant influences from cultures and religions at great distances. There has been reason to point out on several previous occasions how the forms of religion among many "primitive" tribes in North as well as South America have been modified through influences from the religions of the Andes and Mesoamerica. These have been processes of the same kind as those in the Old World when the religions of the Mediterranean put their hallmark on old African cultures or when conceptions belonging to Christianity and Hellenistic paganism transformed the religious world of the ancient Germanic peoples. Like the Old World, the New World has exhibited high cultures which have radiated powerful impulses. "Nuclear America" has become the epithet used by archaeologists for the stronghold of high culture in northern South America, Central America, and Mexico. The religions that took shape in these developed civilizations properly may be called "high religions."[1] In the preceding we have found traces of these religions in those of more primitive tribes, in such features as the cult of the Supreme Being, the sacred chieftainship, and temples built on pyramidal foundations.

Our knowledge of the religions of the high cultures rests on a set of data totally different from that of the religions of tribal peoples. The latter have to a great extent lived well into modern times and have been accessible to research by ethnologists and missionaries, often our contemporaries. Our sources for the high religions, however, consist of ancient Indian manuscripts (sometimes drawn up in an ideographic writing difficult to decipher), archaeological monuments, and the memoranda of the conquistadors from early colonial times. The high cultures themselves, and their religions, perished more than four hundred years ago in the destruction by the Spaniards of the great Indian dominions in Peru and Mexico. Typical of the high religions was their close affiliation with the society, the state structure, the official priesthood. With the overthrow of these institutions the conditions necessary for the continued existence of the religion were lost.

To some extent this argument may perhaps be contested, in that both the Spanish Crown and the Catholic Church still to some degree tolerated the old cultural forms and thereby prolonged the existence of quite a few of the old religious conceptions and customs within this framework. Modern tourists to Mexico and Peru have witnessed the old religious dances still being performed in front of the church doors and the pagan gods and goddesses being addressed in established forms in prayer and cult, even though the rites have nominally been Christianized and the gods have become saints. Ethnologists and scholars of religion have even in our day

---

1. This is a technical term and implies no evaluation of these religions as such.

been successful in collecting substantial data on past beliefs and customs in the mountain districts of Peru, the lowlands of Yucatán, and the central Mexican plateau. It can hardly be denied that these traditions largely date back to pre-Columbian times, even if here, as once in northern Europe, Christian and ancient Mediterranean conceptions induced by Christianity have merged with autochthonous pagan notions.[2] An external guarantee for the continuation of these traditions is undoubtedly found in the absence of any sizable displacements of population after the Indian domains were overthrown. Aymará and Quechua are still found in Peru, Maya in Yucatán and Guatemala, and Nahua groups in the Valley of Mexico.

Still, this adherence to old popular traditions does not mean that the ancient high religions have survived in the forms they had at the time of the arrival of the conquistadors. The characteristic elements of the high religions were upheld by a ruling upper class whose representatives disappeared or lost their positions after the conquest: the Inca clan in Peru, the priests (and the priest-king) of the Maya, the Aztec tribe around Tenochtitlan in the Valley of Mexico. The collapse of the rule of these groups was followed by a regression process with approximately the same consequences as in the corresponding course of events among the Cuna Indians: the "higher" religion, manifested in a complicated cult organization, broke down, whereas the popular religion, which was more widely and firmly supported, survived. We recognize the same situation with the change of religions in northern European countries: the higher gods had to yield to the Christian trinity and the saints, whereas the many beings of popular belief continued their existence among the people (sometimes in slight Catholic disguise). The popular religion of Mexico or Peru does not differ much in structure from the tribal religions with which we were previously acquainted. At most it may be asserted that, unlike tribal religion, the popu-

2. Most Catholic influences derive of course from Spain. For an appreciation of the Spanish components in modern Mesoamerican and Peruvian folk religion see Foster 1960, chapters 10, 12–16.

lar religion is influenced by the religious ideas of the higher or urbanized circles, which often turn up in an almost unrecognizable disguise among the "popular" elements. On the other hand, the popular religion can in no way be said to represent the high religions that once ruled in the same geographic areas.[3]

To understand better the rise, expansion, and exclusive nature of the high religions we must study them in the context of the type of culture and society that characterized the ancient Indian empires and in the context of the changes to which this type of culture was subject.

Americanists were long amazed that the remarkable civilizations of South America and Mesoamerica could rise, without a natural transition, above the surrounding more primitive forms of existence like sky-high towers over low walls. Even if, with the aid of archaeology, they were traced back in time, the impression remained that they or their precursors had abruptly risen out of very simple origins, or no origins at all. In addition, the ancient Andean as well as Mexican cultures seemed to have sprouted forth at approximately the same time, 500 B.C. These mysterious circumstances added fuel to all sorts of speculations about people from another continent having landed on the coasts of Peru, Colombia, or Mexico. The most cherished theory was perhaps that of W. J. Perry, which said that temple builders from Southeast Asia had reached the two American continents by way of the South Pacific.[4] However, the majority of scholars, especially in North America and Scandinavia, long opposed such ill-founded theories and went to the other extreme in their attempts to point out the American roots of the Indian cultures.

Only lately and on the basis of empirical data has it been possible to establish a conceivable connection between the high cultures of the New and the Old Worlds in their initial stages. Investigations carried out by the American archaeologists Meggers, Evans, and Estrada show that the ceramics of the early gathering culture on the coast of Ecuador, the Valdivia culture (3000–1500 B.C.), may be related

3. Cf. Redfield 1941.   4. Perry 1927.

to the almost contemporary Jomon ceramics of south Japan (3000–2000 B.C.). It is interesting from the point of view of the history of religions that in the Valdivia culture there were already stone or clay statuettes of presumably cultic usage. Most of these distinctly anthropomorphic sculptures represent naked women with characteristic high, framing coiffures. Referring to the utilization of similar figures (of wood) among presentday Chocó and Cuna Indians, Meggers and Evans suggest that the Valdivia people employed them for medical cures. Like the Indians on the isthmus of Panama, they later destroyed the figures in the conviction that their potency could only be used once, a suggested explanation for the large number of statuette fragments discovered.[5] The comparison is hardly relevant, however. It seems more probable that the Valdivia statuettes represented the mother goddess. There is much to indicate that they go back to Japanese prototypes and that they signaled the introduction of a new cult and new religious ideas.

Cultural contacts across the Pacific must have continued well into later times. Thus archaeologists have succeeded in tracing East Asiatic influences around Bahía in Ecuador from about 200 B.C., and the Austrian investigator Robert von Heine-Geldern tried to establish in a series of publications that Peruvian metallurgists of the Chavín and the Mochica cultures (just prior to and at the beginning of the Christian era) received their inspiration from the North Vietnamese Dongson culture (700 B.C.–100 A.D.), and that Mexican high culture was influenced by Buddhist and Hindu art forms by way of the Khmer peoples of Cambodia.[6] Whatever our opinion may be of the learned and stimulating, though perhaps somewhat nimble investigations of Heine-Geldern, there is much to be said in favor of the theory that a number of Amer-

5. Meggers, Evans, and Estrada 1965, pp. 108, 157ff. See also Kidder 1964, pp. 474f., and Willey 1966–71 (2), pp. 275f. For parallels to the statuettes among the Cuna, see Wassén 1949. Many American archaeologists are far from convinced that there was contact with the Jomon cultures. See, for instance, E. Wagner in American Anthropologist 77 (2), p. 451, and Lathrap 1973, pp. 1761ff.

6. Heine-Geldern 1966. Cf. also Menghin 1962.

ican cultural elements have come across the sea from Asia, and it looks as if religious and mythological motifs have also taken the same route. For example, it is difficult otherwise to explain how, according to the Danish investigator Hatt, an agrarian mythology characteristic of Indonesia and Melanesia appears in the agricultural districts of pre-Columbian America.[7]

There are many reasons, however, for stating that trans-Pacific conveyance was limited mainly to occasional elements of culture and religion, and did not pertain to the fundamental culture complexes. There is a probable example of culture contact across the seas in the fact that in both Mesoamerica and China jade pearls were put in the mouth of the dead person,[8] but hardly so in the fact that similar methods were used to cultivate the soil in both these places. Even an enthusiastic diffusionist like Gordon Ekholm stresses the fact that agriculture as such in Mesoamerica is too old (5000 or 6000 B.C.) to have been imported from East Asia, where it does not have the same great antiquity.[9] We are led to the conclusion that development on both sides of the Pacific in many respects came to be the same due to similar ecological and technical conditions.

How, then, is the unique position of the American high cultures and their sudden appearance in finished shape to be explained? The question is actually no longer as current as it used to be. Intense archaeological research upon these high cultures has disclosed a series of ancient cultures on the bases of which later civilizations were successively built.[10] A continuous development may be observed from a basic culture of the same type as the circum-Caribbean one to the warlike

7. Hatt 1951. Another striking parallel is that the calendar gods in Mesoamerica have counterparts in the calendars of India: Kelley 1960, pp. 317ff., 334. The cult of the rain gods in China and Mesoamerica has also been adduced in this connection (Lou 1957). Meggers has found a long list of Olmec religious phenomena that have close correspondences in China: jaguar dragons, feathered snakes, rain gods, cult of mountains and volcanoes, etc. (Meggers 1975).

8. Coe 1962.   9. Ekholm 1964.

10. For the gradual development from simple beginnings to high culture see Johnson 1972.

empires of the Incas and the Aztecs. In this context investi-
gators have also been able to establish an inner correspondence—cultural, ecological and historical—between the high
cultures of Peru and Mexico. In the first place, it has become
clear that they are connected through a mutual historical basic
layer called by Americanists "formative" or "preclassic"
(earlier "archaic"). This stratum will be dealt with shortly.
Second, recent investigations have shown that during the
culturally formative period there were lively maritime contacts among Oaxaca, Guatemala, and Ecuador, contacts
which must have meant a lively cultural exchange.[11] There is
every reason to believe, therefore, that religious ideas were
also exchanged in this way.

Consequently, "nuclear America," the term which recently
has come to designate the high cultures in their entirety, is not
only the name of a type of culture but also of a coherent
cultural area (central and southern Mexico, Central America,
the northern Andes, Peru) and of an historic-genetically interrelated civilization. This relationship is most clearly discernible in the formative epoch, but seems to have continued
during the following time—which is otherwise characterized
by increasing differentiation among the different cultural
provinces of nuclear America. In any case, synchronous
development in Mexico and Peru has been considered a
strong argument for continued mutual contacts.[12]

From the point of view of the history of religions it is important to remember that the whole Andean–Mesoamerican
area was once a coherent cultural region where different lines
of diffusion crossed.[13] All parties in this interplay were
perhaps not totally equal. There are reasons to believe that
influences of the greatest number and importance came from
Mesoamerica, at least during the formative period. It also

11. See, for example, Meggers 1973, pp. 46f., 74f., and the map, p. 39.

12. This does not exclude, of course, considerable differences between the
civilizations of Mexico and Peru. See Brundage 1975; see also below.

13. Within this larger whole Mesoamerica constituted one large cultural
unit (Sabloff 1973, p. 1771). We find, for instance, the same gods in
Teotihuacan, Tenochtitlan, and in the Maya area: see, for example, Joralemon
1971. They seem to have been inspired from the Olmec culture (cf. below).

seems probable that this cultural phase first appeared in the Valley of Mexico. Thus the oldest radiocarbon (C–14) datings for the formative period pertain to this region (Zacatenco, 1360 ± 250 B.C.). It can be added that the oldest dates for corn cultivation in America emanate from Central Mexico (5000 B.C.). On the other hand, Mexican metallurgy seems to have originated in Peru (Chavín period). The religion of the high culture attained its peak among the Maya of northern Guatemala and adjoining parts of Mexico and Honduras, but it is impossible to say to what extent the Maya Indians made an impression on Peruvian religion. It seems likely that formative cultures in Mexico created the prototypes of the flat-topped mounds which made up the foundations of temple structures in both Mexico and Peru. And in spite of the evidence of the Valdivia figurines it is not impossible that the classical culture of Mexico brought about the circulation of the miniature statuettes of goddesses—variations, perhaps, of the mother goddess—already existing there during the formative period and generally showing up in Ecuador and Peru in the first centuries A.D. It may be mentioned that some years ago a Japanese expedition found a Mesoamerican statuette at a Peruvian site which is somewhat older than the formative Chavín epoch (the latter dates back to a time between 800 and 400 B.C.).[14]

Correlation among the different parts of nuclear America is also evinced in the close typological affinity between the important periods or cultural phases and their approximate contemporaneity in history (compare above). The American ethnologist Julian Steward has in this complementary pattern of events tried to find grounds for a consistent development in the areas of culture, society, and religion. He has accordingly looked for parallels in Chinese, Mesopotamian, and Egyptian histories of culture and religion. Basic to his reasoning is the supposition that equivalent technical and ecological conditions promote development in one and the same direction, and that similarities between geographically widely

14. To the above, see Willey 1955a, Willey 1955b, Willey 1966–71 (1), pp. 82, 83ff., Coe 1960, Ishida et al. 1960. See, however, Meggers 1973, p. 47, for the reverse interpretation.

diverse cultures and religions are not essentially due to diffusion but rather to analogous conditions.[15] Steward's theory offers an interesting contrast to Heine-Geldern's diffusionism in the attempt to solve the riddle of American prehistoric cultures. Whether we accept it or not, it delineates the large and sweeping epochs in the cultural history of ancient America.

In some agreement with Steward's general views on the development of culture in America, I shall present here the following schematic overview of the great epochs of American high culture. We will consider variations motivated by ecology and history which occurred in different cultural areas. Since our concern is chiefly with the history of religions, technical, material, and social conditions will be touched upon only to the extent that they throw light upon religious and ritual features of the cultures.

The earliest culture worth mentioning in this connection is the formative one, which required an intensified agriculture (preferably with irrigation) and a corresponding population increase which made possible larger villages of concentrated habitation. We have earlier met with this type of culture among the circum-Caribbean peoples and the southeastern Indians in North America. It is thus a matter of a base culture reaching far beyond the borders of nuclear America. Steward has even wished to maintain that the cultures of the South American tropical peoples could be derived from the circum-Caribbean culture, an opinion which must be labeled as exaggerated and which has been strongly repudiated by other Americanists.

Steward has, however, convincingly described the process which led to the type of religion typical of the formative period, a type of religion which was to be refined within the high culture, especially during the succeeding classical period. According to him, the growing population created an ever-increasing need for political integration, and power was put in the hands of a leading class. Among their main tasks was responsibility for an organized and technically adminis-

15. Steward 1947 and 1955, pp. 36ff. Cf. Chapter 10, note 1.

tered agriculture. The scholar Palerm, in cooperation with Steward, has pointed out that

> a strong sociopolitical organization seems to be the only way open to a people with a poorly developed technology to have and use large-scale public works. Human labor is the only substitute for advanced technology; the less technology the more human effort is required, which means greater coercive organization.[16]

According to these scholars the most important responsibility of the authorities in matters of economic productivity was to control irrigation. The age of artificial irrigation in America is, however, a controversial question. Steward seems to have thought that it belonged to the formative period in nuclear America, whereas his countryman Gordon Willey believes that it did not exist in Peru until the end of the formative period and in Mexico not until post-classical times. Remarkably enough, irrigation constructions were in existence by about 500 A.D. (pioneer period) in the Hohokam culture in the southwest region of North America.[17] We must be satisfied with the statement that, irrigation or no irrigation, agriculture in the formative period required a well-developed socio-political organization.[18]

And, according to Steward, this implies the existence of some state structure, albeit limited and local, which in the course of time must have assumed a theocratic character: the supernatural powers protecting agriculture and securing the earth's fertility made their will and wishes manifest through political leaders, chieftains, and priests. These leaders, who acted as mediators between man and the powers and who themselves personified something of the divine, were soon carried away into the sacred sphere—the funeral architecture seems to bear this out. In southern Mexico and in the coast-

16. Palerm 1955, pp. 39f.

17. Willey 1962, 1966–71 (1), p. 221, Meggers 1973, p. 134.

18. The idea that irrigation as such presupposed or gave rise to a central despotic authority, as has been supposed by some scholars (notably Wittfogel and Steward), has been refuted by Mitchell, who has found irrigation systems combined with different socio-political systems: see Mitchell 1976, p. 39.

land of Peru, temples were erected on elevated platforms. These temples undoubtedly served purposes connected with the prosperity of the fields and crops. The builders were probably specialized craftsmen and artists, individuals who, like the priests, were liberated from the peasant ranks through surplus production. These temples are likely to have been both religious and administrative centers for a whole region with a number of habitation sites.

This theory about cultural development during the formative period seems quite plausible, not least in the light of what we know about the rise of the high cultures in the Old World, but it still has not been generally accepted. David Kaplan, for example, suggests that the large construction projects were erected gradually and after general agreement by the people of a stateless society presided over by a nominal chief.[19] Kaplan fails to see, however, that it is a matter of a slowly increasing tendency toward bureaucratic centralism and that those in authority as well as the population in general can have carried through the construction projects in what may be described as an "ideological unity."

The formative epoch both in Peru and Mesoamerica took place in approximately the first millennium B.C., with the reservation that it appeared some centuries earlier in Mesoamerica. The building of temples started about 800–400 B.C., during the latter part of the formative era, in La Venta in Mesoamerica. As a comparison it may be noted that the temple complex in the southeast region of North America did not take shape until about 700 A.D. Temple-building is there part of the Mississippian tradition, with its background in the formative as well as the classical periods in Mexico. As was just mentioned, the construction of temples is probably of Mexican origin.

The cultural landscape of the formative period was characterized by a cluster of villages with a population domiciled around a ritual center. As habitation was so scattered and not concentrated in the temple area, it may seem hazardous to speak of a high culture in this context, since the high culture

19. Kaplan 1963.

was noted for its progressive urbanization. We could, however, join Willey in saying that the cultural profile of the formative period constitutes the threshold of civilization, the high culture.[20] Its organization in the landscape as a "temple culture" suggests that the formative cultural type was decidedly religious-ritual and theocratic in its orientation, as has been suggested (similar to some isolated Mesoamerican communities which remained until the Spanish conquest). We do not know much about the details of this religion but, as mentioned before, it probably had the characteristics of an agrarian fertility religion and the cult must have been controlled by an important priesthood. It is of special interest that archaeologists have found images clearly showing this religion to have been linked to conceptions of female divinities, sphinx-like monsters, and supernatural beings in animal form.

The earliest and most obvious feature in the fertility cult of the formative period is illustrated by the many small female figurines, discussed above. They have sometimes been perceived as magic amulets or talismans, sometimes as religious symbols of the earth or mother goddess. The beautiful and finely embellished statuettes unearthed in Tlatilco in the Valley of Mexico obviously symbolize the corncob and by extension may well symbolize the goddesses of corn: they have the colors of the corn (mostly yellow but also white or red), they have the long "hair" of the corn silk and, like the corn goddesses in North America, they seem to be represented in their maidenly youth.[21]

There is ample evidence that gods and spirits were worshipped in animal form, or in a combined human-animal form. Undoubtedly the artistic images of animals and monsters of this period conveyed religious ideas. Presumably also the larger and smaller human figurines, often of bearded men, found around La Venta in southern Mexico had reli-

20. Willey 1962, p. 6.
21. Cf. Vaillant 1962 and Parsons 1972. It deserves to be mentioned that many fertility gods in Mexico are portrayed as goggle-eyed, just like their counterparts in Sumeria (Grieder 1975, p. 852).

gious significance. (Heyerdahl's thesis that they were meant to represent white seafarers from the Canaries is hardly convincing). They may have represented the sky god or fertility powers, but we do not know exactly.

Among figures of major religious importance created during the preclassic and classic times the jaguar (or other feline) and possibly the snake seem to occupy a first-rank position. In order to come to grips with their significance we must have a quick look at the first two American cultures with wide religious influences, the Chavín culture in northern Peru, which appeared shortly after 1000 B.C., and the Olmec culture in southern Mexico, which flourished after 1200 B.C. The latter is also known by the name of its main center, La Venta in the Veracruz area.

The Chavín culture (1000–500 B.C.) had a great influence in the Andean area. Surprisingly, its remnants evince traits that exhibit influences from the woodlands in the past.[22] The main site, Chavín de Huántar, is characterized by a plaza surrounded by platforms. The structures around the plaza contain columns, pottery, and reliefs with pictures of felines, probably the jaguar (or some other feline, perhaps the puma), condors, and serpents. Sometimes the jaguar has pronounced anthropomorphic features, suggesting the idea of a jaguar-man or jaguar-god.

The Olmec culture (1200–400 B.C.) was the Mesoamerican mother civilization. All later cultures were inspired by it, not least in the field of religion.[23] The appearance of this culture has been designated as a real revolution.[24] It was apparently a fully-fledged theocratic culture, with ceremonial centers, pyramids, and tombs for priest-kings. There appeared here the first efforts to make hieroglyphics, numerals, and a calendar. In the field of art the Olmecs were distinctive because of their giant stone heads and sculptural figures of bearded men

22. Benson 1971.

23. Willey 1962, Coe 1965, Bernal 1969; see also Ford 1969. It has been speculated upon that the prehistoric Olmecs were really Maya Indians (Willey 1966–71 (1), pp. 102f.), which could explain the wide dissemination of their religious concepts.

24. Meggers 1975, p. 17.

and zooanthropomorphic beings, apparently representing gods of earth, fertility, mountains, etc.[25] Furthermore, for the first time we meet here the symbolism of the cross.

Our interest turns to what appears to most archaeologists to be a were-jaguar, a peculiar cross between a man (with a child's face) and a jaguar-shaped animal. The animal lacks the protruding canines characteristic of a jaguar, however—is it perhaps a snake?

This is the position taken by Luckert in a recent work. Just as another author, Drucker, has expressed the opinion that the snake is missing in Olmec art, Luckert says that the jaguar "does not seem to be there."[26] Luckert proceeds from the fact that the Olmecs were earth-oriented planters for whom the snake was naturally associated with fertility. Indeed, at the basis of Olmec religion was a belief in the volcanic earth serpent.[27] It is manifested in carvings and sculptures and in the enigmatic stone heads; in the central ridge of La Venta, ending in a pyramid, is the serpent's face. According to Luckert the serpent cult spread northward and reached a new climax in the great serpent mound of Ohio. The same author concedes, however, that in late Olmec priestly speculation and art a jaguar cult ousted the popular serpent cult.[28]

Whatever the truth of this bold hypothesis (and there is much to support the idea of a serpent cult in Mesoamerica), the fact remains that something like anthropomorphic jaguar figures occurred in the formative religious art of Chavín and La Venta. It is a vain speculation, however, to look for some direct historical connection between the two styles, although it is not altogether improbable. We know, for example, of anthropomorphic jaguar figures in the art of Costa Rica as well, and the later jaguar representations in Peru are anthropomorphic in tendency. In any case, Olmec art inspired

25. Joralemon 1971, pp. 90f. As Proskouriakoff pointed out at the Dumbarton Oaks Conference in 1967, there are probably two artistic traditions in Olmec sculpture, one focused on the jaguar figures, the other on figures of bearded men. Of these the latter tradition seems to be non-Olmec.

26. Luckert 1976, p. 13; cf. Drucker 1952, p. 203. (See also, however, Drucker 1952, p. 194.)

27. Luckert 1976, pp. 28, 44.   28. Luckert 1976, p. 24; cf. p. 130.

the religious art of Mexico. Undoubtedly Olmec art influenced and partly lived on in the Maya art of the classical period and we may even trace it in the classical Teotihuacan art further north.

Among the Maya there exists a jaguar god, depicted for instance on a stucco relief in Palenque; to all appearances he has been the god of the earth and its interior. In the well-known Dresden codex from the post-classical period the sun god is also given certain jaguar traits. This might seem to make the interpretation mentioned above less reliable.[29] Nevertheless, it should be kept in mind that during the Toltec regime in Chichén Itzá the Maya had two military orders, eagles and jaguars, representing the sun in heaven (eagles) and the sun in the nether world (jaguars). The sun, then, bridged the opposition between heaven and the nether world, which these orders probably represented on the ritual level. It may imply that the sun's link with the jaguar god is secondary, which seems probable in a comparative perspective. It is true that certain Americanists such as Spinden and Krickeberg maintain that the sun god was primarily depicted as a jaguar not only among the Maya but also among other Mesoamerican peoples, but their opinion does not seem to be well founded. It would carry us too far here to account for the criticisms that could be brought against their reasonings that are, respectively, much too summary and incomplete, and too speculative.[30]

The connection between Olmec jaguar sculpture and the representations of the rain god in Teotihuacan, the well-known temple northeast of Mexico's capital, is clearly revealed in a diagram included by the noted art historian Covarrubias in his book on Mexican art.[31] In Teotihuacan jaguars are depicted on a relief blowing snail-shell trumpets out of which water is pouring; there is hardly any doubt that here they represent the rain powers.

29. Indeed, in Luckert's interpretation the figure represents a snake: Luckert 1976, pp. 130f.
30. Spinden 1940, p. 467; Krickeberg 1950, pp. 325f.
31. Covarrubias 1957.

Among the late Aztecs, finally, the jaguar or ocelot god, Tepeyollotl, appears as a mountain god and is therefore regarded as one of the earth gods.

All available information, then, seems to indicate that the jaguar god of Central America was above all a chthonic deity, at the same time a rain god and the essence of the earth's fertile power, a fertility god well integrated with the leading ideology of the formative period.[32]

It is doubtful whether the jaguar-like god, the dominating feature of the Chavín style, can be subjected to the same interpretation. This god also survives the formative period; the later classical cultures in Peru, above all the Mochica, depict him with at times remarkable anthropomorphism. The combination of anthropomorphism and theriomorphism in art became distinctive for later cultures as well, such as the culture of the Chimú realm in northern Peru, a combination that surely reflects the nature of those religious conceptions. These data bring to mind the nocturnal werewolf of South American Indians, the jaguar-man.[33] Ancient Peruvian pictorial art allows no certain conclusions, however. Some figural representations from the Tiahuanaco culture, among others, give hints of solar traits in the jaguar beings just as in the post-classical Maya culture. On the other hand, it is tempting to combine, as many Americanists have done, the Andean jaguar god with fertility ideology. Previously discussed examples of a jaguar cult in the marginal areas of high culture in South America (Mojo and other tribes) could be looked upon as representative forms of a secondary development, misunderstood and degenerate, of the original Andean jaguar ideology.

Finally, as was already suggested, there is no certainty whatever that Chavín art portrays a jaguar; it may very well be a puma. In South America the jaguar belongs to the tropi-

32. Cf., for instance, Meggers 1975, p. 14, and Bernal 1969, p. 103. Speculations on the role of the jaguar in Mesoamerican and Andean iconography will be found in Benson 1972a.

33. There seems to be a connection between the ideas of the divine jaguar in the Central American, Colombian, Peruvian, and Amazon areas: cf. Lathrap 1971.

cal lowland, whereas the puma goes into the highlands. With regard to artistic motifs and religious ideology, however, this is of hardly any importance.

The period following the formative one and comprehending the development of America's most splendid cultures has been called the "florescent" (Steward) or the "classical" (Willey) period. This era, largely coinciding with the first millennium A.D., meant a strengthening and refinement in Peru as well as in Mexico of the new powers and ideas of the previous period. This is when art and religion reached their climax and the beginning of scientific pursuits was discernible. In short, high cultures of the same renown as those of the ancient Near East had come into being. At the same time we trace tendencies of regionalism and specialization, tendencies which were gradually to separate the cultures of Peru and Mesoamerica.

The ecological conditions were already different. In Peru irrigation culminated with terrace constructions, the desert territories below the Andes were interrupted by "oasis cultures" with intensive agriculture, and large, concentrated urban formations emerged (the Mochica and Nazca cultures). In the highlands of Guatemala, where the Maya culture had begun to develop during the last centuries B.C., a more primitive cultivation sytem with slash-and-burn agriculture (milpa) had been maintained, preserving a more scattered habitation of non-urban type. Whereas in Peru the temples were in close proximity to urban sites, among the Maya ceremonial complexes and habitation areas were two separate, clearly defined entities. A distinction may be made between, on the one hand, a ritual center with temples and other stone monuments, altars, and ball courts, dominated by priests and other sacred leaders, artists and artisans, and on the other hand, hundreds of small hamlets for the agricultural population, politically and religiously dependent on this center. Further north, in the Valley of Mexico, there was a true city, called Teotihuacan by the Aztecs (which probably meant, more or less, the place where the gods are worshipped), "the most powerful member of a federation of small city states"

(Linné). It was surrounded by villages built of sun-baked bricks. On the outskirts of each village, near the fields, lived the corn cultivators, while priests and chieftains had their living quarters near the plaza in the village center, where the temples were. Teotihucan itself had the same structure, but there the houses of the dignitaries and the temple constructions were far more splendid in their proportions.[34]

Throughout nuclear America theocracy remained during the classical period, apparently growing in strength. Society was formed as a class society with an upper class consisting of priests, chieftains (priest-kings), and warriors. Palaces for these dignitaries were sometimes erected near the temples. The power of the priesthood is also reflected in the colossal size of the temples. Sacred edifices consisting of or containing an altar were built both in Peru and Mexico on top of stepped pyramids. Some of them, such as the pyramid in Cholula and the "sun pyramid" in Teotihuacan, reached enormous proportions. The latter, built of adobe (sun-baked brick) with an external casing of stone has, according to Linné, a volume of one million cubic yards and rises to a height of 216 feet. Today among the Mesoamerican pyramids only those of the Maya Indians have temples preserved on top. Numerous scholars have regarded the pyramid constructions as evidence of a direct link with the pyramid builders of the Old World, especially in the South Pacific and Southeast Asia. However that may be, development seems to move quite smoothly from the low temple foundations ("mounds") of the formative period to the high pyramid forms of the classical period.

If the building of pyramids was mainly an autochthonous process, there is reason to ask what had been its driving forces. Naturally, the commanding dimensions of these buildings may have reflected strivings for social and political prestige, but notions of the celestial grandeur of the gods, perhaps ideas of a mountain of the gods (the world mountain), may also have been inspiring. Unfortunately, we are here reduced to fruitless speculations, just as historians of culture and religion have speculated on the question of the

34. See, for example, Sanders 1962, Bullard 1960, and Linné 1942b.

primal function of Mesopotamian temple towers. Only in the Aztec period do we know with some certainty that at least some pyramids were ritual replicas of the mountain of the gods, the symbol of the cosmic reality in which man is enclosed.[35]

To all appearances, some states in nuclear America were ruled by priest-kings just as in the ancient Near East during the typologically identical period.[36] There is thus reason to suppose that the powerful lord buried in the great Maya pyramid of Palenque was a sacred ruler representing the deity in the cult, and perhaps, like the later monarchs of the Inca or the Natchez Indians in North America, perceived as the son of the sun god. Tombs have been discovered under temples and pyramids among the Maya and the Zapotec, their neighbors in the state of Oaxaca, but none of them is equal to the tomb in Palenque in size and importance.[37]

In any case it is conceivable that the Indians in Palenque, like other agricultural peoples in America, had a ceremonial organization with halves (moieties), and that the same dualism reacted in the political government so that the priest-king was peace chief with a war chief by his side. The division of power between a priest-king and a war-king seems to have existed in various places in Peru and Mesoamerica in classical times, to some degree lingering among the Aztecs in the post-classical period. Their ruler, the "chief of men," conducted warfare and alliance policy, and by his side the "serpent woman"—always a man!—represented Cihuacoatl, the goddess of fertility, and took care of civil and religious matters. In the Andean Mochica culture, as among the Aztecs, the war chief seems to have assumed the leading power, and in accordance with the nature of theocracy the supreme god, whom he probably represented, was portrayed both as a civil ruler and a military leader.

It is possible that our greater knowledge of the classical

35. The idea of the mountain of the gods, or world mountain, is basically a variation of the world-tree idea, sometimes expanded to enclose the world of man, or even the cosmos: cf. Köngäs 1960, pp. 152f.

36. For the typological periods see Steward 1955, pp. 185ff.

37. See Linné 1954 and Ruz Lhuillier 1955. Cf. also Chapter 13.

cultures makes them appear more diversified and variegated than the formative cultures, but undoubtedly conditions at that time were favorable for individualization and intensification within religion, art, and other intellectual activities. The artists created their works for the glory of the gods and the satisfaction of the mighty priests and warriors. The priests were numerous and specialized and they could devote their time to religious speculation, intellectual experiments, and observations of celestial phenomena.

The cultures of Peru and Mesoamerica during this period may to some degree be contrasted. Artistically Peru maintained its position well compared to Mesoamerica. In the coastal cultures works were made in gold and copper (whereas in Mexico metals were not tooled until post-classical times), and ceramics held an eminent position, in the north characterized by modeled figural representations, in the south by brilliant polychrome surfaces. In the highlands of Peru and Bolivia the Tiahuanaco culture flourished, notable for its massive, symmetrical stone buildings. At the same time, however, Mesoamerica witnessed a veritable cultural climax, especially on the Yucatán peninsula and in Guatemala, where the Maya Indians created a splendid culture without equal either before or later in pre-Columbian America. With dramatic suddenness a civilization developed which at once represented artistic exuberance and—unlike the cultures of Peru—intellectual creativity.[38] Stelae, sculptures, frescoes, and construction of the corbeled arch, as well as beautiful temple and palace architecture, give evidence of artistic vitality and refinement, and the existence of hieroglyphics, mathematics, and astronomy (with an exact calendar) reveal high intellectual capacity.

The contrasts between Mesoamerica and Peru must not be overstated. It would be wrong to deny that also in Peru there were certain ventures into a richer intellectual life. According to R. Larco Hoyle, at this time can be found the beginnings of an ideographic writing system among the Indians of Peru. Unfortunately it disappeared completely when the Inca

38. Dramatic, that is, unless the ancient Olmecs were Maya.

dominion came into being. There was no calendar of the Mayan type, but in each temple was kept a sundial with which the priests could make calculations concerning the hours of the day and the seasons, and especially the vernal and autumnal equinoxes.[39]

The religion was also modeled on local or national patterns of tradition. In the Nazca culture of southern Peru a type of religion was developed which was characterized by an advanced burial cult and, presumably in this connection, by ancestor worship (compare the later cult of the dead Inca emperors). A primitive embalming of the dead was practiced: the corpse was cleaned of intestines, dried, and shrouded in masses of cloth. Even today the interested person may easily find round mummy bundles in the dry desert sand along the coast. Some of the deceased were mummified with special care, probably because they had once been religious or secular leaders. Only a few deities are discernible in the art, among them the puma or jaguar god mentioned earlier.[40]

As was already pointed out, the Mochica culture further north in Peru was disposed toward war and its values. The crammed population in the river valleys along the coast continuously demanded more elbow room. The result was a policy of aggression which left distinct marks on the structure and molding of the culture and thus of the religion as well. For modern archaeologists a military pattern is evident from the fortifications (*castillos*) and a wall leading from the Andes down to the sea, from the burial customs—the graves contained men with both weapons and ceremonial regalia—and from the ceramic paintings of fully armed warriors. The warlike activities resulted among other things in the temples being supplied with prisoners who could be sacrificed for harvest and health. Contemporary paintings show unfortunate prisoners of war being thrown from mountain tops, evidently in order to please some deity.

39. Concerning intellectual achievements in classic Andean cultures, see the following note.

40. For descriptions of the Nazca and Mochica cultures, see Steward 1946–59 (2) and Lumbreras 1969.

The gods in the Mochica state were numerous. At the top was seated the jaguar god, depicted as an old man with a wrinkled face, fangs, and whiskers—partly human, partly animal. Sometimes he also assumed other animal shapes. We see him surrounded by his court of theriomorphic servants receiving offerings or appearing in his functions as hunter, fisher, healer, or warrior. This god was obviously conceived in the same way as the earthly war-king of the state: he is so exalted that he is carried in a palanquin (as later was the Inca emperor) and he gives audiences during which subjects kneel with bowed heads. Below this Supreme God were lesser deities in animal form, among them a strange being with the body of a frog but with feline nose and legs. Manioc and beans sprouted out of his body. Apparently he was a god of agriculture, perhaps associated with the immolation myth.

It remains to be added that some of the Mochica ceramic paintings depict scenes of a complicated medical procedure while others immortalize the healing activities of the medicine men.[41]

In Mesoamerica the Maya religion was characterized by a more peaceful adaptation to the cultivator's practical needs and the priest's intellectual (mainly astronomical) endeavors. The deities met with here are rain and fertility gods and exalted beings who exist as stars in the lofty spaces. The particulars of this religion will be examined in Chapter 13.

West and north of the Maya people the Zapotecs and Mixtecs established their cultures (if indeed these peoples were the bearers of the Mitla and Monte Albán cultures in classical times, about which some archaeologists are doubtful). The Zapotec culture at its peak (200–800 A.D.) is of great interest due to its intermediary position of promoting influences between the two great centers of the classical period in Mesoamerica, the Maya culture in the south and the Teotihuacan culture in the north. In later times (that is, in the decades before the arrival of the conquistadors), Zapotec religion was characterized by its dominant priesthood, its

41. See also Benson 1972b, Lavallée 1970.

polytheism with specialized gods—for commerce, wealth and poverty, misfortunes, dreams, omina, and so on—its sacrifices of animals and even humans, and its fertility rites. The latter are of great interest to the phenomenology of religions because of their resemblance to vegetation customs in other places.

Corn, the principal sustenance of the Zapotec as well as of other Mesoamerican peoples, was under the auspices of several gods, among the Zapotec primarily the rain god Cocijo and the harvest god Pitao-Cozobi. A document from Spanish times presented by Father Burgoa and quoted by the Americanist Eduard Seler describes how in order to obtain a good corn harvest in the following year the Zapotec at harvest time cut off the biggest and finest corncob, dressed it in clothes and jewelry, and honored it with prayer and sacrifice, song and dance. When the time came for new sowing these ceremonies were repeated, and at the same time permission was requested from the corncob to carry it out to the field to watch over the growing crops. A priest then brought it to a central place in the field where a hole had been dug, and amidst the scent of incense and the sound of prayers for its gracious protection of the corn plants, it was deposited in the hole.[42]

Similar harvest rites have probably existed extensively all over Mesoamerica. It even looks as if they had a wider range. We find certain analogies to them in the Pawnee rites described above, and we are also reminded of the ancient harvest customs of the northern European peasants, for example, rites concerning the "seed cake" made from the last sheaf. The Norwegian scholar Nils Lid has made great efforts to establish comparisons between Nordic and Mexican fertility religion.[43] We will not discuss here whether these comparisons are altogether correct; the point is that agrarian religions seem to follow certain congruous patterns, the Zapotec rite being a typical exponent of such a pattern.

The religion of the Teotihuacan culture, foremost of the

42. Seler et al. 1904, pp. 300f.; cf. also Linné 1938, pp. 78ff.
43. Lid 1933, pp. 155ff.

high cultures in the Valley of Mexico during the classical period, can only be partially reconstructed.[44] There is reason to believe that it was in part compatible with Mayan religion; as was mentioned, some contact was maintained between Teotihuacan and the Indians of the Guatemalan highlands. In general, the Teotihuacan Indians must have shared with the Maya a religious orientation toward fertility concepts, of which we have just seen examples and which appears naturally in an environment where intense corn cultivation is indispensable for life and prosperity. Sculptures and temple decorations depict a number of figures that could well be interpreted as rain and fertility gods: "the fat god," "the water goddess," the crocodile god, the god with the butterfly head, and others. Rain-producing jaguar gods have already been mentioned. On the whole, cults of water and fertility deities seem to have dominated the Teotihuacan religion.

Some gods are depicted in a manner reminiscent of later Aztec deities. The Aztecs named their fire god Huehueteotl, "the old god," possibly because they had appropriated him from an older culture. To all appearances, this god may be recognized in several figural representations in Teotihuacan, here possibly endowed with the same functions as later in the Aztec realm. The Aztec rain god Tlaloc is also represented in Teotihuacan art, as is Tlalocan, the death realm of the Aztecs. The Tlaloc cult is of ancient lineage and in Teotihuacan it was taken over from the pre-classical civilization. One of the great temples in Teotihuacan is adorned with sculptures and reliefs of the god called by the Aztecs Quetzalcoatl, "the feathered serpent," who was, according to their tradition, the culture hero of the illustrious Toltecs. The Toltecs, described by the Aztecs as the civilized people of the golden age, were at one time believed to have been the master-builders of classical Teotihuacan. As a matter of fact, they could not have had anything to do with Teotihuacan until much later. (On the other hand, they may have been identical to the Mexicans who founded the New Kingdom in Yucatán; see Chapter

44. To the following, see Linné 1934, 1941, and 1942a; Winning 1961.

13.) Quetzalcoatl probably had a more peaceful cult in Teotihuacan than that of which he was the object in post-classical times. According to the myths, he did not receive human sacrifices, only sacrifices of butterflies and snakes. His name also served as the title of the priest-king: here as in other places the sacred ruler was believed to have at least ritual identity with the leading god.[45]

One of the most remarkable gods in Teotihuacan in later times was Xipe Totec, who probably came from the Zapotec and survived well into Aztec times. Like so many other deities of the classical period, Xipe Totec was an agricultural god worshipped in spring in connection with the growing corn. In Aztec times he was known as a bloodthirsty god; humans were sacrificed in his honor and his priest was dressed in the skin of the sacrificial victim. These human sacrifices in Mexico, as well as the ones we have found in Peru, very likely date back to the classical period.

During the centuries called the Dark Ages in medieval Europe (900–1000 A.D.), the classical cultures of America fell to pieces. In general, the havoc of war and devastating migrations seem to have caused the catastrophe. The fall of the Mayan culture could perhaps also be ascribed to ecological circumstances—the maladjustments of a prominent civilization in the tropical lowland—but the problem of its causes is still the subject of lively discussion.

The classical period was followed by the post-classical or, according to Steward's terminology, "imperialistic" period. Both in Peru and Mesoamerica it lasted approximately 500 to 600 years, until the Spanish conquest.[46] It has been said

45. Most archaeologists think that the plumed serpent is first discernible in the art motifs of Teotihuacan, the Zapotec, and the Maya. However, it is not typical for classic Maya and its occurrence in Teotihuacan art has been doubted (Krickeberg 1956, p. 398). On the other hand, there are clear frescoes of jaguars with plumed headdresses in Teotihuacan and in the Maya area. It seems possible to consider the plumed serpent and jaguar as symbols of the union between the powers above and below and thus an expression of ultimate reality, sometimes represented by the Supreme Being or his shadow, the culture hero.

46. Cf. Steward's analysis in Steward 1955, pp. 196f., and Willey's in Willey 1955b, pp. 576f.

of this cultural era that it was characterized by militarism, expansionism, secularization, and urbanization. A military class, absolute in power, was given more importance than the old priestly hierarchy. This change in the social and political structure was effected by intensified martial activity, which had become necessary to secure the supply of provisions. The rapidly growing population could not be supplied from within the narrow borders of the state, and conquest and expansion were the natural resort. In this way two great empires were founded, the Inca realm and the dominion of the Aztecs in Mexico. Along with the increase in population there was also a vigorous urbanization. Tenochtitlan, the Aztec capital (today Mexico City), grew to a population of at least 200,000 (according to some scholars even a million inhabitants), and in northern Peru, Chanchan, the capital of the highly organized Chimú state, had a population of 50,000.

External expansion, however, was counterposed by increasing shallowness in aesthetic and spiritual areas. It is apparent in the art, where the quality and variety of the older period yielded to a standardized mass production. It is apparent also in religion, especially with reference to religious architecture which, in Mexico in any case, declined considerably. It is perhaps not a case of veritable secularization; at least the sources at our disposal do not allow such an interpretation. Probably religion held its old position, although it was increasingly subjected to the demands of militarism and centralized state authority. The cult was no longer mainly focused on fertility gods; it now also incorporated the victorious gods of war and sacrifices to them became just as bloody as those to the vegetation deities, perhaps even bloodier. This is especially true of the Aztec religion, which was a cruel religion from our point of view. The sacred kingdom remained, although infiltrated by military value systems, and it was perhaps more powerful now than during the preceding classical period.

To a certain extent this epoch also was distinguished by the progress of civilization, especially in Peru where an advanced system of administration and a remarkable agricultural economy were introduced. Religion stagnated, however, even if occasional attempts were made to reach a higher knowledge of the divine. It is uncertain whether the arrival of the Europeans meant that the civilizations of nuclear America were thwarted in their ascent toward higher levels. The probability is that they had indeed started their downhill trend by the time of the arrival of the conquistadors.

12

The Religion of the Inca Indians

Inca culture as it appeared at the arrival of the Spaniards was above all the creation of a goal-oriented dynasty and of those who supported it.[1] Similarly, the official religion of the Inca state may be described as a court religion. Even if it had its roots in earlier cultures far back in classical and even pre-classical times, it was distinguished by its close affinity to the Inca dynasty and the individual experiences of the Inca princes. The situation is unique in the history of American religions.

Originally "Inca" referred to an insignificant tribe of the Quechuan language group in the highlands around Cuzco. This city remained the residence of the Inca dynasty even after the great conquests of the fifteenth century. The tribe was organized in two moieties, the "upper" and the "lower," according to a pattern we became acquainted with earlier. Certain traditions maintain that this partition was established

1. On the culture of the Inca Indians see Rowe 1946, Baudin 1947, Mason 1957, Bushnell 1956, Cieza de León 1959, Brundage 1963, Bennett and Bird 1964, Kidder 1964.

by a decree of one of the later Inca emperors, but it was probably of older date and had its origin in the ancient agrarian culture. Besides, the partition of tribes into dualities was common all over the Andean region. Each moiety consisted of a number of *ayllu,* that is, local clans or endogamous groups confined to a clearly delimited territory. Cuzco is said to have originally had eleven such groups. The moieties *hanan* and *hurin* had mainly ceremonial and sacred functions. According to Garcilaso de la Vega the former or "upper" half was under the sovereignty of the monarch while the latter, "lower" half was subordinated to his consort. It is certainly not inconceivable that this ritual opposition between male and female was intended to represent the cosmic powers manifested by the sky god and the earth goddess.

According to Inca tradition, Cuzco was long ago captured by the legendary founder of the dynasty, Manco Capac, and his sister and spouse, Mama Ocllo Huaco. These two were the children of the sun god, Inti, who had let them descend to an island in Lake Titicaca to inform mankind about him and to teach them to live and work in the right manner. This is the origin myth which served as the foundation for the investiture of the Inca emperors, but naturally it tells us nothing of their historical origin. The later Inca dominion, however, kept an official chronology which linked the mythical primeval time with their own age. After Manco Capac and his nearest successors, the Inca sovereigns slowly proceed out of legendary obscurity and into the light of history. They must gradually have consolidated the domination of the Inca tribe in the mountain area north of Titicaca. An earlier historiography has it that from the thirteenth century onward a build-up of all resources took place which a couple of hundred years later led to the rise of the great Andean empire. However, the leading expert on the cultures of ancient Peru, John Rowe, thinks that the Inca dynasty before 1438, when Pachacuti Inca Yupanqui came to power, was of no greater significance than other dynasties in the highlands. The explosive development that followed was, according to Rowe, led by Inca emperors with exceptionally good military and political qualifications.

But it would perhaps be justified to look for the ideological source of Inca imperialism in Pachacuti's father, Hatun Tupac Inca. At the time of his accession to the throne he took the name of Viracocha Inca to honor a deity who had appeared to him in a vision in his youth. As we shall see, this religious experience was to become significant for the son and his creation of an empire. Violent military and political expansion of the Inca dominion followed under Pachacuti and his descendants. During the decades 1460–1490 all land from Quito in the north to the Maule river in the south was brought under the domination of the Inca emperors.

The Inca state was a remarkable formation politically as well as economically. Under the leadership of the Inca tribe, which established itself as a nobility within the large conglomerate of the population (amounting to at least six and perhaps as many as fifteen million people), a state system was constituted which was at once theocratic, monarchic, and socialistic. All land was owned by the state and divided among the "church," the state (that is, the Inca sovereign and .his court, civil servants, and others), and the individual communities or *ayllu*. The members of each *ayllu* were jointly assigned the cultivation and care of all arable land in the home area—church land, state land, and peasant land. Moreover, in the so-called *mita* system they could be recruited for state projects, for example, for military service and the postal system. Transports and military movements were facilitated by a well-developed road system. The intricate but logically organized administration was in the hands of local chiefs, whose tribes had been conquered and incorporated into the Inca empire, and the Inca nobility, who controlled the higher administrative units.

The organization of the administration was pyramidal: leaders of successively higher rank controlled successively larger groups in which the smaller groups were ranked step by step. Contacts between officials took place only vertically, that is, between superiors and subordinates. Highest on the official scale were four governors, each one presiding over a quarter of the state,[2] and at the top of the administration the emperor was enthroned, holding his empire in an iron grip. The government system itself can best be described as "enlightened despotism" because everything, in practice as well as in theory, was done for the public good. Since the emperor was the sacred son of the sun, and according to general belief had been permeated with divine wisdom and power, his deeds were considered to be infallible and intended to give each person his share of good fortune and prosperity.

The aptitude for organization and the remarkable agrarian system of the Inca Indians have made an immense impression on posterity, and we often forget that Inca civilization was built upon older cultures which had already developed many of its more prominent features. It is, for example, fully established today that Inca culture took over important elements from its predecessors, the Tiahuanaco and Chimú cultures. They were superficially discussed in the last chapter but in this context deserve our special attention.

South of the loftily situated Lake Titicaca (12,500 feet above sea level) are the ruins of the temple city of Tiahuanaco, during the centuries immediately preceding 1000 A.D. the center of the culture of the same name. The Tiahuanaco culture is famous for its austere artistic design, its ceramic decor—the jaguar or the puma being a familiar motif since the days of the Chavín culture—and its remarkable architecture, above all manifested in the so-called Sun Gate. Temples and other buildings were erected with monoliths of colossal dimensions, all joined to each other with the utmost precision. The bearers of this culture were probably the ancestors of the Aymará Indians who live in the same region. This is of some interest, considering the fact that some scholars suppose that the Inca tribe was originally a branch of the Aymará which later became incorporated with Quechuan-speakers. However that may be, the Inca people seem to have learned

2. This makes a striking parallel to the administration in other high cultures in the Old World where the kingdom was divided into four provinces linked with the cardinal points.

from their predecessors of the Tiahuanaco culture, directly or indirectly, as is evident in the buildings in Cuzco and its defense fortification, Sacsahuaman. Perhaps also the Inca's principal deity of later times, Viracocha (or Huiracocha), descended from Tiahuanaco as Ph. A. Means, Trimborn, and other scholars believe. According to the myth he first appeared over Lake Titicaca. It seems to be this myth which in a changed form and linked to the sun god became the origin tradition of the Inca dynasty. The central figure on the Sun Gate may possibly depict Viracocha.[3]

The Chimú culture flourished on the northern coastland between 1200 and 1400 A.D., when a powerful dynasty established a firmly organized state on the ruins of the Mochica culture. The capital was Chanchan, the largest city in pre-Columbian South America. The Chimú culture is best known for its handicraft in gold and brilliant feathers. According to the dynastic traditions, the Chimú people travelled on rafts from an unknown land in the south or, according to one source, from "a great ruler beyond the sea," to the coast of northern Peru. This is probably an allusion to a deity, the mythical forefather of the Chimú dynasty. At their assumption of power the Inca princes found the kingdom in the north superior to everything they had seen before in organization and culture, and they were ready to learn. Rowe maintains that the political organization of the Inca state was elaborated by Topa Inca (d. 1493) after he had defeated the Chimú kingdom and carefully examined its structure. Even city planning, methods for mass production, and techniques of featherwork of the late Inca period seem to have been inspired by the Chimú.

Its religion, on the other hand, seems to have made less of an impression on the Inca Indians. Perhaps the distance between the peoples of the mountain areas and of the coastland in lifestyle and spiritual interests was just too great. Presently we will see exemplified the Chimú people's resistance to the Inca religion. There is no reference to a god of creation. There

3. Trimborn 1961, pp. 133f. (after Means 1931?).

was a moon goddess, Si, the guardian of weather and harvest, but the sun played an insignificant part. The sea, Ni, was an important god, as is to be expected in a coastal region. The cult of stones and holy places was common to the coastland and the mountains. There are accounts of ceremonial cannibalism with sexual orgies which might indicate a fertility cult.[4]

A closer scrutiny of Inca religion, that is, the religion which was upheld by the Inca tribe and later made the official state religion of the Inca empire, seems to suggest that it received impulses from other peoples only in the beginning of the Inca epoch (compare what was stated above about Viracocha and his origin). During its later expansion the Inca religion became stilted and inflexible mythologically as well as ritually in a way which seems to have closed the door upon foreign influence. There was indeed a deliberate, government-controlled effort to assimilate defeated tribes into the state by an active missionary policy. (The same aims were sometimes furthered by shifting whole tribes and by forced colonization.) Usually the mission task was carried out by introducing the sky or sun god in the newly gained territory; temples were built to the foremost Inca gods and the new doctrine was preached. At the same time the pantheons of the defeated peoples were brought to Cuzco, where they were installed in the temples and worshipped as lower deities. Each time members of defeated tribes visited the capital they could attend services with their old gods in the temples.

The background just described gives an indication of the complicated religious structure of the Inca state, reflecting as it does the socio-political and ethnic structure. There are three different strata of religion to be discerned, each one of them to some degree contingent on the others.

The first stratum is that of the hereditary religion of the Inca people, privileged in the state cult and enthusiastically propagated by the Inca emperors. It was universal to the whole empire and, at least officially, accepted by everyone. The em-

4. Cf. Rowe 1948, Kutscher 1950.

perors even insisted that the aims of the wars of conquest were to please the gods and spread the faith. We will later give a closer description of this "state religion."

The next religious stratum was represented by the great gods of the defeated states and tribes, who were subordinated to the Inca gods. The defeated peoples were forced to accept such ranking. One exception was the cult of Pachacamac ("the earth creator") in the town of the same name just south of Lima. The veneration of this god and of his huge pyramidal temple was so great that after the conquest of this coastal city the Incas allowed him to be worshipped together with the sun god, and all through later Inca times he was regarded as identical to Viracocha. At the time of the Spanish conquest the temple city of Pachacamac was distinguished as "the Mecca of Peru." Another coastal deity who kept her position after the assumption of power of the Inca Indians was Mamacocha ("the sea mother"), ruler of marine creatures and in certain districts popular among the fishermen. Attempts have been made by Krickeberg to trace the goddess from the sea god of the Chimú culture, but such a development does not seem psychologically feasible.

As a rule the central cults of the indigenous local gods on the outskirts of the empire were transferred to Cuzco. Exceptions made for certain coastal deities are probably due to the fact that they were better adapted to the needs of the coastal population than were the gods of the mountains. The sun cult of the Incas never gained popularity in the coastal area. "The sun burns up our earth," said the rulers around Pachacamac to the Inca prince Capac Yupanqui, who defeated this country.

The third stratum of religion was the "folk religion," the simple faith and cult of villagers all over the Andean empire. From certain points of view it may also be labeled the fundamental structure of religion upon which the other strata were established. The two pivots for the folk religion were life-cycle rites for individuals and vegetation rites for the community. The life-cycle rites (*rites de passage*) usually comprise all the rites performed in connection with the decisive transitions in human life, birth (and name-giving), puberty, perhaps marriage, along with illness and death. Vegetation rites involve rites that refer to changes in the vegetational cycle; all over the Inca empire these have as their object the care of the field crops and the tuber plants. The Peruvian popular religion, then, was a religion for the mundane interests of the individual, the family, and the village community. Its functionaries were partly medicine men summoned to perform some of the life-cycle rites, partly village representatives who attended to the fertility ceremonies (the two categories were, for that matter, not strictly separated). Every village had recourse to a number of *huaca* (sacred places or objects). Each household had its sacred place and each individual its guardian spirit.

The concept of *huaca* was, and still is, peculiar to the Peruvian popular religion. It was not only meaningful for the peasants of the Inca ruler, but was represented in all the lands conquered by the Incas and formed a very important element of the state cult. It lives on today as perhaps the most typical exponent of indigenous Andean religion. The word itself signifies something holy, sacred. In the Inca empire there were thousands of places and things that were *huaca*, especially springs and stones but also houses, graves, mummies, amulets, hills, mountains, and battlefields. All sanctuaries were *huaca*, and the city of Cuzco was one great *huaca*. The higher the mountains were, the more intense was their quality of *huaca*: the mountain cult had a central position in the Inca religion. High in the mountain regions, even up to 20,000 feet above sea level, archaeologists have found altars and mummy bundles of male children and youths who were sacrificed to the mountains or their powers to make them bring good harvests in the cultivated valleys far below.

Also belonging to the *huaca* were the stone piles (*apoceta*) found along the roads at dangerous mountain defiles; the passersby threw stones or chews of coca on them for safe passage, a custom also found in western North America (for example, among the Modoc Indians) and one that has an exact counterpart in the mountain territories of Mongolia and

Tibet (*obo* heaps). The most famous *huaca* were the temple of
the sky gods and the stone stela outside Cuzco which was
believed to be a petrified Inca prince protecting the imperial
family. To the peasants the most important *huaca* were the tall
stones raised in the middle of the fields, which were called
"the watchman of the field" (*wanka*).

Of these three strata of religion in Peru the lowest one has
survived to our time. It is relatively unaffected by the political
upheavals of the centuries, even if much of its practice today
takes place in Catholic guise. The local national religions, on
the other hand, have disappeared. They perished together
with the official religion of the Inca dominion and have left
only traces here and there in popular belief.

We now return to the official Inca religion, which is of great
interest to the modern scholar on account of its association
with the state system and the high level of civilization. It is
fortunate, therefore, that it has been preserved for posterity
in large part through the work of the Spanish chroniclers,
even if the information they have left us is uneven and
our comprehension of the religious conditions cannot be
unambiguous.[5]

Our main sources are partly reports ("Informaciones")
which, shortly after the conquest, were sent to the viceroy of
Peru, and the accounts ("Relaciones") delivered to Charles V
in Spain; partly the compilations of older sources in Cobo,
Oviedo, Las Casas, and others; and, finally, some separate
works: Garcilaso de la Vega's "Los Comentarios reales" (Royal
Commentaries) of 1609 and 1617, Polo de Ondegardo's writings from the middle of the sixteenth century, and Cristóbal
de Molina's extraordinary work, "Relación de las fabulas y
ritos de los Incas," from the same period. The Inca descendant
Garcilaso de la Vega was long held to be the best source; now
we know that his information is in part fabricated and is
furthermore colored by his commitment to the interests of the
old dynasty. The most reliable sources are probably the contemporary although propagandistic reports and the accounts

5. On Inca religion in general see the surveys in Rowe 1946 and the other
works listed in notes 1 and 3 above. For a quick review see Hissink 1960.

of Ondegardo and Molina. Molina has also contributed valuable material to the "Informaciones."

The Inca religion, particularly that of Cuzco and its environs, was a religion intimately connected with the national organization and welfare. This was expressed in three different ways. First of all, the religion protected the national interests: its gods, and their servants the priests, promoted the fertility of the fields, the health and prosperity of the people, wars waged by the political leaders, and obedience to the emperor. Another characteristic feature was that the gods were fairly individualized and organized into a polytheistic divine estate reflecting the political hierarchy; there is a striking parallel here to religious circumstances in the high cultures of the Mediterranean basin and the ancient Near East. A third outstanding feature was state control of the priests, the temples, and the rites. Not only was the emperor a living representative of the sun god but his brother held the highest priestly office. On the other hand, the priests indirectly intervened in politics by way of their functions as soothsayers and diviners.

It has often been said that the ancient Inca religion was a sun religion. This is only partly true. The sun was the first ancestor and protector of the imperial house, but he did not hold the leading position in the imperial pantheon, nor can the "sun temples" or the "sun virgins" (to be described presently) be considered as indicative of the precedence of the sun god since they served many other gods besides him. It seems, however, that the sun god was the principal god of the Inca tribe down to the middle of the fifteenth century, when a remarkable religious reform took place.

Its promotor was the ninth sovereign according to Inca chronology, Pachacuti Inca Yupanqui (1438–1471), the son of Viracocha Inca. The reform implied among other things that religion in the defeated provinces was organized according to the Inca pattern and was coordinated with the Inca religion, and that Viracocha, guardian god of the previous Inca, was elevated to the position of Supreme Being of the empire. In a state with an autocratic government where the sovereign had a divine mission it was not at all difficult to carry through these reforms.

From the religio-historical point of view it was nevertheless a powerful achievement when Viracocha was placed in the center of the official cult, and there is reason to suspect that as a religious reformer Pachacuti may well stand comparison, for example, to the pharaoh Ikhnaton of Egypt, originator of the Aton religion. Like other members of his dynasty and the Inca nobility, Pachacuti must have received a theoretical education in his youth which laid a solid foundation for his advanced theological speculations. Tradition tells that the Inca in his theological contemplations searched for a homogeneous creative principle. The sun god could not be the creator since he regularly rose and set, never rested and, moreover—a sign of his inferiority—was at times concealed by clouds. Pachacuti proclaimed to the priests of the sun that Viracocha was creator and Supreme Being. Local culture heroes and creator figures all through the Inca state were then interpreted as manifestations of Viracocha.

Who was this god then, originally? Opinions are divided. Some scholars have tried to interpret him as an old culture hero; others maintain that he is a half-forgotten sky or weather god who was re-activated. There are reasons for both interpretations. The myths tell how Viracocha travelled around Peru, established cults and taught the people to cultivate the soil and practice various arts. At last he wandered out into the western sea and was lost to the sight of the people. Such narratives of how the culture hero exits from the world after a well-executed task, sometimes with the promise to return near the end of time, are fairly common among the Algonkin and Salish tribes of North America. Other information offered by the Spanish chroniclers describes Viracocha as a god of nature who lives in thunder and storm clouds and who sends lightning and rain. His collaboration with the elements is evident also in the myth of creation. However, Rowe thinks that these characteristics in Viracocha are secondary developments around this—in his view—newly fabricated deity. Viracocha, he points out, means something like "a wise man," "a god," and is the title of a group of deities rather than a name. Thus Pachacuti's Supreme Being was called Teqzi Viraqochan Pachayachachi, "fundamental god, creator of the world." At Urcos in the Cuzco valley was a shrine with an image of the local procreator, who was a *viracocha* and, according to Rowe, came to be identified with the creator whom Pachacuti synthesized.[6]

This is probably not how it actually happened. Gods who are worshipped are not produced intellectually; they appear in visions to their prophets. We know that Pachacuti had visions (among others, a vision of the sun before a famous battle) and his predecessor had beheld a *viracocha* in a vision. The new cult introduced by Pachacuti must have been inspired by extraordinary religious experiences. At the same time he must have drawn on an older tradition which seems to have been obscured by the sun cult. It is not likely that a simple local god was elevated to such a high position that he pushed aside the dominant sun god; on the other hand, a local god of this kind may have been assimilated with the Supreme Being and may thus have influenced his cult. It is probable that the nature god characteristics attributed to Viracocha are genuine and intrinsic, that is to say, that Pachacuti appropriated them together with the conception of Viracocha. It is true that these naturalistic characteristics can be associated with the specialized god of thunder, but no direct genetic connection between him and Viracocha should be assumed for that reason.[7] In all probability Pachacuti restored an ancient belief in a sky and weather god with an unknown name—perhaps the name was too holy to be pronounced or perhaps this being had earlier been called "the god," Viracocha. This sky god, vaguely remembered and pushed aside by the sun god, was restored through Pachacuti's reform and simultaneously provided with creative

6. Rowe 1960.

7. Data from tribal American religions show that the thunder can be personalized as a special god and be part of the functions of the Supreme Being in the same individual's beliefs (cf. Chapter 4). It should be added that there were several regional thunder gods in the Inca realm (Mariscotti 1975).

functions that had earlier been reserved for various figures (culture heroes, among others).

Most probably Pachacuti's reform was induced for political reasons. We have already mentioned how this Inca organized the cult in the conquered provinces and it is certainly not inconceivable that, as Brundage has maintained, the doctrine of the apotheosis of the Inca emperor was dictated by Pachacuti. When the borders of the country were extended to include also the low, sun-baked territories along the coast the sun god was hardly a suitable god to put at the head of the imperial pantheon. The farming peoples at the oases on the coastal plains could be expected to revere Viracocha more than the burning sun god.

Even after Pachacuti's reform Viracocha probably appeared to the individual peasant mainly as a "reposing" god (*deus otiosus*), a deity who only came from his remote heaven to help mankind in times of emergency. As before, the common people probably addressed their prayers instead to the many supernatural beings who protected his work under the supervision of the Supreme Being. In the state cult, on the other hand, Viracocha played a prominent part and regular offerings were made to him so that he would make the country flourish. In Cuzco's "sun temple" stood his statue of pure gold—an anthropomorphic figure with his right arm raised in a commanding gesture and his right hand closed except for the thumb and the index finger. It was this statue and not that of the sun that dominated the famous temple.

During the great sacrificial ceremonies in Cuzco in the month of August, Viracocha was honored as foremost of the gods, and the high priest addressed him with a prayer which deserves to be rendered here in full:

> Oh Viracocha, Lord of the world,
> whether you are male or female,
> you are for certain the one
>   who reigns over heat and creation,
> the one who can work charms with his saliva.
> Where are you?

I wish you were not concealed from these your sons!
Perhaps you are above, perhaps you are below us,
perhaps you are far away in space.
Where is your mighty tribunal?
Hear me!
Perhaps you dwell in celestial waters
or in the waters beneath the world
  and on their sandy shores.
Creator of the world,
Creator of mankind,
great among our ancestors,
before you,
my eyes grow faint
although I long to see you—
for if I see you,
get to know you,
listen to you
and understand you,
you will see me
and get to know me.
Sun and moon,
day and night,
summer and winter,
they wander not in vain
but in prescribed order
to their determined place,
to their goal.
They arrive
to wherever
you lead
with your royal staff.
O hear us,
listen to us,
let it not be
that we tire
and die.
O victorious Viracocha,
ever-present Viracocha!
You are unequalled on earth.
You exist from the beginning of the world
  to its end.

You gave life and courage to man when you said
"Let this be a man,"
and you gave the same to woman when you said
"Let this be a woman."
You created us and gave us a soul.
Watch over us that we may live in health and peace.
You who may be in the highest heavens
among storm clouds
give us long-lasting life,
and accept our offering,
O Creator.[8]

This hymn of the high priest to Viracocha contains some features characteristic of a Supreme Being: the tendency toward androgyny which is often discernible among the high gods of the high cultures and is a symbol of their creative capacity, perhaps also of their perfection or their inexplicable nature; the omnipresence and eternal existence that raise these Supreme Beings over other gods; and, finally, their protecting and supervising functions, here symbolized by the staff or scepter, the cosmic pole.

As has been mentioned, many deities represented in a more specific way some of the functions of the Supreme God; officially he had delegated his duties to a number of supernatural beings. Foremost among these was the sun god, Inti, who dominated the pantheon of the Inca Indians before Pachacuti. Several knowledgeable authors, moreover, have confused him with Viracocha, thereby facilitating their endeavors to represent the Inca religion as a sun religion. The sun god was, as we have seen, supposed to be the first ancestor of the dynasty and was consequently especially cherished by the nobility, but the simple peasants of the highlands were also interested in him, as at those altitudes crops are totally dependent on the heat of the sun. Inti was represented by a large circular face surrounded by rays made entirely of gold. His consort was the moon goddess Mamaquilla, who controlled the festival calendar.

8. This hymn may be found in several works: for instance, Means 1931, pp. 437ff.

Another important god, also mentioned above, was Illapa, the thunder god, who sent the rain. He was represented as a man in luminous clothes symbolizing the lighting, with a war club in one hand and a sling in the other. One of the myths ascribed to this god has a striking resemblance to the Indo-European myth of the dragon guarding the rainwater: when the people were thirsting for rain, Illapa with a stone from his sling broke the jar in which his sister kept the rainwater, whereupon it streamed down over the earth.[9]

The sun, the moon, and the thunder, the gods who protected the Inca farmer's life in the highlands, were the most worshipped powers in Peru besides the Supreme Being. But there were plenty of gods and spirit powers, and several others in addition to those just mentioned were associated with productivity. Star gods watched over the crops, over the llama herds, over the wild animals. The earth goddess Pachamama looked after the well-being of the plants and seems to have also protected the llamas: diminutive metal figures of alpacas were buried in the grazing pastures, presumably to urge the goddess to make the herds increase. In all probability this cult was limited to the rural population even if the goddess as such appeared in the official state cult.

The images and symbols of gods mentioned earlier were kept in temples. The foremost sanctuary was situated, as we would expect, in the capital of Cuzco: it was the famous "sun temple" with images of Viracocha and other major gods. The remnants of this temple today house the Dominican monastery of the city. The temple was surrounded by a wall, and it consisted of a number of square rooms around a central court. The inner sides of the walls were adorned with gold plates. The whole temple complex was the residence of the golden images of the gods and the servants of their cult, the priests and the "sun virgins," who will be described presently. General ceremonies, on the other hand, were not performed in this or in other temples. Such events regularly took place outside on a central plaza. Only the priests and the high state

9. The myth of the thunder god: see, for example, Mason 1957, p. 204. It was first communicated by Garcilaso de la Vega.

dignitaries had access to the temples. Major temples like Cuzco's sun temple were administered by priests of royal blood.

The Inca emperor and his immediate family were on the
borderline between the divine and the human. Their origins
were lost in a mythical age when their ancestors, the children
of the sun god, descended from heaven. According to the
legend the founder of the dynasty had himself become petrified and *huaca*. His successors had been mummified in accordance with an ancient Peruvian tradition. At the mummifi-
cation the intestines were removed and the body desiccated,
whereupon it was shrouded in fine textiles. Each Inca *ayllu*
had its "hero," its founder, who was preserved mummified,
and each Inca emperor was given the same privilege. With
folded arms and in full regal attire, complete with headband,
gold tassel, and gold mask over the face, the dead monarchs
were seated in a row on golden chairs along the walls of *Inti
huasi*, the sun temple. They were served as they were in life;
they even had ladies-in-waiting who whisked away flies with
fans. The imperial mummies were present at each great ceremony celebrated on the plaza facing the sun temple. In the
center before the temple wall the living Inca himself resided
under a canopy, surrounded by high court officials and
priests. On both sides of this central group the imperial ancestors were seated, now as in their lifetimes spectators of the
sacred rites and dances.

The living ruler, *sapa Inca* ("omnipotent Inca") or *intip cori*
("the son of the sun"), was carried about in a magnificent
palanquin and honored like a god: "Supreme Lord, the son of
the sun, you are the one and beloved ruler, all the earth obeys
you." Ecstatic shouts of joy greeted him wherever he went.
The people seldom caught a glimpse of him, however, for he
hid himself and his divinity behind the curtains of the palanquin. Pedro Pizarro, a cousin to the conqueror of Peru, says
that everything that the Inca sovereign touched—clothes,
carpets, food, and so on—had to be burned and the ashes
scattered to the winds lest these holy things be polluted by
some mortal. These taboos remind us of those found in the
sacred kingdoms of many places of the Old World, for exam-

ple in Africa and the South Pacific. Because of the divine birth of the Inca only his own sister could become his official consort, *qoya*. Such marriages between brother and sister intended to protect the purity of the royal blood are well known from, for example, the Mixtec, Hawaii, Persia, and Egypt (during Ptolemaic times). When the emperor assumed power, specially chosen fair young virgins were sacrificed; these sacrifices were repeated if he ever fell seriously ill. At his death his favorite wives and servants were expected voluntarily to be buried with him. Amidst frenzied rites they were poisoned with *chicha* beer and afterward strangled. This reminds us of the Natchez Indians in Mississippi and their similar manner of dispatching those members of the chief's family and his household who wished to accompany "the Great Sun" in death.

In the cult the Inca emperor personified the sun god before the people and the people before the sun god. And just as the Inca was believed to represent the sun god (and the Supreme Being?) *qoya* represented the moon goddess. Together the royal consorts thus impersonated the creative powers of existence.

At the top of the church hierarchy was the high priest, whose office probably was in earlier times that of a peace chief. If that was the case, the military organization of the Inca monarchy is an example of a political order in which the war chief took the lead. One member of the Inca family, most often the emperor's brother, acted as high priest. The highest dignitaries of the foremost temples were also, as mentioned before, of royal rank. The priests were strictly graded according to rank and dignity. The size and venerability of the temple and, of course, the position of the office within the local temple hierarchy were decisive for the esteem and dignity of a priest. Under the highest dignitaries, who also led the religious ceremonies, were the seers and those priests who received confessions; lowest in rank were the temple workmen, who were recruited from the ordinary people.

An interesting group of temple servants were "the selected women," young girls collected from among the people, who were either reserved to be sacrificed to the gods or else entered into a sort of religious order led by an abbess of royal birth, "the consort of the sun." These virgins were often guarded by eunuchs. Because they had been consecrated to the sun and to unswerving chastity they were called "the virgins of the sun." Each major temple had such vestals. Their task was to sew ceremonial clothes, prepare corn beer (*chicha*), and participate in the great ceremonies. They may also, like their sisters in Rome, have guarded the holy fire which was lit anew at each New Year festival—at least that is the opinion of the American ethnologist Loeb, based on Garcilaso's accounts of this matter.[10]

One of the main functions of the higher priests was to officiate at the great annual rites. These rites could serve several purposes at once: they could urge the gods to bring forth rain, cure the sick, and initiate the youth into adulthood. The Inca people had a strictly regulated festival calendar linked to the months of the moon and primarily adapted to the practical and religious needs of the corn cultivator. Of course there were also rites to promote the growth of root crops like potatoes, but the chroniclers have only dealt with the corn ceremonies, perhaps because corn, being new to the highlands, came under the special protection of the Inca and the priestly class (as J. V. Murra maintains).

Each month had its great festival. First came the New Year festival in June, when the new fire was ignited by means of a concave bronze mirror focusing the sun rays to light the tinder. In the third month, the sowing month, the Inca and his priests initiated the agricultural season by digging up the fields around Cuzco with a golden foot plow. The festival of the fourth month was devoted to the exorcism of diseases; that of the seventh month to puberty ceremonies for boys; that of the eighth month to abundant offerings to the major gods on the large court in front of the sun temple, at which time the emperor, his court, and his mummified predecessors

10. Garcilaso de la Vega 1869–71 (2), pp. 155ff.

were present. At this festival, evidently held to promote the fertility of the land and the prosperity of all, an enormous artificial snake made of multicolored llama wool was presented. Could it have been a symbol of fertility?

The great religious ceremonies consisted mainly of ritual dances and processions, prayers and sacrifices, fasting and drinking bouts. Llamas and guinea pigs were usually offered, and occasionally human beings were sacrificed as well. Sacrifices of human beings, though, seem to have been less numerous during the Inca hegemony than in previous periods. The cult in Pachacamac before the Inca period, for example, is likely to have been much bloodier in this respect.

Many priests devoted themselves to divination and curing the sick. They divined with the aid of the intestines of sacrificed llamas, the flights of birds, and the movements of animals, and they engaged in ceremonies and exorcisms to expel the spirits that possessed the bodies of the sick. As physicians, however, they were less important than the popular medicine men who worked with archaic methods corresponding to the diagnoses of intrusion and soul loss.

The priests also contributed to strengthening state control over the individual, even in the domain of personal conscience. People who failed, people who were crippled or had lost their children, were considered malefactors. The gods had punished them for a sin they had committed, perhaps a theft, a ceremonial transgression, or even disobedience toward Inca. He who was guilty of such a crime did well to confess as soon as possible to a priest. The priest could give absolution but at the same time had to subject the delinquent to a certain penalty, for example, some days of fasting or a night's vigil in prayer before a *huaca*. The penance ended with a purification bath in running water.

If the sinner did not make a full confession he fared badly. He was not only stricken with the wrath of the powers in this life but after death he also had to starve and freeze in a place deep in the interior of the earth where there were only stones for food. On the other hand, his friends who had led a virtuous life and confessed their sins, if any, led a happy existence with an abundance of food and drink in the sun god's heaven. The aristocracy, intended for a higher world, ended up there regardless of their way of life on earth.

When the Inca himself died he went to his father, the sun god. It is uncertain whether in recognition of his fortunate destination he could more easily part from this life. Inca Pachacuti's last words indicate a mood of resignation: "I was born and I grew up as a lily in the field. Then came time and old age and death, and I withered away and died."

Dakota Sioux tree burials. Courtesy of the Denver Public Library.

Right: Burial Chamber in the Temple of the Inscriptions at Palenque. Photo by Henri Stierlin.

Tomb A, La Venta. Photo by I. Groth-Kimball, from I. Bernal: *The Olmec World.*

Scenes of human sacrifice as represented on monuments, codices, and wall paintings, Chichen Itza. From S. G. Morley: *The Ancient Maya* (Stanford, California, Stanford University Press); reproduced with permission.

Aztec sacrifice, from Codex Megliabecchiano (Loubat Copy). Courtesy of the Library of Congress.

Colossal Olmec head from Tres Zapotes, now at Santiago Tuxla. Photo by R. Heizer, from I. Bernal: *The Olmec World*.

Colossal Aztec jaguar with hole in back, probably meant to receive human hearts. Photo by Carlos Saenz, from I. Bernal: *The Olmec World*.

Jaguar from one of the carved friezes at Teotihuacan. Photo by Eugen Kusch.

The Temple of the Sun at Teotihuacan. Courtesy of the American Museum of Natural History.

Relief from Palenque. Photo by Henri Stierlin.

Right: Relief panel of a rain priest used as a lintel in the ancient Mayan city of Yaxchilan. Reproduced by courtesy of the Trustees of the British Museum.

Intihuatana at Machu Picchu. Photo by Jean-Christian Spahni.

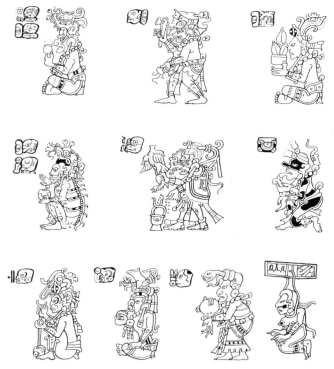

Principal deities of the Maya Pantheon as represented in the codices. From S. F. Morley: *The Ancient Maya* (Stanford, California, Stanford University Press); reproduced with permission.

The sacred cenote or well of sacrifice at Chichen Itza. Courtesy of The Peabody Museum of Archeology and Ethnology at Harvard University.

Aztec Calendar from the Codex Borgia, Messicano I, fol. 30. Courtesy of the Biblioteca Apostolica Vaticana.

13

Mayan Religion

The Maya Indians are still the most enigmatic people of the American continents. With their habitation up to the present day partly in the mountainous areas and lowlands of Guatemala and southern Mexico—today covered by impenetrable rain forests—and partly on the monotonous limestone plateau of Yucatán, these Indians gave rise to a civilization unequalled in pre-Columbian America in its aesthetic and intellectual achievements.[1] Where and when it originated is still undetermined, as is the way in which the Maya developed their art of writing, their arithmetic, and their remarkably exact astronomy surpassing that of the ancient Babylonians.[2] As little is known of the direct causes for the decline and fall of the Mayan culture. Where once priests performed their intricate ceremonies and scholars among them searched for the secrets of the cosmos, there is now nothing left but ruins of

1. General works on Maya culture: Tozzer 1940, Morley and Brainerd 1956, Brainerd 1954, Thompson 1954a, 1954b, Coe 1966. See also Spinden 1917, pp. 65–135.
2. The foundations of these arts were, as we have seen, probably laid by the Olmecs (who were Maya?).

disintegrating temples in a tropical forest. What happened to them—the artists, the intellectuals, the upholders of the finest civilization of Indian America? The Lacandones, remnants of the former Mayan people who even today lead an independent existence, reveal a primitivism in their cultural life which seems most distant from the Mayan high culture.

Considering the difficulties in developing such a prominent civilization in a primitive forest area, where in older times there was only slash-and-burn cultivation (*milpa*), some scholars, such as Steward and Meggers, have suggested that the Mayan culture was brought in its entirety from outside. Other scholars, such as Dumond, have been able to ascertain, however, that slash-and-burn cultivation need in no way be an obstacle for either the domiciliation required in all higher cultures or the surplus production which allows for unrestricted intellectual and artistic endeavors. Furthermore, recent research seems to indicate a gradual development of the classical Mayan culture on the basis of an earlier formative culture. In all probability the Olmec culture provided the foundation on which Mayan culture later evolved. Linguistic data demonstrate that the Mayan peoples, including the Huaxtec on the northeast coast of Mexico, spread from Huehuetenango in northwestern Guatemala, where a corn-farming community was in existence as early as 2600 B.C. The developing Mayan culture may have become crystallized in Petén in northern Guatemala during the first centuries A.D., as the Maya scholar Altschuler has suggested. In any case, Mayan culture did not come into its own until the classical period, roughly the years 300–900 A.D. It was then widespread, partly in the lowlands around Petén, partly in northern Yucatán, with its center and highest flourishing in the lowlands.[3]

Essential for Mayan culture was the collaboration between the slash-and-burn cultivators and the priests, who promoted

3. On the foregoing see Altschuler 1958, Dumond 1961, Vogt 1963, Sanders 1962; see also Sanders and Price 1968. It seems that the beginnings of Maya art took place in southern Guatemala at the start of the Christian era (Meggers 1973, p. 53).

agriculture by means of their ritual activities in the temple cities. Rotating slash-and-burn civilization to some extent hindered the growth of urban developments of the type existing in ancient Peru, but it could stimulate the building of exclusive centers of administration and cult to serve the needs of the farming community. The Mayan culture is not alone in this: Egypt of the Old and Middle Kingdoms, Mycenaean Greece, and Cambodia developed similarly. On the other hand, these temple-city constructions would not have materialized had not the priests had a firm organization and political power. The Mayan territory in the classical period was apparently divided into numerous small states ruled by priest-princes. In post-classical times these states were united in cult amphictyonies or political confederations (for example, the Mayapán confederation, consisting of three city-states in northern Yucatán: Mayapán, Uxmal, and Chichén Itzá).

The question of the relationship between peasants and priests is of great importance to our understanding of the classical culture. There are two conflicting opinions. The first one, held by Maya specialist J. Eric Thompson, among others, suggests that there existed, despite general unanimity as to the aims of the cult and religion, a dualism between the priestly hierarchy and the peasants, who worked for their own sustenance as well as for that of the priests. In support of this thesis it may be mentioned that, according to Bishop Landa, the priests in Yucatán were recruited from the sons of the priests and the younger sons of the aristocracy—in other words, they formed a closed elite. Landa's statements, however, refer to conditions of post-classical times and we do not know to what extent they are applicable to the Mayan culture of the classical period. The second opinion, as it has been presented in later years by scholars like Willey, Saler, and Dumond, amounts to emphasizing a closer association between the cult centers of the classical period and the rural areas than had previously been assumed, and also emphasizing the participation of the peasants themselves in the ceremonial structure. Secondary cult centers were thus established in the villages, and pilgrimages were undertaken to the great temple cities. Perhaps these two opinions can be reconciled to some degree. Presumably there was a gap between priests and peasants, at least toward the end of the classical period, but on the other hand the peasants may not have been totally excluded from the cult system.[4]

In assessing this problem it is important for us to recall what Morley in particular has emphasized, namely that the entire official Mayan religion and in addition such priestly inventions as mathematics and astronomy originated in close contact with the needs of the agriculturalist (that is to say, corn cultivator).[5] Rain and fertility gods occupied the Mayan pantheon and the rites were carefully adjusted to the rhythm of the vegetation year. Mathematical skills became highly significant for chronology and astronomy, which kept pace with the progress of mathematics. With the help of numerology, chronology, and astronomy the learned priest could predict not only sun and moon eclipses and the rise and descent of planets but, what was even more essential, he could also provide weather forecasts and calculate the duration of the harvest year. In this way he joined the practical peasant and assisted him with efficient planning of his food production, which in the long run led to a harvest surplus.

The powerful position of the clergy was not only concentrated at the intellectual and cultic level but was also political. As we have seen above, the Indian states of the classical period were mainly priestly states. They were gentler in nature than the often bloody and tyrannical regimes that replaced them. As far as the Maya are concerned, it seems plausible that the lack of genuinely urban settlements prevented growth of complex political institutions which could serve as a basis for despotism and a rigid state organization. The Maya Indians of the classical period probably were distributed into a number of lesser state structures without a common central authority, but with a priest-king as local potentate: the pyramid grave in Palenque seems to constitute

4. Cf. Willey 1956, Saler 1962.
5. Morley and Brainerd 1956, pp. 183ff.

the last resting-place of such a sacred ruler. We know nothing about the presence of dual moieties among the Maya. Otherwise, for reasons explained earlier, it would seem quite natural for the top administration to have been divided between a priest-king (heir to the peace chief) and a war chief, who would be less important in the comparatively peaceful state. In the epic *Popol Vuh* there are suggestions of a diarchy among the Maya-speaking Quiché in Guatemala. The same epic also relates how, in the beginning of time, two brothers (probably the sun and the moon) attacked the dark powers of the nether world in a ball-game, perhaps a mythological projection of ritual ball-games between sacred moieties.

It is true that Brainerd and other scholars have maintained that the political leader of the Maya combined civil, military, and religious functions, but they base their supposition on the conditions of a post-classical period when the Toltecs had conquered parts of Yucatán. At the arrival of the Spaniards, the Maya Indians were ruled by princes who were the sole representatives of secular power. During the classical period the situation must have been different. Everything points to a person invested with the highest priestly office as having been the dominant figure in a society completely subject to the demands of the religion and the priesthood.

The temple cities of the classical period, the most remarkable monuments in America, give evidence of the powerful position of the priests and the religion, but also of the sober taste and the refined and individualized conception of art that prevailed in leading circles. Even today the temple ruins betray what majestic structures these sacred cities once must have been. Step pyramids with broad flights of stairs rise in ledges above and alongside each other. Crowning the pyramid is the massively built temple with small cell-like rooms below protruding corbeled vaults. An authority like Thompson notes with certainty that the small and dark temple halls are well in tune with the religious pattern: the Maya, he maintains, were an introvert people and their religion was esoteric. In the temple rooms, or at least in some of them, are the altar stones on which the sacrifices to the rain gods were once performed.[6]

In the interior of a number of pyramids, as in the famous pyramid in Palenque (dating from the beginning of the seventh century), archaeologists have found tombs where generally higher potentates have been buried—in Palenque, the priest-king and his court. Recent investigations seem to imply that the majority of pyramids contain tombs and the archaeologist Ruz Lhuillier maintains that in Palenque the tombs antedate the temple buildings. Coe's thesis that the pyramids be regarded primarily as sepulchral monuments seems, however, somewhat limited.[7] It has been suggested lately that the pyramids symbolized ancestral gods, just as the Maya of today believe ancestral gods to be residing in the sacred mountains. This theory is hardly valid: a burial mound is not changed into a god. We must keep in mind that the pyramids, as far as the cult was concerned, were first of all temple foundations. They may have a superficial resemblance to the Egyptian grave pyramids, but in reality they were more closely related to the Sumerian temple towers (*ziqqurat*) which were reproductions of the cosmic mountain. The dwelling of heavenly gods should be situated on high: the temple pyramid can be regarded as a cultic expression of this belief.[8]

In the vicinity of the temples are beautifully ornamented "palaces" on their platforms, long buildings with narrow rooms and heavy walls. They were probably used as storage rooms for cult objects and other sacred necessities rather than as apartments for the nobles. (The priestly class lived in houses thatched with palm leaves near the temple city and the peasants in simpler huts further away.) In some city ruins, high round towers are still standing, no doubt used as astronomical observatories at one time. Between the buildings are large game courts which were once the setting for the ritual ball-games of the sacred moieties. The game was played

6. Thompson 1955. A classic description of the Mayan pyramids will be found in Holmes 1895.

7. Coe 1956. For references to the Palenque tomb see Chapter 11, note 37.

8. Concerning the Mesopotamian temple towers cf. Parrot 1949.

with hips and shoulders, not with rackets as in southeastern North America; this portrayed the interaction of the forces of the universe, above all the movements of the predestinating stars. In post-classical times the ball game tended to become a profane sport.

The temple city also contains buildings where the purifying sweat baths that regularly preceded each sacred ceremony were taken and, not least, numerous raised stelae, which the Mayan priests had marked with astronomical calculations and chronological data.

We modern Westerners cannot suppress amazement at the skill with which the Mayan priests solved mathematical problems and completed astronomical calculations in spite of their lack of proper instruments. As an illustration of their mathematical sophistication may be mentioned their invention of the zero sign, mostly represented by a figure in the shape of a mussel shell. They also made use of a vigesimal system which could be expressed by two sets of numerical symbols, just as we employ both Arabic and Roman numerals. There is now a strong indication that the Olmec, predecessors of the Maya, were the initiators of this numeral system. It seems they were also the first Mesoamerican astronomers and the first ones to attempt a graphic script.

The Maya were able to develop their astronomy with the help of their mathematical knowledge and through the discipline and patience of their observations. Not only do the stelae and observatory towers in their city plan reveal the emphasis they put on astronomical calculations, but the whole layout of the older part of a city like Uaxactún describes an enormous sundial, by which could be determined the spring and fall equinoxes and the winter and summer solstices, bringing to mind Stonehenge in England. The annual cycle was intensively studied. The Maya used two annual chronologies simultaneously. One was a solar year of 365 days, distributed in 18 months of 20 days each, and 5 "unlucky" days when all important functions were cancelled. The other one was a sacred year of 260 days calculated on a system of 20 days repeated thirteen times; the chronology was based on this sacred year. The two annual series coincided after 52 solar years (equal to 73 sacred years) and thus one time cycle was completed. In observance of this event the old fires were extinguished and a new fire was lit. The starting point of the Mayan chronology is the year 3113 B.C., a date which goes back to a mythic primordial time denoting the beginning of the 52-year cycles.[9]

There are not only numerical symbols carved into the stone stelae. On them, as on walls, paneling, altars, and so forth, is also found the hieroglyphic script of the Maya. It is a stylized rebus script with a great number of glyphs appearing in the most bewildering variations and combinations (syllable with affix or infix). Most of the inscriptions are still undeciphered. In certain inscriptions containing data and astronomical calculations there is a high percentage of deciphered signs, but in inscriptions that deal with rites and gods the percentage is low, to the great disadvantage of the scholar of religion.[10]

About 900 A.D. the temple cities of the central lowland were deserted, and therewith the classical period came to an end. Archaeologists have engaged in vivid speculations as to what really happened. Their guesses have included earthquakes, war, climatic changes, and other upheavals. Meggers thinks that in the long run the Mayan culture lacked an adequate resource center. Morley and others have assumed that the recurring forest-clearings gradually converted the primal forest and its soft humus into an extensive grass savanna with a ground soil that was too unyielding for simple farm implements. J. Eric Thompson, on the other hand, believes that the peasants revolted against priestly domination because in their cultic and intellectual activities the priests had become more and more remote from the fundamental religious values that were important to the peasant culture. Cowgill, finally, maintains that depopulation was a result of the new invaders from the north who forced the people to move and concentrated the population in the vicinity of Chichén Itzá. All these alternatives are conceivable, even though Willey, for example, has

9. The Mayan concept of time has been elucidated in León-Portilla 1973.
10. Cf. Thompson 1960, Knorozov 1958.

lately rejected Thompson's attempt to elucidate the problem. To these alternatives will be added one more, introduced by Linné, which is to the author the most plausible one: the tropical forest took over as a result of ever-increasing precipitation. It is true that following local investigations of erosion, sediment, changes of vegetation, and so on, a couple of American scholars decided to reject the "ecological" hypothesis on the grounds that the Mayan territory was subjected to continuous desiccation, but their argument is not convincing. A change toward a more humid climate is proven to have taken place at this time in the Rio Grande area of northernmost Mexico and southernmost New Mexico. Moreover, the climate of northern California was unusually rainy, as is shown by analyses of the annual growth-rings of trees.[11]

In the tenth century conquering peoples pushed down from the Valley of Mexico in the north into northern Yucatán (where the climate was considerably drier on the sparsely overgrown limestone plateau than in the forest region). The conquerors established their center in one of the old Mayan cities, Chichén Itzá. They were a people of quite another disposition than the Maya. In the Valley of Mexico a gradual development had taken place from priestly supremacy to militarism: the warriors, who had been in charge of taking war prisoners to be sacrificed on the altars of the gods, had instituted a new type of society, where violence and power were valued above sacrifice and prayer and where the priests had become servants of the new war lords. The Toltecs, a Nahua group, were the leaders of this change; they were presumably the ones who invaded northern Yucatán, conquered the Maya, and established what Morley with a somewhat unfortunate phrase has called "the new empire."

11. The fall of the classic Mayan culture is, to quote Willey, the mystery of Mesoamerican archaeology (Willey 1966–71 (1), p. 141). On the discussion above, see Meggers 1954, Morley and Brainerd 1956, p. 71, Thompson 1954a, p. 18, Thompson 1954b, p. 87, Cowgill 1964, Willey 1956, p. 781, Linné 1960, pp. 113f.; cf. Kelley 1952. The invasion hypothesis has recently gained in importance: see Sabloff and Willey 1967, Willey and Shimkin 1971. Cf. also Culbert 1973.

The Toltecs expanded Chichén Itzá, and the appearance of other cities was also adjusted to fit the new military pattern. Mayapán, for example, was provided with a new town wall (the cities of the classical period were always unfortified) and the buildings were mostly intended for secular use. It has been estimated that there were forty buildings designed as living quarters to every sacred building. In Chichén Itzá the new art and architecture introduced by the Toltecs reached its peak with the "temple of the warriors," one of the most beautiful buildings of ancient America. Unlike the older Mayan style, there were no exterior stuccos and no narrow chambers. The overwhelmed visitor encounters large pillared halls, one within another, decorated with carved images of warriors and reliefs representing "the feathered serpent," the patron god of the Toltecs. The style is known from Tula, the old Toltec city in the Valley of Mexico. There are scholars who are of the opinion that the Toltecs developed a higher culture in Yucatán than they had previously known and that they exported this new culture to their old home country.[12]

Conquered or intermingled with the foreigners, the Maya Indians slowly regained their influence. This Mayan renaissance, best exemplified in Mayapán (1200–1450), is decadent and unwieldy. By the time the Spaniards arrived the post-classical florescence of the Maya had passed.[13]

This outline of Mayan history is almost entirely based on the findings and research done by accomplished archaeologists. These archaeologists have also been able to give us glimpses of the Mayan religion. Important problems, such as the type of religious pattern of the Maya Indians, their religio-sociological structure, their cult ceremonies, and their gods, can be at least partially clarified with the assistance of archaeologists, but in tracing more specific religious concepts other resources must be explored.

It was mentioned earlier that many inscriptions deal with religious motifs, although it is difficult to grasp their meaning due to our insufficient knowledge of the ancient Mayan

12. On the Toltec era and its consequences see Tozzer 1957, Kubler 1961.
13. Cf. Pollock 1962.

script. These hieroglyphs were drawn partly on monuments (in particular, the stelae), partly in remarkable "books" consisting of folded sheets of paper prepared from the inner bark of fig and mulberry trees. Thousands of these books were no doubt burned by missionaries and conquistadores on the grounds that they contained wicked superstitions; only three collections of texts (codices) remain, all emanating from the same limited region. The manuscripts, "Dresden," "Madrid," and "Paris" (named after the cities where they were later kept), all deal with the art of divination and prophecies and also contain information about important religious ceremonies, for example, the New Year rites. Texts which probably formed part of lost manuscripts were taken down in European writing by educated Mayans during the first centuries after the European conquest. This is how the Books of Chilam Balam originated, "the books of oracle priests prophesying mysterious things," manuscripts that inform us, among other things, of prophecies, myths, and rites. Also significant in this respect is *Popol Vuh,* a document by an anonymous writer of the 1530s which tells us about cosmology, religion, and sacred history according to the Quiché Indians, a Mayan group in the highlands of southern Guatemala. Foremost of all the source documents, however, is Diego de Landa's "Relación de las cosas de Yucatán" from about 1560 (modern edition: Mérida, 1938). It is, in fact, an apology which Landa was forced to write when he was brought to trial by a Spanish court, accused of negligence in his administration.[14]

The difficulty with the Mayan source material is that it dates back to a time when the militaristic Toltec regime put its stamp on the religion of the Mayan people. Conclusions made looking further back in time can be very dangerous under such circumstances, since the Maya of the classical period, which is the era concerning us here, presented quite another religious profile than during later periods.

14. The origins of the Mayan codices have been analyzed in Schellhas 1926. For a good example of a codex see Thompson 1972. The *Popol Vuh,* divided into four sections according to the four creations, was recently issued in a new English edition: Edmonson 1971. See also Landa 1938.

With this disclaimer, we shall nevertheless now attempt a reconstruction of religious conditions during the classical period.[15] As among the post-classical Incas, the structural pattern of Mayan religion in the classical period reflected society within an ecological, economical, and historical framework. The complex and carefully regulated social order of the high civilization corresponds directly to the complex character of the religion, particularly the cult, and also to the formalistic system of classifying the gods, each god being linked to a certain day or a certain cosmological epoch, for instance. To a higher degree than was the case with the Incas, for example, society conformed to the demands of religion. Like high cultures of the Old World at corresponding levels of civilization, religion constituted the primary integral factor of cultural life in all its aspects; architecture and art, as well as astronomy and script-writing, all served religious purposes. The priests based their authority on these conditions. It seems likely that the priests did all they could to further strengthen and promote the religion as well as their own hegemony. As long as there was harmony between the peasants' needs and their religious satisfactions the predominance of the priests would endure. While the rain and corn gods received their due offerings they would bless the soil and its crops and make the peasant feel secure.

In spite of the pressure of culture and society, religion was a deeply personal matter to each Maya Indian. It is true that the rites outside the temple rooms could be witnessed only by a small number of priests and that the higher cult system was entirely in the hands of the priesthood. Even the ordinary peasant had a share in the religious life, however, for he fasted and prayed, and sacrificed at the critical junctures of life and at the seasonal festivals of the crop year. He lit incense of copal (resin) in bowls, just as the Lacandones do to this day. The Maya Indians are and always have been a religious people; certainly their prayers give evidence of a sincere and devoted religiosity. The following version by Sapper is a

15. Surveys of Mayan religion in Morley and Brainerd 1956, pp. 183ff., Krickeberg 1961, pp. 61ff., Anders 1963, Thompson 1970, pp. 159ff.

striking example of a prayer said by the Kekchi Maya in the highlands of Guatemala before the corn harvest:

> You, O God, you my Lord,
> you my mother, you my father,
> you Lord of hills and valleys.
>
> Now and for three orbits of the sun, three days,
> will I commence to reap my corn
> before your mouth, before your face
> you Lord of hills and valleys.
> Show it to me, to my body, to my soul.
>
> A mere trifle of your food, of your drink
>   I give to you;
> it is as nothing what I give to you;
> but I have much and plenty
> of my food, of my drink;
> you have bestowed it on my soul, on my body,
> you, my mother and my father.
>
> I now begin my harvest,
> but today my harvest will not be done
> before your mouth, before your face.
>
> Who knows, how many orbits of the sun,
>   how many days I harvest;
> to look among the weeds is slow proceeding,
> I will not finish soon.
>
> Who knows, when I can pray to you once more,
> you my mother, you my father,
> you angel, Lord of hills and valleys.
> I shall pray to you once more.
> Would I not, you my God.[16]

This prayer has a distinctly archaic ring. That a deity is described as both father and mother probably indicates a heritage from the old high culture; as Baumann has shown, it is unusual for primitive cultivators to emphasize the androgynous nature of the deity. But observations of this kind should not lead us to suggest that the old Mayan religion be reconstructed on the basis of the religious faith and customs

16. Sapper 1897, p. 293 (translated from the German).

of descendants in a later period. Still, there are scholars who assert this possibility. Thus, R. Girard is trying to reconstruct classical Mayan religion with the help of the modern Chorti religion (mainly the mythology) which, in his view, is a direct replica of the beliefs and concepts of the old Maya Indians. Scholars who argue along such lines forget that classical-period Mayan religion formed an integral part of the Mayan society and that the religion was transformed when the social structure and cultural pattern changed shape. The priestly religion perished and "folk religion" lived on, but without the relationship to ceremonial centers that had previously been its distinction. In his famous work *The Folk Culture of Yucatán* American anthropologist Robert Redfield has described the varying forms of folk religion among the Maya Indians of today.[17]

We now return to the religion of the classical Maya Indians. Of primary interest is the official religion, represented by the priests. It seems to have been fundamentally the same all over the Mayan region at the time. It changed character after the arrival of the Toltecs at Chichén Itzá and surrounding areas, when influences from the Valley of Mexico together with a war cult and bloody mass sacrifices produced a new religious spirit. Attention should be given also to this post-classical religion, although its modes of expression were perhaps not genuinely Mayan. Besides, as was stressed earlier, it is difficult to separate in detail this later religious pattern from its older classical counterpart, since the hieroglyphic manuscripts that should inform us about the gods of the classical period derive from post-classical times.

The religion of the classical period is characterized by a great number of gods, most of them in one way or another connected with the harvest yields and the rotation of the agricultural year. Some of them, such as the rain gods, had more distinctly agrarian characteristics than the others. They seem to have been the favorite gods of the cultivators. Consequently, they survived the fall of the priestly civilization

17. Redfield 1941.

and they continue even today. In Yucatán, where numerous examples are found of pagan gods intermingled with Catholic saints, the rain gods (*chacs*) belong to the holy company led by the archangel Michael. On the other hand, as J. Eric Thompson has pointed out, those gods who were associated solely with the priests, the warriors, or the civil hierarchy have perished. This is particularly true of the powerful divine ruler Itzamna, the prototype of the priests, who is today completely forgotten in Yucatán. But for the majority of the deities, it is uncertain to what extent there was a clearly defined borderline between the gods of priests and peasants. In most cases the priests seem to have shrouded the agricultural gods in a more sophisticated attire and equipped them with qualities and attributes pertaining to the daily and yearly chronologies and to astrology.

It is not always easy to identify the gods in sculpture or in kaleidoscopic representations of the manuscripts, nor is it easy to distinguish among them by their functions. It looks as if the gods (for instance, the sun god) changed shape, indeed character, as soon as they moved from one place to another. It is bewildering to meet the same god in the most different circumstances and to find the same function represented by totally opposite categories of supernatural beings.

How is this confusion in definition, these incongruities in the world of gods, to be explained? Each attempt to solve this riddle is of interest for the wider scope of the history of religions, for the Mayan situation is in many ways reminiscent of the conditions in the Greece of antiquity or in the ancient Near East. It appears that two of the foremost causes of what might be called "the mythological muddle" were regionalism, typical of the classical period not only among the Maya but in the whole of America (cf. Steward), and priestly speculation. The gods became differentiated and were developed in different ways in different parts of the Mayan region; a god who showed a benevolent appearance in one place could in another be gloomy and negative in character. One source of confusion in the realm of religious conceptualization was in many cases the importation of a god who was already known in a different form in the area but who carried with him the local characteristics of another area. Finally, many inconsistencies and changes of functions may have come about when the priests' speculatively projected and more polished notions of the divine were confronted with the more robust gods of nature and of the seasonal crop year.

No doubt the priests developed the Mayan mythology according to their own interests. They combined the gods with days, directions, and colors, and they "collectivized," as it were, the concepts of the divine in a way that recalls shamanic speculation among the Dakota. The rain god Chac, for example, is one deity, but simultaneously four *chacs* are mentioned, one in each of the four sacred cosmic quarters, and in addition there are innumerable *chac*-beings in existence here and there under the sky. Even the main god Itzamna is perceived as four beings united in one god. Basic to this kind of speculation, here as in North America, is evidently the notion of the sacred number four. This in turn is directly connected to the concept of the four cosmic directions and the four quarters of the cosmos (it is incidentally possible that the Maya perceived the four cosmic quarters to be placed alternately with the four cosmic directions, i.e., northeast, northwest, southwest, and southeast). Moreover, the speculation does reveal a genuine religious feeling for the unity and multiplicity of the divine nature, for which a comprehensive definition was desired. Perhaps much ground was covered toward that goal. J. Eric Thompson does not reject the possibility that systematization by some speculators was carried far enough to embrace monotheistic conceptions.[18]

Less clear is to what extent the priests contributed to shaping a dualism in the world view of the Maya Indians, the dualism between good gods and evil gods, or good and evil in the gods, and between paradise and hell. The last-mentioned dualism we will return to in a later context; it is of interest even today and was presumably intensified in the course of the sixteenth century through the influence of the Catholic missions.

18. Thompson 1970, pp. *xxivf.*, 233.

The dualism between the gods is difficult to grasp because negative, deadly functions are sometimes attributed to gods who are otherwise benevolently disposed toward man. The dualism was manifested in the opposition between life-bestowing powers and death-bringing powers. The benign gods gave thunder, lightning, and rain, and they cared for the crops. The evil powers brought about drought, hurricanes, and war, which destroyed the corn and caused hunger and other miseries. In a Mayan codex this battle between the forces of the universe is symbolized in a painting which portrays the rain god Chac caring for a young tree while behind him the god of death, Ah Puch, breaks the tree in two. The death powers were usually thought to reside in the netherworld, the good powers to belong to the upper world. But benign powers were sometimes given destructive features; in the manuscripts this could be illustrated by providing the generally benevolent god with the same lower jaw as the skeleton-shaped death god. The ambivalence is in many cases understandable: the rain god, for example, not only sent the fertilizing rain but could also harm the corn by sending hail and dampness. The battle between good and evil, then, was partly a confrontation between the gods, partly (or so one might interpret the matter) between tendencies within a single god.

The dualism of the earlier classical period was perhaps less pronounced. The death god is in any case a less frequent figure in the earlier sculptures. In pre-classical times dualism was presumably associated with the ritual functions of the moieties and the care of the crops. Its earliest sources are found in the dualistic conceptual pattern that we found already in the range of hunting cultures.

Outwardly, as the Mayan gods appear to us in temple sculptures and manuscripts, we find them endowed with special regalia. These are sometimes common to several gods and they bear features derived from the human, animal, and plant realms which are quite often found in harmonious juxtaposition. The rain god is sometimes represented as a human being, but at other times he is a snake; sometimes he shows his face in the jaws of the snake and at other times he holds the snake in his hands. The snake can have two heads, one at each end, and he then recalls the two-headed water monster on the Northwest Coast of North America (they are certainly related in a mythological context). The god who rules the world and its interior is portrayed as a jaguar, but to the sun god may also be attributed the features of the jaguar, namely when he is journeying in the nether world during the dark hours of the night. His sharp teeth, wide-open eyes, and "beard," that is, whiskers, are no doubt taken from the jaguar. We also catch glimpses of other theriomorphic gods: one looks like a frog, another like a bat, a third, evidently associated with the polar star, has a monkey head. Two of these animal symbols, the snake and the jaguar, have been discussed earlier due to their widespread presence in America. The frog also has a wide extension as a mythological motif, especially in South America.[19]

For the purpose of identifying the different gods whose functions and external attributes in the codices are so varied, the German Maya scholar Paul Schellhas classified them by letter symbols: the rain god is god B, the death god is god A, and so on. This classification is still used today and will be followed here. At the same time, we will categorize the gods according to their central functions, as far as these can be established: sky gods, fertility gods, death and war gods, and patron gods for ceremonies and seasons. The categories are, as we see, directly related to the forms of activity and social differentiation of the Mayan society.

It is difficult to say anything with certainty about the position of the sky gods in the Mayan pantheon. Did they appear in the conceptual world of both the peasants and the intellectual elite or were they only present in the priestly religion? Opinions differ. It seems most likely that these high gods existed before the outset of priestly speculation, since their close counterparts exist in different religious manifestations all over the world.

19. For the zoomorphic gods cf. the literature on religious art in Chapter 11. See also, for instance, Preuss 1901.

The dominating sky god, in any case the priests' leading god, was Itzamna (god D), ruler of heaven, also lord of day and night and one of the few gods never to be associated with death and destruction. Oddly enough, J. Eric Thompson identifies Itzamna with the two-headed sky monsters because *itzam* in Yukatec means "lizard." We do know that the cult of Itzamna was above all concentrated in the city of Izamál in northern Yucatán; it would then seem legitimate to assume a connection between the name of the god and of the city. Itzamna is portrayed as a bearded old man with a Roman nose; he is said to have come from the east. His consort is the moon goddess, and he is closely connected with the sun god or he himself performs as sun god—a functional relationship characteristic of American high gods. He is worshipped in ceremonies generally reserved for the rain gods and is an important deity during the New Year ceremony.

Thus far he is established as a typical sky god. But his appearance is complicated by characteristics that pertain rather to the culture hero: he is said to have been the first priest in Yucatán, he is said to have named all the more important places in the Mayan region and to have invented books and the art of writing. Some scholars believe that there existed a sky god Itzamna as well as a culture hero Itzamna and that they were at times regarded as one and the same. This may be the right explanation, at least as far as the identification goes. Let us put it this way: The original name of the culture hero was probably lost when conditions were favorable for the emergence of an all-inclusive supreme divine power, in whom the highest beings of religion and mythology were united.

There is yet another circumstance which seems to attest to such a development. It is said that the sky god Itzamna is the being who infuses the breath of life into man.[20] His function here is in accord with that of a creator, but he is nowhere else referred to as a creator. It is therefore interesting to note that in his functions both as sky god and as culture hero he is in

---

20. Cf. Thurber and Thurber 1959; he is in this capacity a bird.

Yucatán often identified as Hunab Ku, that is, the dimly apprehended creative being, whose name could perhaps be
rendered by "the single existing god." This deity always remains in the background and seems not to have gained a cult,
unless Itzamna, officially represented as Hunab Ku's son, is to
be regarded as the Supreme Being in a dynamic form. We are
here confronted with a kind of trinity, where three mutually
divergent deities—a cult god, a mythological culture hero,
and an otiose creator god—were apprehended as three aspects of one person.[21]

Presumably these combinations of high gods into unities
emanate from the speculative endeavors of the priests. It is
possible that this activity was partly stimulated by Mexican
influence on the Mayan culture in the late classical period,
which may imply a relatively late emergence of the theological fusions in the history of the Mayan realm. We know that
Mexican Indians (Nahua) conquered the Quiché and that
Mexican influence has left a strong imprint on *Popol Vuh*.
According to *Popol Vuh*, the Supreme God is named "the
heart of heaven and earth," Hunrakan, which may be rendered as "the one-legged god"—he is thus a replica of the
Aztec Tezcatlipoca, who is depicted with one leg and one
foot. Now the remarkable thing is that just as the latter is
believed to be present everywhere, "in hell, on earth and in
heaven" (Sahagún), Hunrakan is perceived as both one and
three persons, these three being specified as Hunrakan of the
sky, Chipa of the earth, and Raxa Caculha of the nether
world. It is a reasonable supposition that the linking of
Hunab Ku, the sky god Itzamna, and the culture hero with
the unknown name has emerged in analogy with this, that is,
ultimately following Mexican precedents.[22]

We have noted that Itzamna himself may appear as sun god
(his origin in the east possibly alludes to this). Otherwise the
actual sun god is Kinich Ahau (god G); his jaguar features

21. Itzamna and Hunab Ku may, for that matter, be identical, as Thompson
supposes (Thompson 1970, pp. 203ff.).
22. For a discussion of the Supreme Beings see also Haekel 1959b,
Krickeberg 1949, and Thurber and Thurber 1959.

have already been mentioned. This "lord of the sun's eye" was worshipped especially in Izamál in northern Yucatán. Like Apollo, he was not only the sun god but also the god of the fine arts and patron of poetry and music. His or Itzamna's consort Ixchel (goddess I) is a gloomier figure portrayed with symbols of death and destruction. She is a personification of the devastating floods but presumably also the moon goddess; at least, this is the conclusion reached from her appearances as the consort of the sun god Itzamna. At the same time she is a goddess of women, "our mother," who rules over pregnancy and childbirth and who invented the loom. (As the goddess of weaving she has perhaps been confused with another goddess, Ixchebelyax, unless the latter is to be regarded as a manifestation of Ixchel.) Ixchel's characteristics associate her with the pre-classical tradition of the mother goddess as well as with the concepts of mother and moon goddesses in other parts of the world. Moreover, Mayan priestly speculation endowed her with two additional features: she is represented as the goddess of medicine and of divination.

A third astral god is the god of the pole star, Xaman Ek, with a monkey face (god C), a benevolent deity who guides merchants on their nightly journeys. He is sometimes identified with god M, Ek Chuah, who is ambivalent in character or, as Morley puts it, has a Janus-face: at times he is a malicious war god, lance in hand, and at other times he is the friendly merchant god with the monkey face, his back loaded with goods. He is also the protector of cocoa and the cocoa plantations. In this function he closely resembles the other group of Mayan deities, the fertility and rain gods.

The deities who brought the fertilizing rains and the rich corn fields were far more important to the simple Mayan peasant than the lofty and distant celestial powers. Special reverence was shown to the rain god, "the long-nosed god" Chac (god B), to whom the Mayan corn farmer turned more often than to any other god. The name symbol of the rain god is provided with a T-shaped figure which may indicate tears streaming from an eye, to symbolize the fertilizing rain. All

the way from Argentina to the Pueblo district in the
southwestern United States thunder and rain gods are
depicted as crying gods whose tears, the life-giving rains,
fertilize the crops (according to T. A. Joyce). We have already
mentioned that Chac could also be represented as a snake.
The snake, too, is a rain symbol in many parts of America, as
in many places in the Old World, and it is sometimes identified with the rainbow. There are scholars who have thought
it possible to establish the identity of the snake god Chac with
the Toltec culture hero, the feathered serpent. This is,
however, a dubious conjunction, since the functions of the
two gods are totally incongruous. Furthermore, in his appearance as a snake Chac is never feathered. On the other
hand, there is a possible connection between the long-nosed
Chac and the man-jaguar of the Olmec. If so, "the long-
lipped god" of the Izapa culture on the border between
Guatemala and Mexico has an intermediary function.

As mentioned above, Chac is sometimes represented by
death symbols. These refer to devastating cloudbursts,
floods, and rotting harvests. Perhaps they also stress the fact
that in his capacity as fertility god the rain god also belongs to
the nether world. Although Chac's help was sought daily and
in every possible situation where fields and crops occupied
the interests and thoughts of the Mayans, it was primarily at
an annual temple festival that he became a prominent figure
of the cult. The festival was devoted to the four Chac gods,
each one stationed in one of the cosmic quarters and each one
linked to a special color: red, white, black, or yellow. During
the feast the temple was furnished with new images and
incense burners, and sometimes it was completely rebuilt.
The feast was called "the entrance into the house" and was
apparently an agrarian New Year rite.

Closely related to the rain god was the wind god (god K),
also depicted with some of the serpent's symbols. It is possible that he did not exist separately but only as a manifestation
of the rain god: he was the wind that swept across the fields
just before the onset of tropical downpours. The god is
portrayed with a nose lobed like a leaf. Perhaps this alludes to

gusts of wind, as the German scholar Förstemann has maintained. The Aztec wind god Ehecatl and the culture hero Quetzalcoatl are represented with similar noses. Consequently, some scholars have chosen to regard god K as a variation of Kukulcan, the Mayan counterpart of Quetzalcoatl. This interpretation is doubtful, and if correct is contrary to expectation; it could be applicable only to the post-classical period. On the other hand, the "long-nosed god" appears in Olmec art, where he is bearded as well.

The god of corn, god E or Ah Mun, was a more essential deity.[23] He is portrayed with particular lucidity in the codices, where he appears as a youthful figure with distinctly anthropomorphic features and a corncob as headdress. Above all, he seems to have incarnated the sprouting crops and consequently to have been a Mayan counterpart to "the young god" in the fertility religions of the ancient Near East. There are indications that Ah Mun was represented in the cult by a young man who was sacrificed at the end of the crop year to strengthen the new year's corn. Such sacrifices are well known to us from the areas of other high religions and their peripheral regions, for example, from the Aztecs and the Pawnee (see the discussions in Chapters 10, 11, and 14). Pictures from the classical Mayan period display a man who as the corn god incarnate sprinkles seed over the head of the earth goddess. Other pictures portray the corn god under the protection of the rain god or in combat with the death god.

In all likelihood, god E was a god of all the vegetation, although mainly associated with corn, the primary nutriment. Possibly, as Rafael Girard asserts, he was earlier worshipped in the Olmec region, and was there represented in sculptural arts by the so-called "baby faces." In the post-classical period his image was obscured. It merged partly with the forest god, partly with Chac. Perhaps J. Eric Thompson is right in his assumption that the young corn god

23. Thompson has recently pointed out that the name Yum Kaax used earlier by him and Morley for Ah Mun does not refer to the god of corn but to the "lord of the forest": Thompson 1970, p. 289. Concerning the corn god see also Digby 1955.

was helpless and dominated by other gods, especially the rain and death gods. Spinden, too, is of a similar opinion.[24]

Our sources reveal some additional gods who seem to have been related to agriculture. Some were linked to the earth and its powers, for example, the god of soil, god R, and the earth mother with the snake head as her hood; she was probably identical to the mother goddess Ixchel. Other gods constituted local manifestations of the rain and corn gods. We are also referred to specialized agricultural gods, for example, a god of beans. These lesser deities no doubt existed alongside the corn god, the god of all vegetation. (But there is nothing to support Thompson's hypothesis that the corn god was split up into a number of deities.) The multitude of fertility gods of course reflects the all-absorbing interest of the corn cultivators in the earth and its fruits.

The third category of gods is composed of those who lived under the earth and who personified death and war. Their warlike and destructive aspects doubtless intensified during the post-classical period when militarism and martial activities dominated life. In classical times many of the subterranean gods had probably served concepts of fertility. As we have seen, the sun god, the mother goddess, the rain god, and the corn god were distinctly associated with nether world existence. On the other hand, there is no evidence that the terrifying death god ever had anything to do with the fertility cult. Even if his figure shows clear vestiges of post-classical molding, he is certainly an old autochthonous deity. He was rooted firmly enough to have survived the shift in religions and even today the Indians believe that he hovers around the huts of the sick.

The death god, or god A, according to Schellhas's system, was in the old days called Cizin (he lives on in modern popular belief under another name).[25] Beside the sky god, the rain god, and the corn god, he is one of the most frequently recurring deities in the three codices. This is of course mainly

24. Thompson 1970, p. 285; Spinden 1917, pp. 94, 96.
25. The name Ah Puch, which this god has been given in most scientific works, seems to be wrong: cf. Thompson 1970, p. 303.

due to the fact that he is such a powerful god, the destroyer of life and prosperity. His figure is terrifying: his head is a skull and his ribs and thorny spine project from a body that expresses death and decay. He recalls the North American death god, "the skeleton being" among the Pueblo and plains Indians, and the demon of the man-eaters among the Kwakiutl. The Mayan death god is furthermore depicted with bells of the type found in the sacrificial well in Chichén Itzá. At least in the post-classical period, people sacrificed to this fearful god, the ruler of the ninth and lowest region of the nether world.

In the company of the death god are other gods and demons who either belong to him or, because of their characteristics, are ascribed to his world: the dog, the owl, and, above all, the war deity, god F, who together with the death god seems to have ruled over human sacrifices. His image may possibly be interpreted as having a mask of human skin exactly like that of the Mexican god Xipe Totec. Like Xipe Totec, the war god seems to have been associated with the sacrificial stone knife. The assumption is readily made that god F is wholly or partially an import from the Valley of Mexico, a replica of the dismal Xipe Totec who was worshipped by the Toltec invaders. It would well befit his mission as a war god who, torch in hand, burns down houses and huts. In his destructiveness he partly coincides with the god of the Janus face, god M.

The last category of Mayan gods is composed of patron deities of various kinds, systematized by the priests and presumably bearing their imprint to some degree. The Maya Indians believed that the world consisted of thirteen heavens and nine nether worlds, each one administered by a special deity. The gods who ruled over the nine lower regions were also patron gods of the days of the Mayan calendar. Each twenty-year period (*katun*) was protected by one of the main gods, such as the rain god or the wind god. Each month and each day in the monthly period of twenty days had its own god. Even the numerals 0–13 were represented by gods identical to the above-mentioned prominent gods; number 13, for example, pertained to the rain god Chac. The immediate reason for associating a certain god with a certain day is completely hidden from us. One may suspect that the priests alone harbored the wisdom that motivated the combination.

Not only the gods but also the mythology in the narrower sense of this word, that is, the myths of the gods and the origin of the world, were surely marked by priestly speculation. The functions of mythology in the Mayan community are obviously difficult to establish. On the whole, it is impossible to determine how much was genuine religious faith and how much was semi-believed epic tradition. To the upper classes, not least to the priests, cult and myth probably formed a whole, as is the case in other high religions. The present-day myth of the origin of corn illustrates the close connection between everyday reality, with its interest focused on growth and fertility, and the creative mythical imagination: In the beginning of time the corn lay hidden under a great mountain and only the ants could use it. Then man appealed to the rain gods for help. One after the other, three rain gods hurled their thunderbolts against the mountain, but in vain. Then the fourth rain god, the most powerful one, intervened and with a mighty throw of his thunderbolt split open the mountain rock and the corn was exposed.[26] Together with the previously mentioned Peruvian myth this recalls the Indian (South Asian) myth of Indra's combat with the dragon Vritra, who withholds the fertilizing waters. Its nearest counterpart is found in the myths of numerous gathering peoples concerning the origin of the crops or the fruits.

The foremost collection of Mayan myths is in *Popol Vuh*, the holy book of the Quiché Indians. It consists of four parts, the first two containing myths, the last two dealing largely with the (legendary) history of the Quiché people. The myths include motifs such as the creation of the world and of man, the great flood, the adventures of the divine twins, the origin of fire and of human sacrifice, and so on. The creation story contains the well-known *creatio ex nihilo* motif: In the beginning was only water, but the gods of creation cried "earth"

26. Thompson 1970, pp. 349f.

and the earth came into being. The myth of the creation of man relates how the intelligence of the first four human beings frightened the gods. Hunrakan then breathed a cloud over them in order to limit their vision. (It is a striking parallel to the relationship between men and gods in Greek religion, not least with regard to the hubris motif.) The myth of twins, common in American mythology, relates how the two brothers Hunahpu and Xbalanque, probably symbolizing the sun and the moon, fight against the powers of the nether world in a game of ball.[27] This is very likely the mythic prototype of the ritual ball-game.

We are much better informed as to the importance of the cult in classical and post-classical times. In an agrarian civilization such as the Mayan, the main vegetation and rain gods were quite naturally integrated with the ritual of the agrarian festival year, especially with the New Year ceremonies. They began during the five last "inauspicious" days of the old year when all work was interrupted and everyone stayed at home as much as possible. In the New Year festivities were included religious dances, and sacrifices of incense and food and drink to the image who was believed to protect the new year. The most pious people sacrificed their own blood by piercing their tongues or ears till the blood dripped. The drops of blood were collected in a stone vessel and poured over the image of the god. During these days houses were thoroughly cleaned and old utensils were thrown away and replaced with new ones.

The New Year rites were the first in a well-planned festival calendar which covered the months of the year. Only a few months, says Landa, lacked ritual festivals. There were offerings to the gods and dances performed in their honor in order to obtain rain and corn, flowers for the bees, a good cocoa harvest, success in hunting and fishing, cure of diseases, good fortune in war, and—enjoyable diversions. Each festival focused on gratifying one specific god, except for the New Year festival, which was addressed to all the gods. If a festival aimed at promoting a particular economic aspect by ritually

27. Otherwise the moon is female: cf. Thompson 1970, p. 234.

celebrating its patron god, only those actually involved in this economy took part. Thus at the festival of the bee god in the month of *tzec* only the keepers of the beehives assembled. Like other ceremonies, this one was concluded by a boisterous drinking bout with an intoxicating honey wine. (Catholic priests later complained that unrestrained drinking was the most distinctive feature of the Maya festivals; first fasting, then excesses in food and drink!) Especially important were the ceremonies at sowing time, which still exist in some places. The Maya Indians of British Honduras (Belize), for example, observe sexual abstinence at harvest time, keep a vigil, and fast as long as thirteen days. In pre-Columbian times there were also offerings to the gods, especially to Chac and Itzamna. Chac is sometimes invoked even today, but generally prayers are addressed to the Christian trinity and saints before the altar of the village church.

Offerings were of various kinds: animals killed at the outset of the festival, agricultural products, flowers, feathers (especially of the famed quetzal bird), pearls, and jadeite. Copal incense may also be considered as a kind of offering. If the offerings were bloody, the idols were usually smeared with the blood of the sacrificed animals. In times of extreme need human beings were sacrificed, too, particularly if the land had been wasted by severe drought, but human sacrifice was not very common until the post-classical period.[28]

The priests, the functionaries of the cult, were held in high esteem. In outward appearance they were distinguished from ordinary people by their ostentatious dress, which at least in post-classical times might consist of jaguar hides, ornaments of jadeite, and quetzal feathers. The priests were ranked in a hierarchy of classes. The highest official in classical times was the priest-king, in post-classical times the high priest. His influence on worldly matters was restricted to participating in the great council, which nominated a new chief upon the death of the old one. The high priest, who was closest to the chief in rank, was succeeded in office by his son. His family

28. Helfrich 1973, p. 181.

was regarded as foremost in the country after that of the chief. One Mayan group, the Cakchiquel in southwestern Guatemala (neighbors of the Quiché), had two elected high priests, one responsible for the sacrificial cult and the other for astrology and the art of divination. If there was a single high priest he combined these functions at the same time as he supervised the entire priesthood and taught future priests.

The other priests were divided into sacrificial priests ("sun priests") and prophets (*chilan*). The latter were recruited from priests with visionary powers, those who could fall into a trance either spontaneously or through narcotics. It was their main task to predict future events and, especially important, to establish auspicious times for the holy rites. The role of the prophets in Mayan culture indicates as much of an emphasis on augury, divination, and prophecies as in ancient Babylonia. Among the sacrificial priests may be counted those who tore out the heart from the body of the sacrificial animal. They were assisted by four elderly temple servants, remarkably enough called *chac*.

The priests also listened to the people's confessions of committed sins. Confession was a traditional institution among the Maya as among the Inca Indians. If there was no priest available the confession had to be addressed to the next of kin. The confession was made in order to remove a disease, for diseases were supposed to derive from crimes in the past—above all, theft, murder, adultery, and false testimony—provided these crimes were not committed deliberately, in which case there was no need for confession! What could be a clearer indication that crimes were regarded as thoughtless negligence toward the divine order, as taboo transgressions. It caused amazement among the first Catholic missionaries to find the institution of confession on pagan ground. The similarities of Catholic and Maya beliefs led them to the conclusion that the apostle Thomas must have preached the gospel to the Maya Indians.

From the Quiché Thompson gives an interesting example of a scapegoat of the same kind as the ones met with in the religions of the Near East and Africa: A very old woman was taken out to a crossroads outside the city, followed by everyone from that area. The people surrounded her and loudly confessed their sins all at once. When they had finished, a priest went up and hit the old woman on the head with a stone until she died. Then the people piled stones over her body and returned home convinced that they and all their neighbors were cleansed of their sins.[29] A more literal way of removing sins is hardly imaginable.

In many respects the religion of the classical period was retained during the Toltec regime, and above all, we may assume, in the true farming districts far from the cities. But the official cult changed, the domination of the priesthood was replaced by that of the military and old sacred actions lost their sanctity (for example, the ball-game) at the same time as the fertility gods declined somewhat in importance and reputation in favor of the gods of war and human sacrifice. We described earlier how the temples at this time were decorated with pillared halls and carved reliefs depicting warriors and sacred beings, especially the feathered serpent who was the culture hero of the Toltecs.

Monuments from the classical period show that the concept of the feathered serpent was already known to the Maya. Only from the tenth century is the snake combined with Kukulcan, imported by the Toltecs, whose image was soon to embellish practically every wall and sculpture in Yucatán. Kukulcan is a direct replica of Quetzalcoatl of the Valley of Mexico, a god who was worshipped by the Toltecs and other Nahua peoples in the centuries before Aztec ascension to power and who was in fact the city god of Tula, the powerful center of Toltec culture. Kukulcan is translated "the feathered serpent," just like Quetzalcoatl, which is a strong indication that the two gods were identical. Dethroned by Tezcatlipoca in Tula, Kukulcan became the ruler of Chichén Itzá. Landa describes in his "Relación" how their great ruler Kukulcan was among the Itzas (the Mexicans) who occupied this city.

They say that he arrived from the west; but they differ

29. Thompson 1954b.

among themselves as to whether he arrived before or after the Itzas or with them. They say that he was favorably disposed, and had no wife or children, and that after his return he was regarded in Mexico as one of their gods and called Quetzalcoatl; and they also considered him a god in Yucatán on account of his being a just statesman.[30]

Behind this narrative with its euhemeristic tendency we may trace the legend of how Kukulcan moved from Tula to Chichén Itzá.

In a way Landa was perhaps right: Kukulcan may have been personified by an historical person, because the Toltec king and high priest bore the title of "the feathered serpent" and was probably the god's representative on earth. However that may be, Kukulcan came to dominate Chichén Itzá and the largest, most central temple in the city, now called Castillo, was his principal sanctuary. The other temples in the city were also consecrated to him. In Chichén Itzá as well as in the other city-states of Yucatán the cult of the Mexican god seems to have been reserved for the reigning Toltec families. The people (that is, the Maya Indians) still worshipped the old gods even if Kukulcan little by little also gained a foothold among them.

Kukulcan seems to have been a highly complex god. As a founder of cities and of the state he was also a culture hero. He is said to have introduced image worship and human sacrifices. As Morley and Brainerd have pointed out, this tradition meets with some support in archaeology. At least we know that the sacrificing of human beings was intensified after the Toltec conquest and that simultaneously plastic clay images of the gods were more numerous than before. It is difficult to determine whether the blond, golden-haired god from the north was directly connected with these tendencies. Furthermore, it is possible that Kukulcan embodied the role of wind god, just as his namesake in the Valley of Mexico did. Surely he was foremost among the gods, and of course he was the war god.

30. Tozzer 1941; also quoted in Morley and Brainerd 1956, p. 80.

Kukulcan was surrounded by other gods, all deriving from the Valley of Mexico. There were in his retinue a number of gods who were later to occupy the Aztec world of religious conceptions, as for example the somber Tezcatlipoca, the sun god Tlalchitonatiuh, the headless corn and snake goddess Chicomecoatl, and the rain god Tlaloc, all in war costume and all recipients of human sacrifice. (Tlaloc also appears in Kaminaljuyú near the Pacific Coast, where he was introduced through influences from Teotihuacan.) There was little response to these gods from the ordinary people. On the contrary, it looks as if the cult of Chac grew stronger among the peasants during this time. The foreign aristocracy, on the other hand, included the Mayan rain gods in their pantheon, as is evident from temple paintings and wall reliefs. Perhaps their intent was to appease the peasants.

The Mayan priests also seem to have been accepted by the Toltec rulers. At the same time, certain priestly functions were transferred to the military orders, or perhaps it was the case that priests were required to belong to those orders. The latter were modeled on Mexican prototypes and were probably related to the male warrior societies found in other parts of America. Two orders are famous, those of the eagles and of the jaguars, symbolizing the sun in the sky and the sun in the nether world, respectively. Presumably they were both, at least initially, accommodated in the cultic system of the sacred moieties. The friezes around the pyramid of the Temple of the Warriors in Chichén Itzá show members of the warrior societies in eagle and jaguar attire presenting the hearts of sacrificed human beings to the god of the rising sun, Tlalchitonatiuh. Here, then, we find these societies engaged in a function which was generally entrusted to the priests.

Human sacrifices were innumerable at this time. Practically every god seems to have received such offerings. There were three procedures: tearing out the heart of the victim, shooting him with bow and arrows, and finally—in the cult of the sacrificial well in Chichén Itzá—throwing him into the sacrificial well. Spanish accounts and depictions from the Toltec period reinforce each other. The victims to be sacrificed were war prisoners and it is no overstatement to say that the need for human sacrifices in many cases inspired the warfare. The basic idea of the sacrificial rites was probably ultimately related to the value system of the militaristic ideology: bloodshed as an integral part of the achievement of duty. The myth provided the priests with a rationale for performing the sacrifice. It stated, for example, how the sun god after his nightly journey in the vacuous land of the dead had to be fortified with human blood at dawn in order to be able to continue his orbit across the world of the living.

Human sacrifices were often followed by ritual cannibalistic meals. Having torn out the heart from the breast of the victim, the priest gave it to the *chilan*-priest, who smeared the image of the god with the blood and then wrapped himself in the flayed skin of the dead person. In this gruesome attire he danced before the assembled audience. If the sacrificed man had been a brave warrior, his body was cut up and pieces of his flesh were eaten by the aristocracy and the warriors. His hands and feet were reserved for the executive *chilan*-priest. In these ritual meals one looks in vain for any fertility symbolism.

On the other hand, the sacrifices in the sacred *cenote* (giant well) in Chichén Itzá must be designated as rain and fertility rites. When drought, hunger, or epidemics endangered the existence of the city population, live people, perhaps mostly young girls, were thrown into the deep limestone well (the distance from the rock ledge down to the water surface was about sixty-five feet, the depth of the water another sixty-five feet or more). It is said that the sacred rite took place at the hour of dawn when the sun rose from the realm of the dead. We know from archaeological investigations that copper, gold, and jade, as well as other precious metals, were sacrificed to the powers in the deep well. Analyses of the findings indicate that the sacrificers came from near and far— undoubtedly the holy *cenote* was a Mecca to pilgrims from all over Mesoamerica. Many of the victims were hunchbacks or were otherwise deformed; according to a widespread Mexican belief such people could avert accidents.[31] The fact that all these recovered sacrificial objects can be dated to the post-classical period indicates that the *cenote* cult in the manifestations known to us was introduced by the Toltecs.

We have seen how the members of the ruling aristocracy were buried under the pyramids. It is reasonable to assume that in such a distinctly agricultural civilization as that of the Mayan classical period, these dead were invoked as caretakers of fertility. The dead in general, who were buried in the earth close to or even underneath the houses, were obviously credited with similar fertility powers on a more restricted level. A Maya Indian is said to have stated that the Indians bury their dead in the earth "to enrich the soil with their dead." "The earth gives us food; we should enrich it."

The deceased were also thought to dwell in a far-off land of the dead. The lid of the famous stone sarcophagus in the Palenque pyramid (discovered in 1952) depicts among other things a mighty world tree.[32] It is probably identical to the tree in the Mayan paradise, the holy ceiba (that is, the wild cotton tree) where, in the shade of its powerful foliage, the good people rest after their worries in life. Like the gods, the tree of paradise could also be represented as fourfold. One such tree was supposed to grow in each one of the four quarters of the world and to carry the specific color of that cosmic quarter. There are reliefs in Palenque and Piedras Negras which portray the world tree with birds perched on its branches. The tree on the Palenque sarcophagus is especially interesting: its top is crowned by an eagle and its roots are resting on earthly monsters. In this composition, as we have seen before, is expressed a dualism between the powers of heaven and earth.

Landa's version of the Mayan belief in a life after death is

31. On the sacred role of hunchbacks in nuclear America, see Linné 1943, Ponce Sangines 1969. Humpback gods also appeared in, for instance, Hohokam and Hopi cultures in North America.
32. Ruz Lhuillier 1954.

incomplete and is colored by his own Catholic expectations. There is a paradise with its delights, including an abundance of food and drink in the shadow of the holy tree, and there is Mitnal, a subterranean hell for the wicked where hunger, cold, and sorrow torment the unfortunate ones. The death god presides over this gloomy world and in this context he is named Hunhau. He is known under other names as well. We know nothing of the ruler of the paradise, but it is likely that god F, god of war and human sacrifice, dwelt in the land of the blessed, since warriors who had fallen in battle and those who had been sacrificed came to this land. Women who had died in childbirth and suicides were also admitted to paradise. It was a death realm for those who were snatched away in their prime in some supernatural, inexplicable way or for supernatural purposes. It is said that many who were sick and weak shortened their lives in order to enjoy the privileged existence of suicides beyond the grave. There they were protected by Ixtab, goddess of all who had hanged themselves. She is represented with a noose around her neck.

The old Maya Indians have passed on to the land of the shadows, to the death realm of the warriors or to that of ordinary people—thus Landa's dualism between "paradise" and "hell" may be read—and the brilliant Mayan culture is gone with them. Their descendants live on, however, and much of the popular religion of the classical period seems to linger in their religious concepts. As in other parts of Catholic Latin America, a gradual fusion has taken place between pagan gods and Christian saints. They have become identified with each other, the original Mayan traits only dimly visible under their Christian guise: the Virgin Mary, for example, is the mother goddess Ixchel. Also, the old gods, for example the mountain gods, are mentioned together with the Catholic saints in the prayers of the medicine men before the symbol of the holy cross.[33]

33. The ancient beliefs are most vigorous today, for instance in prayers and offerings for good weather, good crops, and good health at old sculptures of

The Maya Indians of today make no essential distinctions regarding all these categories of supernatural beings. They are all included in one religious totality which is nominally Christian and yet to a very large degree a continuation of the ancient religious heritage of the Mayan people.

---

the gods (Lee 1972), in tales of the old gods (Blaffer 1972), and in beliefs in witchcraft and nagualism (Hermitte 1970). For religious acculturation see Oakes 1951.

14

The Religion of the Aztecs

The Maya and the Aztecs, Mexico's best-known cultures, are sometimes compared to the Greeks and the Romans of the Old World. Like the Greeks, the Maya created a civilization which on the aesthetic and intellectual level overshadowed other cultures in the surrounding civilized world of that time. Just as Hellenistic culture conquered the Roman empire from the inside, primitive Aztec culture was transformed through the Mayan influence. It is as inaccurate, however, to deny unique characteristics to the Roman culture as it is to deprive Aztecs of the honor of having formed their own cultural profile. They were experts on political and military organization, just as the Romans were, and they were skilled engineers and city planners. It is true that their religion was in many respects a reflection of the military pattern of their culture—the many cruel human sacrifices eloquently speak for themselves—but it also comprised spiritual values which even today excite our admiration. Their love of flowers, dance, and poetry, for example, belongs to the surprising side of Aztec culture.

According to Aztec traditions, their people had once come

from the north, and philologists certify that they are distantly related by language to the more primitive Shoshoni and Paiute Indians of the Rocky Mountains, the Great Basin, and California (the so-called Uto–Aztec language family). Most probably they were initially a primitive conquering tribe who settled on the shore of the Texcoco lake in the Valley of Mexico at the beginning of the fourteenth century. Here they absorbed the inherent culture of the post-classical type upheld by the peoples in the Valley of Mexico at this time; they gradually expanded their domination to include a number of surrounding tribes, for example, the Mixtec and their partially supplanted predecessors the Zapotec. (Other neighbors, like the Tarascans and the Huaxtec of Mayan lineage on the Gulf Coast, the Aztecs never succeeded in subduing.) The Aztecs, it seems, were to some extent influenced by their conquered neighbors, but the classical heritage reached them mainly through the civilizations which they replaced physically, that is, the Teotihuacan and the Toltec cultures.

Teotihuacan, Mexico's foremost pre-Spanish urban settlement, was built by a people unknown to us. It flourished during the third to the seventh centuries A.D. By the ninth century the city seems to have been destroyed by invaders; it was never again restored to its earlier grandeur. Much later, when the Aztecs came to power, the city had been abandoned by its former population. It was looked upon with reservations by the conquerors and it played no part in their lives. Even if the city itself had lost its significance, the culture it represented lived on. In the middle of the fifteenth century the ruler of Texcoco (east of the lake with the same name) still regarded himself as heir to the priest-king of Teotihuacan.[1] And, as we found earlier, a number of religious conceptions and divine beings from this city survived in the Aztec pantheon. Some of these gods, for example Quetzalcoatl and Yacatecuhtli (the god of the merchants), seem to have been taken over via the Toltecs.

1. On Teotihuacan see the references in Chapter 11, note 44. Late excavations and reconstructions in Teotihuacan are presented in Bernal 1963.

The Toltecs, like the Aztecs, belonged to the Nahuatl group within the Uto–Aztec language family. From their unknown ninth-century origins—it is controversial whether they arrived from the northwest or from the far south—they invaded the fertile Valley of Mexico, which at that time (and long afterward) was full of lakes and forests and had a pleasant climate. The civilization that they founded in Tula lasted, according to the chroniclers, from 856 to 1168 A.D. It largely implied a continuation of the earlier classical civilization but was in addition characterized by the impetuosity of the conqueror and his more disciplined, martial way of life. The harmonious priest-state of the classical period gave way to a military dictatorship and expansive, dynamic statesmanship; religion was integrated with the lifestyle of the warrior; human sacrifice and the death cult spread. It is the same civilization which in the tenth century disrupted the Mayan Chichén Itzá, a city that was probably remodeled with Tula as its prototype. Here as in Tula the Toltecs built their characteristic four-sided columns with reliefs of warriors, and their enormous temple halls, the roofs of which rested on caryatids representing the feathered snake Quetzalcoatl, the best-known Toltec deity. In many respects the Toltecs were the principal instructors of the Aztecs. In the Aztec annals this was the golden era which disappeared when Quetzalcoatl at the head of his followers emigrated from Tula; conviction was strong, however, that one day the lost paradise would return with him. With Cortez and his conquistadors Moctezuma II, the last great Aztec king, thought that he beheld Quetzalcoatl and his retinue.[2]

It was most likely the constant assaults of a primitive Nahua group in the north, the Chichimec, that forced the Toltecs to move south.[3] Possibly a simultaneous deterioration

2. It now seems probable that Quetzalcoatl was also an historical person, or rather, the king wearing this god's title (cf. below). The exodus from Tula might have been, as our sources indicate, the outcome of a civil struggle between the adherents of the gods Quetzalcoatl and Tezcatlipoca; the followers of the latter were the winners. However, a more probable motive for the emigration was military assault from the north.

3. Aztec history: see Vaillant 1962.

in climate added to the retreat of the Toltecs, since we know that at this time deserts spread in all directions in North America. One of the intruding primitive tribes was the Aztecs, "the crane people," who at some time in the thirteenth century set out from their mythical homeland in the north, Chicomoztoc ("the seven caves"). This name was later used by their medical practitioners to designate the uterus. This implies that like many other American peoples the Aztecs believed themselves to have risen from the womb of the earth (the mother goddess). On their arrival in the Valley of Mexico they called themselves "Mexica," the name which later came to designate the foundation of their dominion and then the modern state that took over their traditions.

In the beginning the Aztecs constituted a small group among many others in the Valley of Mexico and they were at times held in submission to stronger peoples of that area. About the year 1325 they settled on some small islands in the Texcoco lake, where they had taken refuge from their hostile neighbors, and here they founded the city of Tenochtitlan, upon whose ruins the modern capital of Mexico is built. According to their own traditions, they settled in a place that had been assigned to them by Huitzilopochtli, the patron god of the Aztecs. Huitzilopochtli is said to have led his people the long way around through the Mexican deserts. In a vision he told the priests that their new home was to be built on the place where they saw a gigantic eagle kill and devour a snake. The legend tells that this vision became reality on the island in the middle of the Lake of the Moon, the lake of Texcoco. The eagle was a representative of the sun god, Huitzilopochtli, and the scene with the eagle fighting the snake is in motif identical to a myth known throughout North America: the combat between a celestial bird, the eagle, the thunderbird, and the monster of the underworld or of water, often a double-headed or horned serpent.

The newly arrived Aztecs were soon involved in a conflict among the small city-states for hegemony over the Valley of Mexico. In this densely populated area with its homogeneous economy and transport system there was a natural tendency toward political unity. For some time the Tepanec west of the Texcoco lake established a strong domination. In approximately 1430, after the Tepanec were overthrown by the vassals in Tenochtitlan and (the city of) Texcoco, the Aztecs began their rise to power. The king of Texcoco, the remarkable Nezahualcoyotl ("the hungry coyote," d. 1472), first assumed all power in his sway, but by about 1460 the Aztecs became dominant. (Texcoco retained its sovereignty until 1516 but became increasingly dependent on Tenochtitlan.) The Aztec ruler Moctezuma I, his daughter's three sons, and his grandson Moctezuma II established an "empire" eventually extending over a vast domain from the Atlantic to the Pacific and from the semideserts in the north to the border of Guatemala. When the conquistadors arrived, this kingdom numbered between five and six million inhabitants.

At the same time Tenochtitlan grew to a metropolis with canals, avenues, palaces, and temples. The annals tell how the famous calendar-stone, a world history with calendar symbols around an effigy of the sun, was chiseled and brought to Tenochtitlan. This huge stone, still extant, weighs twenty tons. In the 1480s the "great temple" was erected, a duplex temple in honor of the war god Huitzilopochtli and the rain god Tlaloc; resting on its huge pyramidal base, it commanded the whole of Tenochtitlan. At the inauguration no less than 20,000 prisoners taken during a campaign against Oaxaca are said to have been sacrificed. The kings of Tenochtitlan and Texcoco commenced the temple festival by tearing the hearts out of the breast of two prisoners, whereupon the priests were given the task of completing the bloody executions. On later occasions as well, massacres took place before the image of the war god; thus Moctezuma II once sacrificed to him 12,000 prisoners-of-war. That sacrifices of such dimensions called for extensive military activity is easily understood. Indeed, some scholars maintain that the cult of sacrifice was the principal reason for the continuous expansion of Aztec dominions.

The reign of Moctezuma II (1501–1520) signaled the beginning of the deterioration of the state government and was in the light of subsequent experiences perceived as a long descent to the inevitable holocaust. Auguries of various kinds portended the impending ruin of the realm, and the mystically inclined ruler spent a great deal of his time anxiously pondering the strange natural phenomena reported to him by augurs and seers. Nevertheless, in 1507 the inauguration of the new 52-year cycle was celebrated in the usual fashion. However, at that time rumors of the arrival of white men in the coastal regions were already circulating. One after another the suppressed peoples rebelled, and soon Moctezuma was feuding with his closest neighbors. In 1519 Cortez began his march on Tenochtitlan. Supported by the revolting tribes and after many and considerable difficulties, he succeeded in establishing himself as commander of the city and thus as ruler of Mexico.[4] Just as the Inca empire could be crushed because of centralization in the political and administrative apparatus—Pizarro needed only to secure the Inca in person to demolish the whole state structure like a house of cards—Cortez could deliver a deathblow to the Aztec dominion as soon as he had won over the tribute-bound tribes to his side. The Aztecs had made themselves unpopular through their tribute system, and doubtless their gory cults had aroused the displeasure of the suppressed tribes. From a religious point of view Tenochtitlan was not the Rome of the New World, even if Moctezuma II with his interest in religion kept a sanctuary where gods were represented from all the lands conquered by the Aztecs.

The swift expansion and violent fall of the Aztec empire gives expression to a "rhythm" of civilization also reflected in the potent dynamics of their art and the dramatic manifestations of their religion. It is plausible, as Professor Linné has suggested to me, that the wild and colorful world of the Aztec gods was partly stimulated by visions aroused through the priests' peyote consumption.[5] But basically the religious pattern remained in harmony with the whole atmosphere that

4. Díaz del Castillo 1950, 1956.
5. Furst makes the hypothesis that to a great extent Aztec religion was influenced by psychedelic experience: see Furst 1972, Introduction.

permeated this culture. From a religio-historical point of view, then, there is reason to examine the causes for the political and military development and to explore the Aztec power structure.

From their predecessors, the Toltecs in particular, the Aztecs must have appropriated a militaristic ethos, the source and background of which we have earlier attempted to explain.[6] This ethos seems to have been reinforced by contemporary ecological and economic conditions in the Valley of Mexico. As was mentioned before, this was a most fertile valley, but a great number of socio-political groups were crowded there and in time their numbers increased. The population density and the limited amount of arable land gradually necessitated an intensified economy. On the lakes were built artificial islets, *chinampas* ("floating gardens"), which could give rich corn harvests. In the fifteenth century an aqueduct was constructed, with a dam nearly ten miles long, for the irrigation of the extensive territories around the Texcoco. Nezahualcoyotl was the instigating force for this project. The population increase was such, however, that no reforms were sufficient. Food had to be imported at an accelerating rate and the only way of securing necessary provisions in the long run was to sack neighboring peoples.

Such considerations were no doubt basic to Aztec war expeditions. Aztec armies opened trade routes to distant lands, forcing the neighboring tribes to accept their thoroughfare. They defeated other peoples in order to confiscate land from their territories and hand it over to Aztec dignitaries; the peasants who lived on confiscated lands were instructed to plow the fields for the benefit of Aztec landlords. They made the defeated peoples pay tribute: clothes, jewelry, and provisions were brought in great quantities to the famous market in Tlatelolco near Tenochtitlan, a market that aroused the amazement and admiration of the conquistadors. To protect this economic exploitation Aztec garrisons were stationed in

6. Aztec culture has been described in the following works: Vaillant 1962, Burland 1948, Rivet 1954, Krickeberg 1956, Armillas 1964, Coe 1962, Soustelle 1961.

the conquered area. In other respects the captured city-states were left intact.

This signified that these states retained their political constitution as well as their religion. Unlike the Inca emperors, the Aztecs did not act as missionaries. This was no doubt due partly to an inherited polytheistic tolerance and partly to their respect for Toltec tradition: they considered their predecessors, the Toltecs, to have established the norms in the field of religion. The basic elements of the Toltec religion, above all the Quetzalcoatl cult, were widespread and accepted both by the Aztecs and tributary tribes. The Aztecs showed less tolerance, however, when it came to providing Tenochtitlan gods with sacrifices. Huitzilopochtli and his retinue claimed human blood to strengthen their power to victory and captured warriors of the opposing armies were kept to become sacrifices at the altars of the gods. From their predecessors the Aztecs had taken over the custom of waging war to procure human sacrifices for the temples, but the enormous proportions that the Aztec sacrificial cult reached seem connected with the fact that the victim-procuring wars were coordinated with, or, perhaps more accurately, became a function of war campaigns organized for economic purposes. The appetite of the gods grew with the increase in military achievements. If the number of sacrificial prisoners was not sufficient, as was sometimes the case, it became necessary to apply old tactics which had been in use in the area well before the arrival of the Aztecs: in agreement, or rather by injunction to an agreement with a neighboring city, "a flower war" was arranged, a bloody mass combat where prisoners were taken, later to be sacrificed to the gods.

The military success of the Aztecs was in no slight degree due to the fact that wars were considered an obligation to the gods, above all to Huitzilopochtli, and were therefore waged in a "constructive spirit," as it were. War was a civilizing enterprise; the consequences of this viewpoint are clearly evident in their socio-political organization.[7] One of its

7. Besides the references in the foregoing note, see Carrasco 1961.

characteristic features was the fusion of civil and military duties, and the king (*tlatoani*, "the speaker"), the highest functionary of the state, had supreme authority in both domains. At the same time he was the people's representative before the gods and the gods' representative before the people, and was therefore accountable for the successful outcome of civil as well as military enterprises. In short, he was a sacred monarch.

The Aztec monarchy no doubt arose from a primitive institution of chieftainship which in the Valley of Mexico was soon to be permeated by the ideology of sacred kingship dominant among adjacent peoples. The dynastic system grew strong with time and, in the interest of the religious and historic traditions, was linked to the Toltec kings. Like his Toltec predecessors, the Aztec king was supposed to be descended from Quetzalcoatl, king of Tula. This may imply that in the cult both Toltec and Aztec rulers have represented this god of the classical era. It is noteworthy in this context that the Aztec royal mantle had the bluish-green color of the quetzal bird.

The Aztec monarch was elected within the ruling dynasty by a special crown council consisting of older noblemen, high priests, and renowned warriors. The new sovereign was usually one of the nearest relatives of the deceased king, for example, a brother or a son. He was installed with an enthronement ritual which brings to mind the coronation ceremony practiced in the Near East. Among other things, it included the monarch's penance before the gods, his gratitude to them for having chosen him (the decision of the crown council was thought to be inspired by the gods), his pledge to the gods to support their worship, and his inauguration speech to the people. The main part of the ceremony took place in Huitzilopochtli's temple, where the king was brought by the high priest. Here he lit the sacred incense before the image of the god, here he vowed to defend the god's temple, and here he stayed four days and nights fasting and meditating. When speaking to the people, the king appeared in official vestments with a diadem of gold and turquoise, a shimmering quetzal-feather mantle, and a scepter in the form of a snake. He called himself the "father and mother" of the Aztecs and he assured his people that during his reign they would enjoy "the fruits of the fields in abundance." As far as we know, the Aztec rulers did in fact care for the good of the people. They were known for their compassion and generosity, qualities that are certainly in no way characteristic of their Spanish successors.

Reports of the conquistadors confirm that the king was believed to have a divine commission and was treated like a god. Bernal Díaz del Castillo tells in his interesting account of the conquest how, at his first meeting with Cortez, Moctezuma arrived from his palace in a palanquin. He stepped down from it and proceeded on foot under an embroidered, feathered canopy with noblemen sweeping the road before him and spreading pieces of cloth to prevent his feet from touching the ground. In his palace he ate behind a screen so that only the women serving him and a few noblemen standing behind his chair could see him. At the audiences even the highest court dignitaries were obliged to stress their inferiority to the ruler by wearing coarse robes of cactus leaves and by entering barefoot. They approached him with bent heads and withdrew backwards and bowing.

It was thus quite natural that the Spaniards regarded the Aztec ruler as a king in the European sense, although he had been elected to his office (elected kings existed in Europe at this time, as well, for example, in Sweden, Poland, and Germany).

During the post-classical period the older sacred diarchy gradually expired; the Zapotec Mitla seems to have been the only political center to keep this form of government until the Spanish conquest. It is possible, however, that a reflection of the old dualism between war chief and peace chief can be traced in the Aztec distribution of power between the king and the vice-regent, the latter called "the snake woman," *cihuacoatl*. This title was also the proper name of an important deity, an earth goddess who was the special patron goddess of women in childbirth. Perhaps the vice-regent represented her in the cult. We know that the office was established during the reign of Moctezuma I (1440–1468), that his brother was its first incumbent, and that later it was inherited by his descendants. The title itself is older; already at the end of the fourteenth century we find an Aztec king referred to as *cihuacoatl* before his accession, and princes in other Nahua groups seem to have used it.

The functions of the two highest dignitaries of the Aztec state were mainly distributed in the following way. The *tlatoani*, as chief of state and the highest representative of military, civil, and sacred affairs was primarily referred to as *tlacatecuhtli*, that is, "the chief of men (the warriors)," war chief. The vice-regent, *cihuacoatl*, on the other hand, was apparently chief of state when the king was absent on war expeditions and also during interregnum. He organized the military expeditions and acted as supreme justice; this last function seems to have been particularly characteristic of his office. In the sacred hierarchy the king was at the head, as supreme priest of sacrifices, while "the snake woman" supervised temples and priests. This outline does not correspond to what we think of as the older diarchic organization in the Valley of Mexico, but should rather be considered as an incomplete copy of the form of government of the classical tradition.

Next to the two highest leaders existed a solid military-civil-sacred organization where individual merits as well as noble birth predetermined leading positions. Different opinions have been put forward as to the real structure of the society; today it is apparent that older scholars such as Bandelier and Vaillant have overstated the extent of the egalitarian principle in the Aztec community.[8] The organization was extremely complex and cannot be described in detail here. Of immediate religio-historical interest are the priest-

---

8. The much-debated issue of whether Aztec society was a class-structured society or a democracy built on clans may now be resolved in favor of the first alternative. All high offices were filled from among the members of the royal house. The land belonged to the princes and to the clans (*calpulli*), and within the latter the aristocratic families owned more than the commoners. The twenty clans of Tenochtitlan each had its own part of the city with a plaza, a temple, and a marketplace. Cf. also Linné 1948.

hood, to which we will return in a later context, and the military orders.

Only warriors of merit were admitted into the military orders, for it rested upon their members to act as commanding officers during the campaigns. The most remarkable tasks of the members were of a ceremonial and ritual nature. According to some sources, there were three orders: eagles, jaguars (or tigers, or panthers, "ocelots"), and arrows (or wandering arrows). It is uncertain, however, if the "arrows" were an organization on a par with the "eagles" and "jaguars," for they are seldom mentioned. The two former orders, on the other hand, are often referred to. Evidently they were in ceremonial opposition to each other, on the ritual plane together embodying the creative and the destructive principles in the universe. In all probability they originated from the sacred moieties in an older cultural phase. The eagles represented the light and heavenly powers, the jaguars the dark and chthonic ones. The Aztecs had taken over this dualism from the Toltecs—we have already seen the same orders appear in Chichén Itzá—and, just like their predecessors, they connected it with the sun and its twenty-four-hour phases. The eagles were the attendants of Huitzilopochtli, the god of the daytime sky and the shining sun of day, whereas the jaguars served Tezcatlipoca, the god of the nocturnal sky and the nocturnal sun of the underworld. The two orders performed in dramatic rites describing how the sun was killed in the evening but was reborn the following morning. The attire of the orders, the eagle's plumage and the jaguar's hide, respectively (the warrior's head looked out between the jaws of the jaguar), symbolized the powers they served.

The military orders demonstrate how tenaciously the idea of sacred dualism lasted into the Aztec period (we will come back to this later). They also reveal the close connection between warlike and religio-ceremonial enterprises in the Aztec community. Vaillant has suggested that the civil servants became military leaders in war. To this could be added that both civil and military functionaries had cultic authority, or at least that at some time in life such authority was given. In the temple schools (*calmecac*) and under the supervision of the priests, the sons of noblemen as well as of commoners were trained, their education covering both religious instruction— this was the main subject—and military training (there were also special military schools for more advanced training). To the Aztecs, war, civil administration, and temple service were closely-related functions.

Militaristic pursuits and lifestyle did not exclude an Aztec emphasis on continuing and, in their special way, shaping the cultural legacy of the classical period and of the Toltecs. A great deal was given to them: ideographs, the annual calendar (with 52-year cycles), architecture, and many other things. Everything that they took over, however, was amalgamated with their own cultural background and permeated by their restless disposition and fatalistic view of life. The Spanish conquerors marveled at the monumental capital: its temples on top of high pyramids, the palaces of the king and the high dignitaries with their beautifully ornamented frescoes, the plazas, the straight streets and canals. Along the canals and on the roads built on bridges connecting Tenochtitlan with the mainland, products of all kinds were carried, and the marketplaces offered a variety of turkeys, corn, beans, squash, sweet potatoes, and other country produce, and in addition fine specimens of the Nahua people's excellent handicraft, featherwork and objects in gold and wood.

Behind this splendid façade was a culture with frightening aspects marked by sterility and pessimism. The whole of existence was circumscribed by taboos and punishments, foreboding and augury stressed the hazards of human life, and death was everywhere imminent. What were those great human sacrifices, if not expressions of fright and desperate exertion? At least for the moment they released the people from their doubts, but they cannot have been altogether gratifying. The conquistadors were nauseated and disgusted by the raw blood stench that met them from the walls and pavements of the temples. Sahagún, a competent chronicler of the Aztec world, tells us that even the inhabitants of

Tenochtitlan were repulsed. Aztec religion revealed some of the dark sides of the culture, but it also opened up other perspectives.

Posterity is comparatively well-informed about this religion.[9] Its outer cultic form as well as its myths, ritual texts, and doctrines are preserved in manuscripts from the time of the conquest. Before the conquistadors attacked Tenochtitlan they wandered about as invited guests in *tecpan*, the walled-in temple city in the heart of the capital, and many of their valuable observations from that time have been preserved. Noteworthy in this context is the travelogue written by Bernal Díaz del Castillo. Here the manners and customs of the Aztecs are described, not least among them eyewitness accounts of human sacrifices at the temples.[10]

Other important sources are the numerous codices—manuscripts with ideographic writing of a mixed pictographic and hieroglyphic character, exactly as among the Maya Indians—in which the Aztecs and their neighbors the Mixtecs recorded important events from the time of the Aztec state. The German scholar Eduard Seler devoted a great deal of his life to collecting, interpreting, and publishing these documents.[11] The manuscripts he synthesized were later classified according to their artistic style into four main groups: the Tenochtitlan group with, among others, Codex Borbonicus from the early colonial time; the manuscripts from the Cholula and Tlaxcala district (especially Codex Borgia from the thirteenth or fourteenth century), which are of great artistic beauty and constitute excellent sources for the ritual and magic of the Aztecs and their predecessors; the Mixtec group with, among others, Codices Vaticanus B, Cospi, and Zouche–Nuttall; and finally Codices Fejérváry–Mayer and Laud, the provenances of which are still unknown. There are several other manuscripts, for example, the Mixtec Codex Vindobonensis (in Vienna), which contains interesting information on myth and religious belief.[12]

9. Cf. Radin 1920.   10. See Díaz del Castillo 1950, 1956.
11. Seler 1902–23.
12. See Nowotny 1961, Spranz 1964. See also Krickeberg 1956, pp. 273ff. Usually American specialists consider Codex Borgia, Vaticanus B, Cospi,

Additional sources were written by descendants of the Nahua princes in the Valley of Mexico. One of these authors was Juan Batista Pomar, grandson of the last independent monarch in Texcoco. He wrote an account published in 1582, entitled "Relación de Texcoco." Among Spaniards who have produced manuscripts on Mexican religion after the conquest are, in addition to the conquistadors, Sahagún and Juan de Torquemada (d. 1625), whose "Monarquia indiana" contains valuable information about the Aztec cult, for example.

The most important source for Aztec religion was compiled by Bernardino de Sahagún (d. 1590), a Franciscan monk who arrived in Mexico from Spain in the year 1529. The conquest was just completed (the last Aztec king Cuauhtémoc was murdered in 1524) and the old religion was still a living reality although the temples had been leveled to the ground. Sahagún decided to collect all existing knowledge of myths, doctrines, and rituals; he established himself as the first ethnologist and historian of religions of the New World. Having first learned the Aztec language, he interviewed with the aid of native assistants the leading and most conservative Aztecs. Thus a whole corpus on Aztec religion came into being, often containing varying statements by different informants around the same theme. The great work, which was to be called "Historia general de las cosas de Nueva España," contains some material on the political organization of the Aztecs, their economy, and so forth, but it largely deals with the gods and their origins, ceremonies, divination and augury. The manuscript, written in Aztec, is located in Madrid, but a revised and somewhat abridged Aztec text together with its translation into Spanish by Sahagún are kept in the Laurentiana library in Florence under the name of Codex Florentino. The latter Aztec text has recently been translated and published in English by two American specialists on the Aztecs.[13]

Fejérváry-Mayer, and Laud to belong to the so-called "Borgia group." They are the only definitely pre-Conquest manuscripts from the Aztec area.

13. See Sahagún 1950–69. On the person Sahagún, see, for instance, Moreno 1938. Sahagún's work has also been discussed by, among others, P. Radin, A. J. O. Anderson, and L. N. d'Olwer.

The Aztec religion has long attracted the interest of scholars in religion and culture and it has been analyzed in many learned works.[14] Its human sacrifices have been compared to corresponding customs in the ancient Near East and its fertility rites have been associated with agrarian seasonal rites in Germanic Europe. The cruelty of the religion has fascinated and horrified a wide circle of readers. Efforts have also been made to understand Aztec religion from within, as it were, in its own setting and context. Some of the earlier speculations in the field today appear naïve and inadequate, for example, Seler's astro-mythological interpretations. The opinions of scholars have often been widely divergent and are still incompatible. Alfonso Caso, Mexico's most distinguished ethnologist and archaeologist in later times, assures us that the impact of religion among the Aztecs was so tremendous that "it is no exaggeration to say that their entire existence revolved around religion and that there was not a single act, public or private, that was not tinged by religious sentiment." On the other hand, a younger Mexican archaeologist and scholar in religious studies, Laurette Séjourné, maintains that, following the tenth century with its upheavals in Mesoamerica, the kingdom on earth became more important than the kingdom in heaven and the gods were replaced by the military organizations. There is probably more than a grain of truth in both of these viewpoints.[15] There are two tendencies in Aztec culture, one religious, almost mystic, and one profane or militaristic and secular; the tension between these tendencies elucidates many of the oppositions in the religious pattern.

The balance and harmony of Mayan religion is frequently contrasted to the frenetic, "Dionysian" character of Aztec religion, and rightly so. But we must not forget that the Aztecs were endowed with a twofold heritage, half primitive from their place of origin in the north, the other half classical

14. General works on Aztec religion: Caso 1958, Soustelle 1940, 1966, Spence 1945, Séjourné 1956, León-Portilla 1956, 1963, Krickeberg 1961, pp. 36ff., Beyer 1965, Burland 1967, González Torres 1975, Lanczkowski 1970a.
15. Caso 1958, p. 90; Séjourné 1956, pp. 16, 35, 45.

with the same substructure as that of the Maya, but reshaped by the Toltecs and other pre-Aztec cultures in the Valley of Mexico. Séjourné suggests that the classical heritage is represented by what she calls the "Quetzalcoatl-doctrine," a striving linked to the god Quetzalcoatl to reach inner purity and perfection, even a union between man and the cosmic soul. The primitive heritage, on the other hand, displays a degenerate mysticism with a profane, this-worldly objective of power and conquest. To this end the ritualized human sacrifices were a fit political means. To Séjourné the baptism of children and adult confession are manifestations of the spirituality and individualism that distinguished the classical culture. The profane tendencies, she declares, derive from the magic which, according to Aztec tradition, belonged to their mythical primordial time when Huitzilopochtli's sister practiced it. The Aztecs, we are told, had no religion at all to begin with, but knew only sorcery and magic.

Séjourné has quite rightly stressed the double historic heritage of the Aztecs, but she has carried her theses too far. There was no Quetzalcoatl-doctrine but instead a lingering range of ideas from the classical and Toltec period, to which indeed Quetzalcoatl belonged, but also such a blood-curdling god as Tlaloc. The militaristic and "profane" attitude had grown out of this civilization in the early post-classical time, which is evident in the Toltec culture, among others, but it was certainly strengthened later on by the spirit in the small, closely-knit ethnic group of Aztec immigrants. We know nothing of the spiritual world of these first Aztecs. Their view of life was hardly "magism": Séjourné's theory of a magic primeval period in the history of mankind recalls a concept of the science of religions at the turn of the century which is incompatible with modern ethnological facts. Nor was this period pre-theistic.[16] The Aztec immigrants had the tribal god

16. However, this is apparently the conviction of Danish historian and sociologist of religions A. Hvidtfeldt. He translates the word for god, *teotl*, with "mana," supernatural power. This seems acceptable in and by itself (although, as demonstrated by the examples he adduces, simply "supernatural," or "imbued with supernaturality," would be a better alternative). But he means that as time went by objects permeated with "mana," for instance,

Huitzilopochtli who remained their foremost god until the Spanish conquest. One of his names, Mexitl, forms part of the name Mexico, meaning Huitzilopochtli's city. As we have seen, he was thought to have appeared there in the distant past, in the form of an eagle, to the people whose patron he was.

The nature of this oldest Huitzilopochtli is ambiguous.[17] Possibly he was a god associated with game and hunting, a master of deer of the type common in northwest Mexico and the southwestern United States. His image in Tenochtitlan was adorned across the forehead with the skull of a deer. It is noteworthy that deer were extinct in the Valley of Mexico long before the appearance of the Aztecs there. They had disappeared in the early classical period. Also, the Chichimec god Mixcoatl seems to have originally been a master of animals.

In the Aztec religion, such as it was when the conquistadors arrived, the classical and intrinsic heritages had merged into a kind of religious unity, a configuration of religion. But just as in the case of the Maya Indians, it was a most complex religion where local gods borrowed each other's traits, and astral and calendrical speculations became confused with the gods and even deprived individual deities of their specific qualities. At the same time they were provided with warlike attributes and linked together with a death cult sprung from the war experiences which added confusion to the religious structure. Deities appropriated and "conquered"

---

masks and images, were personified as gods. This process of personification was operating during the days of the Aztec kingdom: see Hvidtfeldt 1958, pp. 52ff., 76ff., 97ff., 118ff., 140. However, it cannot be proved that this development took place; it seems to be an improbable—and unnecessary—construction. Moreover, Hvidtfeldt's theory does not take into account the fact that most Aztec gods had been taken over from the civilizations that preceded the Aztecs in the Valley of Mexico. As a contrast to this theory we may mention another one created by the well-known linguist Morris Swadesh. He assumes that the Nahua either imported the name for god, *teotl*, from some other people, associating it with their own word for the sun, *tootl*, or that they retained an old word for the sun, *teot*, as a name for god. See Swadesh 1964, pp. 539ff.

17. Cf. G. Brotherston's discussion of Aztec beliefs about Huitzilopochtli in Hammond 1974.

by the Aztecs were molded in accordance with the symbols of the kingship, the priesthood, and the warrior profession into what seems at a cursory glance to be a homogeneous world of gods. But basically, as Spinden and Linné have pointed out, it was a chaotic pantheon.

There might have been reason to expect an active monarchical god superior to the other gods, in a civilization with such an advanced social structure. This was not the case. Huitzilopochtli was the city god of Tenochtitlan and the most powerful god of the Aztec tribe, but he was no Supreme Being. Tezcatlipoca has been regarded by some Aztec scholars as the head of the Aztec pantheon, for he carries among other titles those of "our Lord, our Creator and Former through whom everything exists that exists," but the same titles also pertain to Quetzalcoatl. Presumably none of these gods was in himself a Supreme Being, but for reasons that will be declared presently they all expressed certain aspects of such a being.[18]

In the mythical pantheon fashioned by priestly speculation there is a deity called Ometeotl, "the god of dualities," "he who created (or conceived) himself," "the creator of man, the mirror that unveils things." This god is said to be intangible, invisible as the night wind. As his name indicates, he is usually perceived as a duality, a divine couple, Tonacatecuhtli–Tonacacihuatl (respectively, "the lord" and "the lady of our flesh"), or Ometecuhtli–Omecihuatl ("the dual lord/ lady"). From this god or these deities emanated the whole of creation: it was brought forth by the androgynous Ometeotl or by his polar sexual characteristics manifested in a divine couple. Without doubt this cosmogonic mythology represents the philosophy of the priests. This does not preclude the possibility that Ometeotl may have initially been a folk deity who, however, never acquired a position in the official cult system. There are records attesting to the fact that in situations of emergency the people worshipped this highest god.

18. To the following, cf. Haekel 1959b and Dietschy 1940–41.

However that may be, a spiritualized cult of a Supreme Being was introduced, or possibly reintroduced, by the Texcoco king Nezahualcoyotl (d. 1472). The god in question, Tloque Nahuaque, was said to reside above the nine heavens; he was invisible, and he was represented by no cult image. His empty temple room crowned a pyramid containing nine burial levels representative of the nine heavens. Even if the concept of such a god were rooted in the heritage from Teotihuacan and the Toltecs, a heritage of which the inhabitants of Texcoco were especially proud, it was through Nezahualcoyotl, "the first personality known to us in the history of ancient Mexico" (Linné), that the idea took shape. Nezahualcoyotl was a remarkable man. If we may trust the chroniclers, he made Texcoco a center of science and art. He compiled an excellent library, built new temples to the gods, and surrounded himself with a splendid court. He was a poet, a philosopher, a statesman, and a city-builder. Although he could devote himself to bloody sacrificial rites in the temples of Texcoco and Tenochtitlan, he created the most abstract cult divinity known in Mesoamerica until that time.

Independently of Nezahualcoyotl's reform, there seems to have been in the Aztec state an ever-increasing theological tendency to include all gods in one homogeneous deity. The German scholar Hermann Beyer thought he could prove this fifty years ago and today's Mexicanists are mostly of the same opinion.[19] This striving toward monotheism probably answers the question of why so many gods appear endowed with qualities that ought to have been reserved for the Supreme Being. We have already seen how the creative primal couples have been depicted as manifestations of the Supreme Being. Other gods also, especially Huitzilopochtli, Tezcatlipoca, Quetzalcoatl, and Xolotl, were made participants in the nature of the Supreme Being. This is probably due to the fact that they were all identified with a religio-mythological figure, quite well known in America, who had a shifting relationship to the sky god: the culture hero.

19. See, for example, Caso 1958, p. 8, Séjourné 1956, p. 29, Burland 1967, pp. 130ff. However, Keen goes against this opinion: see Keen 1971, pp. 484f., 504.

Of these four gods, three were city gods and were, along with the rain god Tlaloc, the mightiest and most renowned in the Aztec state. Huitzilopochtli, Tenochtitlan's city god and the special patron of the Aztecs, was worshipped as a powerful war god and, as we soon shall see, he also shouldered the mantle of the sun god. Tezcatlipoca was the city god of Texcoco and, like Huitzilopochtli, was an old Nahua god who had roots in early Chichimec culture. His name means "the smoking mirror," and his symbol in Texcoco was an obsidian mirror wrapped in fine blankets. The mirror, which reflected the night sky, was an instrument of divination through which the magicians could look into the future. It was also a kind of tribal medicine recalling, for example, the Arapaho sacred flat pipe wrapped in blankets. It is noteworthy that other deities of the Valley of Mexico were also represented by medicine bundles: Huitzilopochtli was represented by the oracle pack which the Aztecs had brought with them during their early wanderings, and "the cloud snake" Mixcoatl was symbolized by the bundle containing his image, which a Chichimec warrior carried on his back during their peregrinations. (The Danish historian of religions Hvidtfeldt suggests, somewhat surprisingly, that Mixcoatl originated out of the white stone fetish in the medicine bundle.)

Like Huitzilopochtli, Tezcatlipoca was a god of princes and warriors, connected with the sky and the sun. At the same time his figure was as composite as might be expected of a tribal god. He was portrayed as the invisible god, the protector of magicians, the god of providence and destiny, everywhere present and omniscient; as the eternally young god who abducts the beautiful flower goddess; and as the culture hero who has discovered fire and protects the school of the young warriors.

The nature of Quetzalcoatl, "the feathered snake," city god of the old Toltec city Cholula, was equally complex.[20] As was mentioned earlier, this god held an important position in the Toltec pantheon and archaeological excavations have shown that he was present also in the classical period in Teotihuacan.

20. Concerning Quetzalcoatl see Lanczkowski 1962, Kirchhoff 1955, Beyer 1908.

His image is found also on Mayan temples of the classical period. Quetzalcoatl may be described as the guardian patron of the priests: he is surrounded by sanctity and purity, and the school of priests and youth (*calmecac*) is under his protection. He is also the bearded old god, the creator and benefactor of mankind, their cultural hero. He discovered corn, he taught men handicrafts and astronomy and gave them instructions for organizing the calendar. He also instituted the religious ceremonies. In certain functions he was accompanied by his brother Xolotl, a clever magician, the god of all monsters.

The attentive reader cannot help noticing that Tezcatlipoca and Quetzalcoatl largely appear as each other's opposites, one dark and destructive, the other a figure of light and a helper of man. (Beyer's attempt to connect Quetzalcoatl with the night sky seems barely convincing even if later the suggestion elicited the support of an authority like Krickeberg.) Actually, the two deities constitute a correlation of opposites with a long history. The Toltecs witnessed a cosmic opposition (which perhaps had a ritual background) between Quetzalcoatl and Tezcatlipoca; according to the legend the latter assumed supremacy toward the end of the Toltec era.[21] This dualism was also maintained by the succeeding Nahua cultures. In the Mixtec–Aztec tradition the cosmic battle is waged between Quetzalcoatl on one side and Tezcatlipoca or Xolotl on the other. In later Aztec tradition Huitzilopochtli also appears in Quetzalcoatl's function: as the god of the day sky he opposes the night-sky god Tezcatlipoca. Perhaps Huitzilopochtli also appropriated Quetzalcoatl's outward attribute, the plumage, although the luminous quetzal feathers were replaced by colibri feathers. Huitzilopochtli means "the colibri to the left." Two colibris adorned Huitzilopochtli's huge statue in the great temple in Tenochtitlan.

The cosmic dualism between the gods is without doubt a reflection of social, political, and ceremonial structure (dual chiefs, sacred moieties, and so forth) but it is more than this. It also expresses an ethical evaluation, the contrast between

21. Cf. above, note 2.

constructive and destructive forces, sometimes accentuated in the contrast between good and evil. We recognize the pattern from the beliefs of tribal Indians where twin gods represent the highest symbols of the positive and negative sides of existence. The latter part of Quetzalcoatl's name, *coatl*, means both "snake" and "twin." In all probability, he and his adversary constitute a mythological pair of twins. It is also said that the two (later also Huitzilopochtli) issued from the womb of the great earth goddess Coatlicue. Similar to other American twin gods, both Quetzalcoatl and Tezcatlipoca have the characteristics of the culture hero. Unlike such gods, however, they are not mere anemic mythological beings but rather the objects of cult and worship. In the high culture with its elaborate theological system the integration between myth and rite is almost complete and the culture heroes are included in the actual supernatural course of events and are identified with leading national gods.

This theological and speculative activity has, among other things, resulted in all higher deities being comprehended in the solar, lunar, and astral categories of mythology.[22] For example, scholars have almost unanimously agreed that the myths about Quetzalcoatl reflect the phases of Venus. The detailed account of how he fled from Tula to "the black and red country" and how he promised to return from the east in the year that bore his name cannot be associated with historical data in this form, although Moctezuma and his subjects believed in a historical interpretation. (It is another matter that modern archaeologists have glimpsed behind this narrative the story of "the Toltec emigration.") It is also well known that Heyerdahl identified the bearded Quetzalcoatl with the roaming white men who appeared in America, according to him, long before Columbus. No, the tale of Quetzalcoatl links up with Venus's disappearance as an evening star and its return as a morning star. Tezcatlipoca, the god of the night sky, is, among other things, represented by the constellation of the Big Dipper. In the picture gallery of the codices he is depicted with one foot replaced by an obsidian mirror, the

22. See especially González Torres 1975.

symbol of the night sky. The scene alludes to the myth of how the earth monster tore off the foot of the god, a myth which, at least according to two interpreters (Caso and Soustelle), illustrates the sinking of one of the Big Dipper stars beneath the horizon in southern latitudes. The myth recalls, by the way, the Teutonic myth about Tyr, whose arm was devoured by the Fenris wolf, and the Celtic tradition of how Nuadu, leader of Tuatha Dé Danann, lost his hand (compare also the discussion about Hunrakan in Chapter 13).

Huitzilopochtli, finally, is the sun. In the morning he is born out of the earth goddess, and he strikes down the powers that try to destroy her: he decapitates the moon and puts the stars to flight. Then he is carried in a palanquin across the heavenly vault by warriors who have fallen or died on the sacrificial stone, recalling the voyage of the Egyptian sunboat. During the afternoon the bold warriors are relieved by women who have died in childbirth, and in the glow of evening the god is led back to earth. The myth comes amazingly close to the twenty-four-hour cycle of the Egyptian sun god.

Our exposition has shown how the Mexican world of gods, in addition to a clear monistic (and monotheistic) tendency, was also distinguished by its dualism, a dualism that recurs in many forms. There was the dualism between male and female, manifested by "the world parents." There was the dualism between peace and war, good and evil, represented by the twin culture heroes. There was the dualism between light and darkness symbolized by the couples Huitzilopochtli–Tezcatlipoca and Huitzilopochtli (the sun)–the moon. There was also the dualism between heaven and earth, expressed in the enmity between the sun god Tonatiuh in eagle shape and Tezcatlipoca in jaguar shape. The eagle, as mentioned above, is the representative of the heavenly luminous powers; in the codices the world parents are also depicted with sweeping crowns of eagle feathers. The jaguar stands for the earth and the underworld. According to the American archaeologist Ekholm, the jaguar symbolism was to a great extent replaced during the classical period and later by the snake symbolism which (still according to Ekholm) was imported by sea from Southeast Asia.[23] In any case, we may ascertain that the oppositions eagle–snake and eagle–jaguar have occurred in Mesoamerica and have had the same general significance. On the cultic plane the opposition between heaven and earth has been dramatized in the ceremonial games between eagle- and jaguar-warriors.

The many-faceted cosmic dualism was above all attached to the twin gods; they incarnated all of the oppositional pairs mentioned above. At the same time, they represented a unity beyond duality and could be merged in the Supreme Being which, as we have seen, epitomized all in one but was also experienced in its polar aspects. We have already observed that the differentiation between a male and a female creative being took shape within the framework of the undiversified creative deity Ometeotl. As for the identity between the latter and the culture heroes, on the other hand, we are faced with a process of fusion contingent upon the similarity in function of the two divine categories: the Supreme Being and the culture hero are reciprocal in function although their ranges of activity are located on different levels, those of religion and of mythology. As we have just seen among the Aztecs, effacement of the borderline between these two levels made fusion inevitable. We pointed out that both Quetzalcoatl and Tezcatlipoca could be addressed with words denoting their character of Supreme Being and creator. Quetzalcoatl was portrayed as an old, bearded god; Ometeotl too was represented as an aged deity, Huehueteotl ("the old-old god"). Like Ometeotl, Quetzalcoatl was a wind god and in this capacity called Ehecatl, and like Ometeotl, he was invoked as Tota-tonan, "our father, our mother." While he appeared, according to Codex Borgia, either as an eagle or a snake, he was both of these beings simultaneously. In his person the opposition between the dominions of eagle and snake was dissolved: he was the feathered serpent. Similarly, Tezcatlipoca was regarded as identical with the Supreme Being. He was omniscient, omnipresent, and invisible like Ometeotl and, like

23. This reconstruction is of course in conflict with Luckert's hypothesis, which presupposes a reverse development (see Chapter 11).

him, he was the nocturnal wind, intangible and amorphous. The cosmogonic myths maintain that he who was the god of the night sky had also been the sun god at one time.

This tendency, thoroughly discussed above, toward systematics and homogeneity in the theology, with all its mythological ramblings and loose associations, has no doubt marked priestly speculation and thus the official religion. But it was hardly characteristic of the popular religion even if one or another theological myth took hold within it as *gesunkenes Kulturgut* and then emerged in a misunderstood, fragmentary, or transmuted form. The constellation of three deities, an androgynous creative god—culture hero or Supreme Being—his consort, and "the messenger" culture hero (often sun, moon, and morning star) seems, however, to have been prevalent among the Nahua tribes and was perhaps originally common to the Mesoamerican peoples.[24] Moreover, ever since ancient times different tribal gods have been regarded as manifestations of a Supreme Being within their local domains.

To unsophisticated people, the peasants, here as in other parts of Mesoamerica the rain and fertility gods must have been the most essential ones. These were also included in the official pantheon of the Aztecs and there is no easy distinction to be made between them and the recently discussed sky gods. Tlaloc, for example, the god of rain and thunder, occurs in the mythology as a sun god as well, and his statue was placed as a counterpart to that of Huitzilopochtli in the great double temple of Tenochtitlan.

Tlaloc, "he who calls forth vegetation," is a very old and popular god in Mexico. Chac of the Maya Indians, La Venta's jaguar-masked divinity, and the most reproduced god of Teotihuacan were all rain gods and hence the foremost guarantors of good harvest and general well-being. In the Valley of Mexico Tlaloc was the principal agriculture god. He was a benevolent god when he sent the fertilizing rain, but he

24. The same constellation of ideas probably diffused to North America: cf. Hultkrantz 1965a, p. 106.

could also become angry and would then instigate catastrophes of various kinds—drought, floods, and lashing hail which mowed down the corn. The only way to avert his anger was to sacrifice children to him. Like Zeus for the Greeks, Tlaloc was "the cloud herder" who gathered the rain clouds around the mountain tops, and in caves in the interiors of mountains were the great water reservoirs where he collected rainwater. It was probably his association with mountains (there is still a mountain range with the name Tlaloc) which was given mythological expression in his marriage to a mountain goddess. Like Chac, he was not only one but many gods, or surrounded by many gods, *tlaloque,* who distributed the rain about different mountains. Assembled in his kingdom, called Tlalocan, were those who had died from diseases thought to be connected with the water.

As god of rainwater, Tlaloc was closely linked to Chalchiuhtlicue, the goddess of the lakes and the sea, and she was sometimes represented as his wife. Fishermen and others living from the products of the sea and the lakes addressed their prayers to her. Huixtocihuatl, the patron goddess of salt merchants, may have been identical with her.

Although Tlaloc produced vegetation through the rain, he did not personify it. Other deities, male and female, represented the crops in their entirety, or else single significant ones, such as corn and the maguey plant from which the intoxicating agave juice *pulque* was prepared. Not unexpectedly, flowers too had their own gods in this flower-loving culture. But the predominant goddess of vegetation was Chicomecoatl, a corn goddess, evidently inherited by the Aztecs from the Toltecs and their predecessors. Although primarily a patron goddess of corn, she was in general a fertility goddess of the farmland, "the goddess of sustenance" as the chroniclers put it, and she extended her influence to human fertility as well. A more specialized corn deity was Cinteotl, "the corn god," who allegedly was the son of the earth goddess; the myth here illustrates how corn grows out of the earth womb. Furthermore, corn had different patrons for different stages of growing. The goddess Xilonen, "the person of the unripe corncob," represented the young corn and her colleague Ilamatechutli the ripe yellow corn.

In the floating gardens (*chinampas*) the flower prince Xochipilli was worshipped together with his charming wife, the flower goddess Xochiquetzal. Xochipilli was also the god of summer warmth, games, and dancing, and he moved about in a palanquin which was a corn plant (he was also closely associated with Cinteotl and appears to have shared his wife with Cinteotl and Tlaloc). The flower goddess Xochiquetzal was likewise a representative of summer's delight, a symbol of beauty and love. In this capacity, moreover, she was the patron goddess of the courtesans who lived with young unmarried warriors and whose protector was Tezcatlipoca. According to the myth, Tezcatlipoca had abducted Xochiquetzal and made her his mistress.

Mayahuel personified the maguey plant; like the Ephesian Diana she had a large number of breasts—no less than four hundred—with which she nourished her equally numerous children, the gods of drinking. One of them, Tepoztecatl, was said to have been born of a virgin (Mayahuel) who had become pregnant in a mysterious way.

Whereas these fertility deities, except for Chicomecoatl, were more or less specialized in their functions as masters of individual plant species, the red god Xipe Totec, "our lord, the flayed one," represented the whole vegetation. His attire was a human skin symbolizing the new growth that covers the earth each spring. Inherited from the ancient Zapotec civilization and in the 1470s admitted into the Aztec pantheon, Xipe Totec became the god of spring and was associated with such vernal activities as sowing and planting. We will return later to the gruesome cult that took place in his honor.

The close link that exists between plants and the earth we just saw symbolized in the relationship of the corn god and the earth goddess as mother and son. The earth goddess was, on the whole, a goddess connected with child-bearing and delivery: one of her manifestations was Cihuacoatl, "the snake woman," the patron deity of women in childbirth, referred to earlier (the vice-regent bore her title). Another was Coatlicue, the divine mother who had given birth not only to the gods but also to mankind (compare below the myth of Huitzilopochtli's birth). A third was Tlazolteotl or Toci, who is portrayed in realistic art as giving birth to the corn god. Coatlicue has been immortalized in a colossal statue of expressive force which constitutes a remarkable monument to the artistic skill of the Aztecs. She is depicted without a head, or rather, with two snakes emerging from her neck and forming a face. Her necklace is composed of sacrificed hands and hearts and her skirt of intertwined serpents. An interesting detail is her flat breasts, according to the myth the result of her constant nursing.

The earth goddess was thought to feed on human corpses and this was perhaps why she was called "the dirt devourer" (Coatlicue) or "the deity of dirt" (Tlazolteotl). But she received this title also because she consumed the sins of mankind: she cleansed human beings from the dirt and guilt they had brought upon themselves by not paying attention to right behavior and right observances. He who was conscious of his sin confessed before the earth goddess. This usually happened only once in a person's lifetime, when he had reached a mature age. The confession of sins was a frequent feature in the Aztec religion; this has been described in full detail by Sahagún. It seems to have been a permanent element in the religions of the American high cultures in general.[25]

The borderlines between the various earth goddesses are practically nonexistent. All were manifestations of the same deity, Mother Earth, and all were associated with the dead. Furthermore, Mictlan, the world of the dead, was situated in the lower regions. The twofold concept of the mother goddess, on the one hand birth- and life-giving, on the other death-awaiting, was as well known in Mexico as in the *oikoumene* of the Old World. Like Tlaloc, she has survived the change in religions, albeit transformed in shape. Just as the mother goddess of the Mediterranean was transformed into

25. Cf. the presentation in Chapters 12 and 13.

the Virgin Mary, the Aztec earth goddess Tonantzin ("our mother") was christened the Holy Virgin of Guadalupe. In Tepeyac, now situated on the northern outskirts of Mexico City, an Indian had a vision of the Holy Virgin in 1531. Since then Tepeyac has been a pilgrimage resort for pious Catholics. Among other functions, the Guadalupe Madonna is the patron of motorists.[26]

The majority of the people, the common folk, believed not only in the gods of rain, fertility, and earth, although those meant most in their struggle for survival. Death gods and a host of death demons were always at hand, and we shall hear more of them later on. The spirits who dwelt in nature outside the populated areas were less frightening but still feared. The mountains, we know, had their patron deities, *tlaloque,* who have survived in Christian guise into modern times. We hear of a particularly powerful mountain god in ocelot shape, Tepeyollotl, who was of southern origin and was worshipped in caves. From the interiors of glowing volcanoes Xiuhtecuhtli spouted eternal fire. Like Ometeotl, he was also called "ancient god," Huehueteotl. Perhaps this epithet alludes to the seniority of the fire god in the Mexican region, where he is found by the pre-classical period.[27] Perhaps he was, as Burland suggests, a manifestation of Ometeotl and was therefore represented as an aged deity. He was frequently depicted as an old man (for example, in Teotihuacan). Xiuhtecuhtli was also supposed to represent the cosmic fire and the cosmic pole on which the universe was thought to rest. He brought the souls of the newly born to the earth and the spirits of the dead to the death realm.

Other types of deities are also known to us, several of them initially non-Aztec. In the northern parts among the hunting Chichimec their god Mixcoatl, "the cloud snake," was worshipped as the patron of hunters (in astral speculations he was perceived as the god of the Milky Way); as was mentioned above, he is likely to have been a master of animals.

26. See Wolf 1958, Bushnell 1958, Hellbom 1964.
27. Preuss oriented the whole Aztec pantheon around the concept of fire: see Preuss 1903.

He was represented by a white stone fetish. The merchants had their Mercury, the pathfinder Yacatecuhtli, presumably the same god as the one who, under a different name, guided the journeys of Mayan tradesmen. A popular figure was Huehuecoyotl, "the ancient prairie wolf," the trickster of the Otomí Indians.

The number of gods was legion for each area and each locale had its own deities. Great god figures appeared in many shapes, as was evident in our description of the earth goddess, for example. In addition, priest and astrologers established a mythology which was adapted to the needs of astral speculation, orientation to the cosmic quarters, and the calendar. There were estimates of 400 southern and as many northern star gods; each week, each day, and each hour was granted its patron deity. It was up to each individual to conform to the multiplicity of omens belonging to different days and different gods. The sacred calendar (13 weeks of 20 days each, that is, 260 days) was divided into four parts, each one corresponding to one of the four quarters of the world. Nadir and zenith were represented by the two world parents, and the points of the compass were governed by their sons Xipe, Tezcatlipoca, Quetzalcoatl, and Huitzilopochtli. Time, space, and planets were joined in a curious but meaningful totality by the Aztec priest-philosophers.

Knowledge of astrology and familiarity with the calendar and the rituals were among the skills taught in the priestly schools, the *calmecac*. As was mentioned above, not only priests and scholars but also warriors, administrators, and judges were educated in these schools. They were open primarily to *pilli*, the sons of leaders of the community; other children were given more elementary education in clan schools. The priests seemed in general, then, to have belonged to the upper class, although Sahagún also speaks of priests recruited from the ranks of the poor. Each novice was ordained to the service of Quetzalcoatl, the primal priest, the patron of priests, the founder of the cults; his help was needed for each who was to undergo the training of the priestly school. Training in the *calmecac* was extremely hard: it included ascetism, self-torture, vigils, and heavy labor. In this way the novice was prepared for the strains during war (priests were expected to distinguish themselves in battle) and during periods of religious fasting. Of course the future priest also underwent periods of intellectual training: he learned the ritual songs, the script and the calendar, astrology and oneiromancy. The great majority of the neophytes became minor cult servants, flute and drum players during rites, or assistants at sacrifices. At most they were employed as priests in the small clan temples (each clan constituted a territorial unit and had its own temple). Large temples had many priests— nearly five thousand in the main temple in Tenochtitlan alone—all with quite specialized functions. Each priest was named after the god he served and embodied.

There were also priestesses. Quite often they were women who had taken a vow to live in celibacy for a certain number of years within the temple walls, in return for which and by divine grace they might recover lost health or enter a happy marriage. Their service was primarily devoted to the cults of the earth and fertility goddesses.

The temple priests filled the conquistadors with disgust. Their hair was tangled and matted from the smearing of sacrificial blood, their ears were torn by all the self-inflicted bloodshed in praise of the gods, and their smell was, to put it mildly, disagreeable. The Spaniards found it peculiar that a high civilization could possess such repulsive cult functionaries. That they were also entrusted with its intellectual heritage appeared even more incredible. To the Aztecs it seemed obvious that those who were close to the divine and its secrets should also be imbued with the essence that was ascribed to the gods. As their titles suggest, the priests were cultic representatives of the gods; to emphasize this identification they were sometimes covered with the skins of sacrificed persons who in special rituals had performed in the role of the deity.

There were two high priests at the head of the Aztec cult system who were both titled *quetzalcoatl*, the supreme cultic servants of Huitzilopochtli and Tlaloc. Their title reminds us that Quetzalcoatl was the priest-god, and it throws some light on the story of the Toltec emigration under Quetzalcoatl, as it was comprehended in Yucatán. Huitzilopochtli and Tlaloc were the two gods worshipped in the great temple in Tenochtitlan and they can be said to have represented the two main aspects of Aztec existence, militant imperialism and peaceful struggle for food. It was therefore quite natural that the high priests of these very gods were entrusted with the chief supervision of matters concerning the cult. They were regarded as equals and were addressed with the greatest reverence. They seem to have deserved such appreciation, for only he who was humble, meek, and good was considered worthy of the office of high priest.

Under these two high priests, cultic affairs were administered by a secretary-general for church and schools; he supervised the temple service throughout the whole kingdom, as well as education in the *calmecac*. He had two secretaries at his disposal, one for temple concerns and one for school affairs. Temple taxes were controlled by a treasurer. Gifts to the temple were, among other things, used for building homes for the poor and hospitals for the sick.

The cult was adapted to the ceremonial calendar, the regulations of which had to be followed meticulously.[28] We have already observed that the Aztec calendar was the Mesoamerican one, with an ecclesiastical year of 260 days and a solar year of 365 days. As each day and "week" of the ecclesiastical year had its own god, and consequently its particular characteristics and omens, it was the priests' duty to make sure that each god in turn was granted his ritual and his tribute. The general public observed the significance of the different days and, for safety's sake, consulted the divination priests who were numerous (in the temples as well) and who had re-

28. The festival calendar is described in the Florentine Codex, Book 2 [Sahagún 1950–69 (3)], The Ceremonies. Some rituals, as for instance the sacramental eating of Huitzilopochtli's image, are described in the same work, Book 12: The Conquest of Mexico [Sahagún 1950–69 (13)]. For the correspondences between the ritual calendar and the Gregorian calendar see Vaillant 1962. There is a general review of the Aztec festive calendar in Bancroft 1883 (2), pp. 502ff.

ceived a thorough education like the other priests. The ritual calendar proper, however, was supplemented by the solar year, consisting of 18 months of 20 days each (360 days altogether) and rounded off with five inauspicious days when all important functions were cancelled. Just as the inhabitants of India postulate cycles of time, Aztecs calculated according to the Mesoamerican custom with cycles of 52 years. The termination of each such period resulted in a cosmic predicament which had to be removed, partly through proper ritual actions. The last time this happened was in 1507.

The ceremonies of the solar year first of all reflected the changes in vegetation. In the beginning of February (Aztec month I) the ground was dry and the priests tried with special rites to persuade Tlaloc to send rain. Then came the time of sowing and planting (II), when Xipe Totec ruled. A slave was sacrificed and one of the earth priests was clothed in his flayed skin, thus reproducing Xipe's own attire. This ceremony was a symbolic allusion to the earth in spring covered anew with vegetation. In the middle of March (III), when the drought once more became severe, young children were sacrificed to Tlaloc. Masses of children met with their fate on the mountaintops; the more they cried, the more Tlaloc was pleased and the more willingly he sent rain. In the beginning of April, when the new corn was sprouting (IV), Cinteotl and Chicomeocatl were honored. During the successive months rain and fertility ceremonies of different kinds followed (among them phallic dances) and when the corn had tasseled in June (VIII) an eight-day celebration was held in honor of the goddess Xilonen: the women loosened their hair and a priest carried on his shoulders a young slave girl, a personification of the goddess, whose head was later to be cut off. The ceremony depicted the severing of the green corncob from its stalk. In conclusion, there was a feast during which the new corn was eaten for the first time that year. This was evidently a firstling rite.

In August (X) the ripening of the corn was encouraged through rites to the fire god, Huehueteotl, the giver of warmth and heat. On one day war prisoners and their captors participated in a sacred dance; the next day the prisoners were led up to a platform where a great fire was lit. Each one of the attending priests got hold of a prisoner, tied his hands and feet, and hoisted him onto his back. Then a macabre dance took place around the fire and one by one the miserable prisoners were thrown into the flames. Before their life was extinguished they were dragged out again, whereupon the priests opened their burnt chests and tore out their hearts. Next to the child sacrifices to Tlaloc, this was probably the most cruel sacrificial rite in Mexico. In connection with the sacrifice to the fire god a felled tree was raised in the plaza and at its top was placed a dough image of the tree god Xocotl. The young men competed to see who could climb the trunk of the tree first and he who won broke the image and threw the pieces down to the people on the ground, who ate them greedily. The ceremony signified ritual communion with the deities of vegetation and ritual anticipation of the partaking of the first ripe fruits. By the end of August (XI) came the time of the harvest festival. The priests and priest-esses of Chicomecoatl danced around a woman who represented Toci ("our grandmother"), the mother and earth goddess. At midnight she was brought to the temple and beheaded, and after the dead body had been flayed a priest donned her skin. Seated in front of the temple steps, the priest then acted as if he were a woman in childbirth: he represented the earth goddess giving life to the corn god Cinteotl (compare what has been said above about the birth of the corn god). The rite seems to have been a recapitulation of the vegetation process up to ripening and harvest.

We will observe that the Aztec ritual imitated nature, depicting the life cycle of domestic plants as well as their mythic prototype, the primordial course of events on the divine plane. The close relationship among myth, rite, and daily routine so typical of many old cultures in the Near East (compare, for example, the *Ras Shamra* texts) was, then, just as distinctive for religions on the same level of civilization in the New World, a fact that hints at a uniformity in the evolutionary pattern. Human sacrifices in Mexico occurred in the classical period, especially in agrarian ceremonies, but they were probably more numerous and more frequent in the post-classical period, presumably as a reflection of the enormous sacrifices to the war gods. These latter sacrificial rites were also included in the calendar and belonged primarily to the later phases of the year, to fall and winter. It would, however, be erroneous to assume that the rituals for Huitzilopochtli and Tezcatlipoca, the foremost war gods, were characterized solely by human sacrifices. Sacramental meals with vegetarian food were also part of their cult, which indicates that they were masters of life and fertility as well.

The most dramatic ritual was performed in honor of Tezcatlipoca. In the fifth month (April) the bravest and best-looking of the prisoners was chosen to incarnate the god. For a full year he was taught courteous manners by the priests. Dressed in the god's attire he walked through the streets with his attendants, playing his clay flute and receiving the same distinctions of honor as those of a king. Later he was married to four young girls who impersonated and were dressed as four goddesses (among them Xochiquetzal and Xilonen). At the end of the year, when the festival day in the fifth month again drew near, ceremonies, dances, and banquets were arranged in honor of the god-man. At last he was brought in a procession and then by canoe to a temple on a lake shore. He bid farewell to his wives and his attendants, who tried to console him and reconcile him to his fate. Then he slowly mounted the temple steps, at each step breaking off a piece of his flute. Having reached the temple platform, he was seized by the waiting priests. They took off his festive robes, stretched him across the sacrificial stone, pushed a knife into his chest, and tore out his heart. The corpse was carried down the steps and his head was put up on the great scaffold of skulls in the vicinity of the temple. This shows, says Sahagún, "that those who enjoy wealth and pleasures in this life will end in poverty and in sorrow."[29]

It was in his role as the sun god completing the yearly cycle

29. A recapitulation of this interesting rite will be found in Caso 1958, pp. 68f.

that Tezcatlipoca was thus incarnate as a man. In the fifth month the sun passed through the zenith for the first time since the winter solstice, and then the old Tezcatlipoca died in the form of a captured warrior; we must remember that he was the protector of the young warriors. At the same time he was reborn in another warrior, also a prisoner, who had been chosen to take the place of the deceased immediately following the bloody execution. In this way the sun god set out on his New Year cycle and the rainy season began.

Similar sacrificial ceremonies with divine personifications are also found in the cults of Huitzilopochtli and Quetzalcoatl. In Cholula, east of the capital, Quetzalcoatl's image was mounted on top of Mexico's largest pyramid (there is now a church on the old temple platform). Every year a feast was held there in his honor. A handsome slave boy was brought and dressed in the divine attire, with a feathered cloak and a jewelled headband. For forty days he moved about in the city, receiving the homage of the people. With the approaching end of his allotted time the priests prepared him for his imminent death. His anguish was moderated by drugs, and when the forty days were up he was sacrificed at midnight before the image of Quetzalcoatl. The god was sprinkled with the blood of the victim and his heart was eaten by the priests. When the sun rose, the priests danced in a frenzy, delighted that Quetzalcoatl had gained new life and that they themselves had shared in the god's life in ritual communion. Apparently this worship of Quetzalcoatl bears a strong resemblance to the Tezcatlipoca cult. This is natural enough when we recall that these two gods were at once complements of and contrasts to each other, a twin pair representing the functions of the Supreme Being in differentiated forms. Both gods were worshipped as a Supreme Being and both represented the sun and the cosmic year.

Tezcatlipoca as well as Quetzalcoatl (the latter to a lesser degree) also received human sacrifices at other times— Quetzalcoatl, for example, each time his planet Venus was in a weak calendrical phase. Of course, not only human beings were sacrificed. Ordinary human food such as pigeons and quails and, in addition, clothes and flowers were regularly placed on the altars of the gods. Four times during the day and three times at night incense of copal and rubber was burnt before their images.

Strangely enough, even so gruesome a figure as the war god Huitzilopochtli received flower offerings. The ninth month (corresponding to the change from July to August) was dedicated to him and his image was then decorated with wreaths and flower garlands. We also know that he was the principal figure in a sacramental meal: his image was formed in dough, shot at with a stone arrow (!) by *quetzalcoatl,* the high priest, then cut and eaten by youthful representatives of different parts of Mexico (compare the Xocotl rite described above). Especially characteristic of the Huitzilopochtli cult were the blood sacrifices, the sacrifices of human beings; not without reason has this god been called the god of sacrifice. During Cortez's war of conquest captured Spaniards were sacrificed to Huitzilopochtli. The prisoner was placed with his back on a sacrificial stone in front of the god's image, his arms and legs firmly held by black-robed and black-painted priests while a sacrificial priest in red attire lowered a knife to his chest, slit it open, and pulled out the heart. The heart was then held up before the idol and eventually placed in the censer where it was left to burn. The body was thrown down the temple steps, flayed, cut up, and sent as powerful food to the high dignitaries. Moctezuma, among others, had his share.

The conquistadors have left exhaustive descriptions of Huitzilopochtli's and Tezcatlipoca's two temples on the great pyramid in Tlatelolco. Cortez ascended the huge stairway on November 12, 1519. At the top, on a platform the size of a plaza, he was welcomed by Moctezuma, who had prepared for the visit by sacrificing some youths and who was now, as always after such sacrificial rites, in good spirits. After some hesitation Moctezuma allowed Cortez to visit the two temples. In one of them was a colossal stone statue of Huitzilopochtli decorated with precious stones, gold, and pearls, and circled by golden snakes. His face was broad, his eyes were terribly savage, and in his hands he held a bow and arrows. In the other temple was a statue of Tezcatlipoca. The hearts of eight people sacrificed earlier in the day were burning in the censers. The temple walls and the pavement were black with clotted blood and the stench was unbearable. Moctezuma explained to the shocked Cortez that cessation of human sacrifices would cause the destruction of the whole cosmic order.[30]

Alarm and anxiety about the continuance of the cosmos was, then, the ultimate cause of this fearful custom, here carried to absurd lengths. At the opening ceremony of the great double temple in Tenochtitlan in 1487 no less than 20,000 people were sacrificed. The victims stood in line and the blood poured in streams. 50,000 people are said to have lost their lives annually, stabbed on the sacrificial stone, shot with bow and arrow, beheaded, burnt, or killed in gladiatorial games. Drowning was part of the Tlaloc cult, arrow shooting in the Xipe-Totec ritual: at certain sacrificial feasts in honor of Xipe-Totec the prisoner was tied to the upper part of a fence-like scaffold and shot at with arrows until he died. The blood that flowed down on the ground was supposed to make the soil fertile and magically hasten the rains. Gladiatorial combat was reserved for imprisoned chieftains and brave warriors. The victim was tied with a rope to a large circular stone, *temalacatl,* and armed with a wooden sword with a blade of feathers. Five combatants opposed him, among them eagle and jaguar warriors, armed with swords with obsidian blades. One by one the prisoner had to overpower them, which supposedly was his chance to escape being sacrificed

30. Speaking about the sacrifices, the Dominican friar Diego Durán, who settled in Texcoco in the middle of the sixteenth century, remarks: "This was their goal: to seize yet not to slay; to do no harm to man or woman, to a home or cornfield, but to feed the idol" (Durán 1971, p. 93). Durán gives many examples of the people (or at least the upper classes) also being fed with the meat from human sacrifices. Michael Harner thinks that Aztec cannibalism—too often overlooked—was a response to growing population pressure and a need for protein. He concludes that "the Aztecs were unique among the world's states in having a cannibal empire" (Harner 1977, p. 131). It is not explained, however, why nutritional cannibalism had to be performed only in connection with sacrifices.

on the altar of the god. The likelihood of the escape was of course exceedingly small.

Mythology sanctified human sacrifices. The myth of the creation of man tells us that the creator Quetzalcoatl poured his blood over them. Consequently, said the priests, mankind must feed the gods with their hearts and their blood. Another myth relates how the earth goddess was cut up and the earth and everything upon it was formed from her limbs. Human sacrifice was traced back to this primal sacrifice; that is, each sacrifice reproduced the original one.

The cosmic equilibrium that these enormous sacrifices were supposed to secure was particularly threatened when the 52-year cycle came to an end. At one of these critical transitions the world was expected to collapse. During the last days of the closing cycle all fires were extinguished and all household utensils were broken. In excitement and fear the people waited for what was to come. On the last night priests searched the starlit sky from a temple on top of a volcano. When the Pleiades reached the meridian the priests knew that the world would last for another cycle. A man was sacrificed and in his opened chest the priests lit a new fire with a fire-drill. Messengers were soon running with torches from the new fire to the temples lighting their fires anew, from the temples the flame was passed on by individual family members to the domestic hearths. At dawn new utensils were put in place and feasts and sacrifices succeeded each other. A critical date had been lived through. Fear of what could happen at the end of the 52-year period was fostered by the knowledge that four earlier worlds, "four suns," had perished in great catastrophes.

One of the rites connected with the 52-year cycle, the *volador* rite, is still popular in Mexico. Four men dressed as birds (that is to say, gods), climb up a high pole which has four ropes attached to a ring at the top. The ropes are then rolled up. Each man takes his rope and throws himself out in the air, which sets the ring in slow rotation, and the ropes are successively lengthened. Thirteen times the men swing round the pole and with each turn they come nearer to the ground. The thirteen rounds of the four men signify the orbit of the sun during the 52-year cycle.[31]

The cosmic background to Aztec ritual is even more apparent when the symbolism and mythological setting of the temple site and the temple pyramids are taken into consideration. The sacred area of Tenochtitlan, *tecpan,* was surrounded by a wall ("the snake wall") decorated with snake heads. Inside this wall were situated, from east to west, the great pyramid with a double flight of stairs leading up to the temples of Huitzilopochtli and Tlaloc, the gladiator stone, the head scaffolding, and the ball-game court. In the northwest part of the temple area stood the pyramid called "the eagle house" and the famous calendar-stone was raised in its immediate vicinity. The cult of "the eagle house" indicates that Aztec pyramids, as perhaps Egyptian pyramids once had been, were built to symbolize the universe. On the day "4 earthquake," a precarious day of the year when the issue at stake was ritually to tie the sun to a new annual cycle, a war prisoner was sacrificed to Tonatiuh, the sun god. The prisoner, however, as he ascended the flight of stairs with measured steps, was believed to be the sun himself, and the pyramid must have represented our world. The same symbolism probably applied to the great pyramid. It was called "the (cloud-) snake mountain" and was evidently a cultic replica of the world mountain leading up to heaven, the dwelling-place of the gods, and a ritual representation of our world over which the sun follows his orbit.

As we recall, there was an enormous statue of Huitzilopochtli housed in the temple room on top of the Tlatelolco pyramid. The myth about the birth of this god gives us an insight into the cosmic ideas behind the disposition of his temple site in *tecpan.* It relates that Coatlicue, the great earth goddess, mother of the 400 southern star gods and the moon goddess Coyolxauhqui, lived on "the cloud mountain." Once while she was participating in a cult service on the mountain a ball of feathers fell on her and made her

31. Cf. Larsen 1937.

pregnant. (The feather ball here stands for the divine celestial element.) The stars were infuriated by her disgraceful condition and decided to kill her. But the foetus in her womb calmed her. The moon goddess, wishing to warn her mother of the murder conspiracy, rushed ahead of her star siblings toward the top of the snake mountain, passing the head scaffolding and other places that can be identified within *tecpan*. At that moment Huitzilopochtli was born; he came forth armed with shield and spear. Unaware of his sister's good intentions, he cut off her head and chased the star gods down the snake mountain.

This myth, which in symbolic form renders the eternal interplay of sun and moon, day and night, supplies a conception of the world which is reflected in microcosmic form in the planning and architecture of the temple site. Consequently, the myth must have had a cultic foundation. The complete world-encompassing course of events has been located in *tecpan*. As Seler and Krickeberg have shown, the buildings and monuments had their significance as a reflected image of the universe. Their exact symbolic connotation may still be disputed. To Krickeberg the pyramid or the sky mountain is a symbol of heaven. It is unlikely that the Aztecs shared this view. As Krickeberg has also implied, they considered the pyramid to represent the framework of our own world and the temple at its top to be the heavenly abode of the gods or the god.[32]

It should be added that in the Mexico City area a stone head about one meter high was found, representing the severed head of Coyolxauhqui. Most probably it once adorned the topmost platform of Huitzilopochtli's temple pyramid.

As we know, it is told that each morning when the sun is born anew and he has chased away the moon and stars he is brought to mid-heaven in a palanquin by warriors who were killed in battle or on the sacrificial stone. In the afternoon he

32. The myth of Huitzilopochtli's birth may be found in the Florentine Codex, Book 3: The Origin of the Gods [Sahagún 1950–69 (4)], pp. 1–5. The ritual interpretation, first discussed in Seler 1902–23, (2), was later developed in Krickeberg 1950.

is carried to the land of the sunset by women who have died in childbirth. This myth, which we have had reason to compare to the ancient Egyptian myth in which the dead pull the sun boat, unites the luminous supernatural powers with the privileged dead. For the masses, however, fate was not that gentle, and a bleak, shadowy existence in the nether world, like that related in the Odyssey and the Gilgamish epic, awaited them.

The Aztec concepts of life after death may thus be summed up. Determining factors for a man's destiny in the next existence were his social position and the circumstances surrounding his death. On the other hand, we do not hear of any retribution after death based on his conduct in this life. This might have been expected, since the confession of sins and penance, for example in the form of asceticism or temple service, were not unusual occurrences. Perhaps they were important only for happiness and success in this world.[33]

The dead were distributed among a number of death realms, one of which, Mictlan, was intended for the majority of the people. Mictlan, situated in the north, belonged to the lower regions and was ruled by Mictlantecuhtli and his consort Mictecacihuatl. Mictlantecuhtli was a frightening skeletal figure, surrounded by bats, spiders, and owls. The journey to his kingdom led through nine subterranean worlds and took four years. As in other Indian tales of journeys to the land of the dead, especially among North American Indians, there were numerous obstacles on the way: a river difficult to traverse, mountains, icy winds, man-eating beasts, and so on. Amulets buried with the dead protected them from these perils.

The other death realms were lighter in tone. Those who were drowned or struck by lightning or had died from leprosy came to Tlaloc's paradise, Tlalocan, in the south, where they enjoyed a pleasant existence with an abundance of fruit, corn, and beans. There existed no sorrow in this land, writes Sahagún. Tlalocan has a long history in the Mesoamerican

33. Cf. Lanczkowski 1970b.

conceptual world. There is an exceedingly beautiful temple painting from Teotihuacan in the early classical period which depicts the delights of this paradise. The painting illustrates this fortunate land with its lake, rivers, and cacao trees as the abode of a multitude of dancing, singing, and swimming people, all full of life and motion.

Another paradise was "the house of the sun," the kingdom of the sun god in the east. Those who had the privilege of arriving there were warriors who had fallen in battle and prisoners who had been killed on the sacrificial stone. The sun summoned them and invited them to share his joy. They could enjoy the fragrance of marvellous flowers, they feigned combats with each other, and when the sun rose in the east they greeted him by beating their shields with loud shouts of joy. After a four-year existence in this blessed kingdom of dreams the dead were reborn on earth as colibris, the birds of Huitzilopochtli.

The sun also had a propitious land in the west, "the corn house." There gathered the women who had died in childbirth. In the afternoon they escorted the sun on his way, at night they sometimes returned to earth and their ghostly apparitions frightened women and small children.

Just as there were nine night gods and thirteen day gods, so were there nine hells and thirteen heavens. In the highest heavens, the twelfth and thirteenth, dwelt the two creators, Ometecuhtli and Omecihuatl. There also were the deceased infants and the unborn souls of the next human age. The latter were nourished by a large heavenly tree, a conception known in various forms in Indonesia and northern Asia, for example.

We do not know how generally accepted this differentiated conception of the death realm was and to what extent it represented the hopes or fears of the people, or whether it merely constituted a mythological padding of vague beliefs. It is beyond question that concentration on death and death motifs has been conspicuous in later Mexican popular belief (and in modern Mexican art as well). The sacrificial hecatombs during the Aztec period no doubt encouraged thoughts of death, but this does not necessarily indicate general acceptance of a belief in life after death. Aztec poetry gives evidence of a more inquiring, sometimes skeptical, attitude. In one song the poet avows:

> I cry, I am sad, I am only a singer.
> If only once I could wear flowers,
> adorn myself with them in the land of the spirits.
> Grief lies heavy on me.
> Only like a flower is man honored on earth,
> just for a short moment he rejoices
>   in the blossoms of spring.[34]

34. This plaintive poem is from Garibay 1953, p. 176. Cf. a similar poem in Leander 1971, p. 47.

Bibliography

Abbreviations

AA   American Anthropologist
AE   American Ethnologist
AMNHB   Bulletins of the American Museum of Natural History,
         New York
APAMNH   Anthropological Papers of the American Museum of
         Natural History, New York
AR   Anthropological Records, University of California
ARBAE   Annual Reports of the Bureau of American Ethnology,
         Washington, D.C.
BBAE   Bulletins of the Bureau of American Ethnology, Washing-
         ton, D.C.
CA   Current Anthropology
ES   Etnologiska Studier, Göteborg
FFC   Folklore Fellows Communications, Helsinki
HR   History of Religions, Chicago
IAE   Internationales Archiv für Ethnographie, Leiden
ICA   Proceedings of the International Congress(es) of Ameri-
         canists
INM   Indian Notes and Monographs, Museum of the Ameri-
         can Indian, New York
JAFL   Journal of American Folklore
JSA   Journal de la Société des américanistes, Paris
MAAA   Memoirs of the American Anthropological Association
MAES   Monographs of the American Ethnological Society, New
         York
OCMA   Occasional Contributions from the Museum of An-
         thropology of the University of Michigan, Ann Arbor

PAES	Publications of the American Ethnological Society, Seattle and London
PM	Primitive Man, Washington, D.C.
PMP	Papers of the Peabody Museum of American Archaeology and Ethnology, Cambridge, Massachusetts
RHR	Revue de l'histoire des religions
SCA	Smithsonian Contributions to Anthropology, Washington, D.C.
SEMMS	Statens Etnografiska Museum (Sweden) Monograph Series, Stockholm
SEMNS	Statens Etnografiska Museum (Sweden) New Series, Stockholm
SR	Smithsonian Reports, Washington, D.C.
SSCR	Stockholm Studies in Comparative Religion, University of Stockholm
SWJA	Southwestern Journal of Anthropology (since 1943 Journal of Anthropological Research), Albuquerque, New Mexico
TRE	Theologische Realenzyklopädie, Berlin, de Gruyter
UCPAAE	University of California Publications in American Archaeology and Ethnology, Berkeley
UWPA	University of Washington Publications in Anthropology, Seattle
VFPA	Viking Fund Publications in Anthropology, New York
YUPA	Yale University Publications in Anthropology, New Haven
ZE	Zeitschrift für Ethnologie, Berlin, Braunschweig

Bibliography

Aberle, D. F.
    1959   The Prophet Dance and Reactions to White Contact. SWJA 15 (1): 74–83.
Albers, P., and S. Parker
    1971   The Plains Vision Experience: A Study of Power and Privilege. SWJA 27 (3): 203–233.
Alexander, H. B.
    1916   North American Mythology. Mythology of All Races, vol. 10. Boston: Marshall Jones.
    1920   Latin American Mythology. Mythology of All Races, vol. 11. Boston: Marshall Jones.
    1953   The World's Rim: Great Mysteries of the North American Indians. Lincoln: University of Nebraska Press.

Altschuler, M.
1958   On the Environmental Limitations of Mayan Cultural Development. SWJA 14 (2): 189–198.
Anders, F.
1963   Das Pantheon der Maya. Graz: Akademische Druck- und Verlagsanstalt.
Anderson and Dibble. See Sahagún
Angelino, H., and C. L. Shedd
1955   A Note on Berdache. AA 57 (1): 121–126.
Armillas, P.
1964   Northern Mesoamerica. Pp. 291–329 in Prehistoric Man in the New World (ed. by J. D. Jennings and E. Norbeck). Chicago: University of Chicago Press.
Bahr, D. M., et al.
1974   Piman Shamanism and Staying Sickness. Tucson: University of Arizona Press.
Bancroft, H. H.
1883   The Native Races of the Pacific States. 5 vols. San Francisco: A. L. Bancroft.
Barbeau, M.
1952   The Old-World Dragon in America. Pp. 115–122 in Indian Tribes of Aboriginal America (ed. by S. Tax). Chicago: University of Chicago Press.
Basso, K. H.
1970   The Cibecue Apache. New York and London: Holt, Rinehart and Winston.
Baudin, L.
1947   Les Incas du Pérou. Paris.
Baumann, H.
1955   Das doppelte Geschlecht. Berlin: Dietrich Reimer.
Beauchamp, W. M.
1898   Indian Corn Stories and Customs. JAFL 11: 195–202.
Benedict, R. F.
1922   The Vision in Plains Culture. AA 24 (1): 1–23.
1923   The Concept of the Guardian Spirit in North America. MAAA 29. Menasha, Wisconsin.
1932   Configurations of Culture in North America. AA 34 (1): 1–27.
1935   Patterns of Culture. London: George Routledge & Sons.
Bennett, W. C., and J. B. Bird
1964   Andean Culture History. 2nd ed. New York: American Museum of Natural History Handbook no. 15.
Benson, E. P.
1971   (ed.) Dumbarton Oaks Conference on Chavín. Washington, D.C.: Dumbarton Oaks Research Library and Collection.

1972a   (ed.) The Cult of the Feline. Washington, D.C.: Dumbarton
        Oaks Research Library and Collection.
1972b   The Mochica: A Culture of Peru. New York: Praeger.
Bernal, I.
1963   Teotihuacan. Mexico: Instituto nacional de antropologia e
        historia.
1969   The Olmec World. Berkeley: University of California Press.
Beyer, H.
1908   Der "Drache" der Mexikaner. Globus 93.
1965   Mito y simbolismo del México antiguo (ed. by C. Cook de
        Leonard). Mexico City.
Bianchi, U.
1958   Il Dualismo religioso. Rome: "L'Erma" di Bretschneider.
Birket-Smith, K.
1943   Kulturens vägar. 2 vols. Stockholm: Natur och Kultur.
Blaffer, S. C.
1972   The Black-Man of Zinacantan: A Central American Legend.
        Austin and London: University of Texas Press.
Blom, F., and O. La Farge
1926-27 Tribes and Temples. Middle American Research Institute
        Publ. 1–2. New Orleans: Tulane University.
Blumensohn, J.
1933   The Fast among North American Indians. AA 35 (4): 451–
        469.
Boas, F.
1897   The Social Organization and the Secret Societies of the
        Kwakiutl Indians. United States National Museum Report
        1895: 311–738.
1915   Mythology and Folk-Tales of the North American Indians.
        Pp. 306–349 in Anthropology in North America (by F. Boas
        et al.). New York: Stechert.
1917   The Origin of Death. JAFL 30: 486–491.
1966   Kwakiutl Ethnography (ed. by Helen Codere). Chicago and
        London: University of Chicago Press.
Böning, P. E.
1974   Der Pillánbegriff der Mapuche. St. Augustin: Steyler.
Boglár, L.
1971   Chieftainship and the Religious Leader. Acta Ethno-
        graphica (Hung.) 20 (3–4): 331–337.
Bogoras, W.
1902   The Folklore of Northeastern Asia, as Compared with That
        of Northwestern America. AA 4 (4): 577–683.
Bourke, J. G.
1889   Notes on the Cosmogony and Theogony of the Mojave In-
        dians of the Rio Colorado, Arizona. JAFL 2: 169–189.

Bouteiller, M.
1950   Chamanisme et guérison magique. Paris: Presses Universitaires de France.
Brainerd, G. W.
1954   The Maya Civilization. Los Angeles: Southwest Museum.
Brinton, D. G.
1868   (1976) Myths of the New World. New York (: Rudolf Steiner Publications).
Brown, J. E.
1953   The Sacred Pipe. Norman: University of Oklahoma Press.
1970   The Unlikely Associates: A Study in Oglala Sioux Magic and Metaphysics. Ethnos 35: 5–15.
1976   The Roots of Renewal. Pp. 25–34 in Seeing with a Native Eye (ed. by W. H. Capps). New York: Harper and Row.
Brundage, B. C.
1963   Empire of the Inca. Norman: University of Oklahoma Press.
1975   Two Earths, Two Heavens: An Essay Contrasting the Aztecs and the Incas. Albuquerque: University of New Mexico Press.
Bullard, W. R., Jr.
1960   Maya Settlement Patterns in North Eastern Petén, Guatemala. American Antiquity 25: 355–372.
Bunzel, R. L.
1932   Introduction to Zuñi Ceremonialism. ARBAE 47: 467–544.
Burland, C. A.
1948   Life and Art in Ancient Mexico. Oxford: Oxford University Press.
1967   The Gods of Mexico. London: Eyre and Spottiswoode.
Bushnell, G. H. S.
1956   Peru. Ancient Peoples and Places, vol. 1. London and New York: Praeger.
Bushnell, J.
1958   La Virgen de Guadalupe as Surrogate Mother in San Juan Atzingo. AA 60 (2): 261–265.
Carrasco, P.
1961   The Civil-Religious Hierarchy in Mesoamerican Communities: The Pre-Spanish Background and Colonial Development. AA 63 (3): 483–497.
Caso, A.
1958   The Aztecs: People of the Sun. Norman: University of Oklahoma Press.
Castaneda, C.
1968   The Teachings of Don Juan. New York: Ballantine Books.
1971   A Separate Reality. New York: Simon and Schuster.
1972   Journey to Ixtlan. New York: Simon and Schuster.

1974   Tales of Power. New York: Simon and Schuster.
Catlin, G.
    1841   Letters and Notes on the Manners, Customs, and Condition of the North American Indians. 2 vols. London.
    1967   O-kee-pa: A Religious Ceremony and Other Customs of the Mandan (ed. by J. C. Ewers). Centennial edition. New Haven: Yale University Press.
Cieza de León, P. de
    1959   The Incas of Pedro de Cieza de León. Norman: University of Oklahoma Press.
Clements, F. E.
    1932   Primitive Concepts of Disease. UCPAAE 32 (2): 185–252.
Coe, M. D.
    1956   The Funerary Temple among the Classic Maya. SWJA 12 (4): 387–394.
    1960   Archaeological Linkages with North and South America at La Victoria, Guatemala. AA 62 (3): 363–393.
    1962   Mexico. New York: Praeger.
    1965   The Jaguar's Children. New York: Museum of Primitive Art.
    1966   The Maya. New York: Praeger.
Coe, R. T.
    1976   Sacred Circles: Two Thousand Years of North American Indian Art. London: Arts Council of Great Britain.
Cooper, J. M.
    1933   The Northern Algonquian Supreme Being. PM 6 (3–4): 41–111.
Count, E. W.
    1952   The Earth-Diver and the Rival Twins. Pp. 55–62 in Indian Tribes of Aboriginal America (ed. by S. Tax). Chicago: University of Chicago Press.
Covarrubias, M.
    1957   Indian Art of Mexico and Central America. New York: Knopf.
Cowgill, G. L.
    1964   The End of Classic Maya Culture: A Review of Recent Evidence. SWJA 20 (2): 145–159.
Culbert, T. P.
    1973   (ed.) The Classic Maya Collapse. Albuquerque: University of New Mexico Press.
Curtin, J.
    1899   Creation Myths of Primitive America. London.
Czaplicka, M. A.
    1914   Aboriginal Siberia. Oxford: Clarendon Press.
Dähnhardt, O.
    1907   Natursagen, vol. 1. Leipzig and Berlin.

Dangel, R.
1927 Der Schöpferglaube der Nordzentralkalifornier. Studi e
materiali di storia delle religioni 3. Rome.
Darwin, Ch.
1890 (1839) Journal of Researches into the Natural History and
Geology of the Countries Visited during the Voyage round
the World of HMS "Beagle" under the Command of Cap-
tain Fitz-Roy. London.
Denig, E. Th.
1930 Indian Tribes of the Upper Missouri. ARBAE 46: 375–628.
Deursen, A. van
1931 Der Heilbringer, Eine ethnologische Studie über den Heilbringer bei den nordamerikanischen Indianern. Groningen:
J. B. Wolters.
Devereux, G.
1957 Dream Learning and Individual Ritual Differences in
Mohave Shamanism. AA 59 (6): 1036–1045.
Dewdney, S.
1975 The Sacred Scrolls of the Southern Ojibway. Toronto and
Buffalo: University of Toronto Press.
Díaz del Castillo, B.
1950 Historia verdadera de la Conquista de Nueva España.
México.
1956 Discovery and Conquest of Mexico. New York.
Dietschy, H.
1940-41 Mensch und Gott bei mexikanischen Indianern. Anthropos
35–36.
Digby, A.
1955 The Maize God and the Crossed Band Glyph. ICA 30:
41–44.
Dixon, R. B.
1905 The Northern Maidu. AMNHB 17 (3): 119–346.
Dockstader, F. J.
1954 The Kachina and the White Man. Cranbrook Institute of
Science, Bulletin 35. Bloomfield Hills, Michigan.
Dorsey, G. A.
1905 The Cheyenne, vol. 1. Field Columbian Museum of Natural
History, Anthropological Series 9 (1). Chicago.
1907 The Skidi Rite of Human Sacrifice. ICA 15: 65–70.
Dorsey, J. O.
1894 A Study of Siouan Cults. ARBAE 11: 351–544.
Dozier, E. P.
1970 The Pueblo Indians of North America. New York: Holt,
Rinehart and Winston.

Driver, H. E.
1941 Girls' Puberty Rites in Western North America. AR 6 (2): 21–90.
Drucker, Ph.
1940 Kwakiutl Dancing Societies. AR 2 (6): 201–230.
1952 La Venta, Tabasco: A Study of Olmec Ceramics and Art. BBAE 153.
Du Bois, C.
1935 Wintu Ethnography. UCPAAE 36 (1): 1–148.
Dumond, D. E.
1961 Swidden Agriculture and the Rise of Maya Civilization. SWJA 17 (4): 301–316.
Durán, Fray Diego
1971 Book of the Gods and Rites and the Ancient Calendar (ed. by F. Horcasitas and D. Heyden). Norman: University of Oklahoma Press.
Dusenberry, V.
1962 The Montana Cree: A Study in Religious Persistence. SSCR 3.
Edmonson, M. S.
1971 The Book of Counsel: The Popol Vuh of the Quiche Maya of Guatemala. Middle American Research Institute Publ. 35. New Orleans: Tulane University.
Ehrenreich, P.
1905 Die Mythen und Legenden der südamerikanischen Urvölker. ZE 37, Supplement.
Ekholm, G.
1964 Transpacific Contacts. Pp. 489–510 in Prehistoric Man in the New World (ed. by J. D. Jennings and E. Norbeck). Chicago: University of Chicago Press.
Eliade, M.
1961-62 Mythologies asiatiques et folklore sud-est européen. 1: Le Plongeon cosmonique. RHR 160 (2).
1962 Le Créateur et son "ombre." Eranos-Jahrbuch 30: 211–239. Zurich.
1964 Shamanism: Archaic Techniques of Ecstasy. New York: Pantheon Books.
1969-71 South American High Gods. 2 parts. HR 8 (4): 338–354; 10 (3): 234–266.
Fenton, W. N.
1941 Masked Medicine Societies of the Iroquois. SR 1940: 397–430.
1953 The Iroquois Eagle Dance, an Offshoot of the Calumet Dance. BBAE 156.
Fewkes, J. W.
1897 Tusayan Snake Ceremonies. ARBAE 16: 267–312.

1903   Hopi Katcinas. ARBAE 21: 3–126.
Findeisen, H.
1957   Schamanentum. Stuttgart: Kohlhammer.
Fletcher, A. C.
1904   The Hako: A Pawnee Ceremony. ARBAE 22 (2).
1910   Wakonda. Handbook of American Indians. BBAE 30 (2): 897–898.
Fletcher, A. C., and F. La Flesche
1911   The Omaha Tribe. ARBAE 27.
Fock, N.
1963   Waiwai: Religion and Society of an Amazonian Tribe. Nationalmuseets Skrifter, Etnografiske Raekke, vol. 8. Copenhagen.
Ford, J. A.
1969   A Comparison of Formative Cultures in the Americas: Diffusion or the Psychic Unity of Man. SCA 2.
Foster, G. M.
1944   Nagualism in Mexico and Guatemala. Acta Americana 2 (1–2): 85–103. Washington, D.C.
1960   Culture and Conquest: America's Spanish Heritage. VFPA 27.
1976   Disease Etiologies in Non-Western Medical Systems. AA 78 (4): 773–782.
Frazer, J. G.
1910   Totemism and Exogamy. 4 vols. London: Macmillan.
1955   The Golden Bough. 3rd ed. (reprint). 13 vols. London: Macmillan.
Furst, P. T.
1972   Flesh of the Gods: The Ritual Use of Hallucinogens. New York and Washington: Praeger.
Garcilaso de la Vega
1869-71   The First Part of the Royal Commentaries of the Yncas. 2 vols. (ed. by C. R. Markham). London: Hakluyt Society.
Garibay, A. M.
1953   Historia de la literatura nahuatl. Mexico.
Giddings, R. W.
1959   Yaqui Myths and Legends. University of Arizona Anthropological Papers no. 2. Tucson.
Gjessing, G.
1948   Guden med det éne øye. Viking 1948: 31–55.
Goeje, C. H. de
1943   Philosophy, Initiation and Myths of the Indians of Guiana and Adjacent Countries. IAE 44.
Goldenweiser, A.
1910   Totemism: An Analytical Study. JAFL 23: 179–293.
1937   Anthropology. New York: Crofts.

Goldman, I.
1975   The Mouth of Heaven: An Introduction to Kwakiutl Religious Thought. New York: Wiley.

González Torres, Y.
1975   El Culto a los astros entre los mexicas. Mexico: Sep/Setentas.

Grebe, M. E., S. Pacheco, and J. Segura
1972   Cosmovision Mapuche. Cuadernos de la Realidad Nacional 14: 46–73.

Grieder, T.
1975   The Interpretation of Ancient Symbols. AA 77 (4): 849–855.

Gunther, E.
1926   An Analysis of the First Salmon Ceremony. AA 28 (4): 605–617.
1928   A Further Analysis of the First Salmon Ceremony. UWPA 2 (5): 129–173.

Gusinde, M.
1930   Das Brüderpaar in der südamerikanischen Mythologie. ICA 23.
1931-37   Die Feuerland-Indianer. 2 vols. 1: Die Selknam (1931); 2: Die Yamana (1937). Mödling bei Wien.

Haeberlin, H. K.
1916   The Idea of Fertilization in the Culture of the Pueblo Indians. MAAA 3 (1).
1918   Sbetetda'q, A Shamanistic Performance of the Coast Salish. AA 20 (3): 249–257.

Haekel, J.
1938   Zweiklassensystem, Männerhaus und Totemismus in Südamerika. ZE 70: 426–454.
1947   Schutzgeistsuche und Jugendweihe im westlichen Nordamerika. Ethnos 12 (3): 106–122.
1952   Die Vorstellung vom Zweiten Ich in den amerikanischen Hochkulturen. Pp. 124–188 in Kultur und Sprache, ed. by W. Koppers. Vienna: Herold.
1955   Zur Problematik des heilegen Pfahles bei den Indianern Brasiliens. ICA 31: 229–243.
1958   Kosmischer Baum und Pfahl in Mythus und Kult der Stämme Nordwestamerikas. Wiener völkerkundliche Mitteilungen 6, 1 (1–4): 3–81.
1959a   Purá und Hochgott. Archiv für Völkerkunde 13: 25–50.
1959b   Zur Problematik des Obersten goettlichen Paares im alten Mexiko. México Antiguo 9: 39–76.

Hahn, R. A.
1973   Understanding Beliefs. CA 14 (3): 207–229.

Hale, H.
1888   Huron Folk-Lore. JAFL 1: 177–183.

Hallowell, A. I.
1926 Bear Ceremonialism in the Northern Hemisphere. AA 28 (1): 1–175.

Hammond, N.
1974 (ed.) Mesoamerican Archaeology: New Approaches. Austin: University of Texas Press.

Harner, M. J.
1962 Jívaro Souls. AA 64 (2): 258–272.
1972 The Jívaro: People of the Sacred Waterfalls. Garden City, N.Y.: Doubleday.
1977 The Ecological Basis for Aztec Sacrifice. AE 4 (1): 117–135.

Harrington, M. R.
1921 Religion and Ceremonies of the Lenape. INM 19.

Harris, J. R.
1906 The Cult of the Heavenly Twins. Cambridge: Cambridge University Press.

Hartmann, H.
1973 Die Plains- und Prärieindianer Nordamerikas. Berlin: Museum für Völkerkunde.
1976a Ein Maistanz in San Ildefonso Pueblo. Baessler-Archiv 24: 5–39.
1976b Schutzgeistvorstellungen bei Pueblo-Indianern. Baessler-Archiv 24: 317–332.

Harva, U. (before 1928 Holmberg)
1922-23 Der Baum des Lebens. Annales academiae scientiarum fennicae, ser. B, vol. 16. Helsinki.
1938 Die religiösen Vorstellungen der altaischen Völker. FFC 125.

Hatt, G.
1951 The Corn Mother in America and in Indonesia. Anthropos 46: 853–914.

Heine-Geldern, R. von
1966 The Problem of Transpacific Influences in Mesoamerica. Pp. 277–295 in Handbook of Middle American Indians, vol. 4 (ed. by R. Wauchope). Austin: University of Texas Press.

Heinen, H. D., and K. Ruddle
1974 Ecology, Ritual, and Economic Organization in the Distribution of Palm Starch among the Warao of the Orinoco Delta. SWJA 30 (2): 116–138.

Heizer, R. F.
1947 Francis Drake and the California Indians, 1579. UCPAAE 42 (3): 251–302.

Helfrich, K.
1973 Menschenopfer und Tötungsrituale im Kult der Maya. Monumenta Americana 9. Berlin: Mann.

Hellbom, A.-B.
1964   Las Apariciones de la Virgen de Guadalupe en México y en España. Ethnos 29: 58–72.
Hermitte, M. E.
1970   Poder sobrenatural y control social en un pueblo Maya contemporáneo. Mexico: Instituto Indigenista Interamericano.
Hewitt, J. N. B.
1902   Orenda and a Definition of Religion. AA 4 (1): 33–46.
Hickerson, H.
1960   The Feast of the Dead among the Seventeenth Century Algonkians of the Upper Great Lakes. AA 62 (1): 81–107.
1962   Notes on the Post-Contact Origin of the Midewiwin. Ethnohistory 9 (4): 404–423.
Hissink, K.
1960   Alt-Peru: Beispiel einer Hochkultur. Pp. 90–103 in Völkerkunde (ed. by B. Freudenfeld). Munich: C. H. Beck.
Hoffman, W. J.
1891   The Midewiwin or "Grand Medicine Society" of the Ojibwa. ARBAE 7: 143–300.
Holmberg, A. R.
1950   Nomads of the Long Bow: The Siriono of Eastern Bolivia. Smithsonian Institution, Institute of Social Anthropology Publ. no. 10. Washington, D.C.
Holmberg, U. See Harva.
Holmer, N. M., and S. H. Wassén
1953   The Complete Mu-Igala in Picture Writing: A Native Record of a Cuna Indian Medicine Song. ES 21.
Holmes, W. H.
1895   Archaeological Studies among the Ancient Cities of Mexico, vol. 1. Field Columbian Museum of Natural History, Anthropological Series 1 (1). Chicago.
Howard, J. H.
1960   When They Worship the Underwater Panther. SWJA 16 (2): 217–224.
1968   The Southeastern Ceremonial Complex and Its Interpretation. Missouri Archaeological Society Memoir 6. Columbia, Mo.
1974   The Arikara Buffalo Society Medicine Bundle. Plains Anthropologist 19 (66): 241–271.
Hudson, Ch.
1976   The Southeastern Indians. Knoxville: University of Tennessee Press.
Hultkrantz, Å.
1953   Conceptions of the Soul among North American Indians. SEMMS 1.

1954   The Indians and the Wonders of Yellowstone. Ethnos 19: 34–68.

1956   Configurations of Religious Belief among the Wind River Shoshoni. Ethnos 21 (3–4): 194–215.

1957   The North American Indian Orpheus Tradition. SEMMS 2.

1961   The Owner of the Animals in the Religion of the North American Indians. Pp. 53–64 in The Supernatural Owners of Nature (ed. by Å. Hultkrantz). SSCR 1.

1962   Die Religion der amerikanischen Arktis. Pp. 357–415 in Die Religionen Nordeurasiens und der amerikanischen Arktis (Die Religionen der Menschheit, ed. by C. M. Schröder, vol. 3). Stuttgart: Kohlhammer.

1963   Les Religions des Indiens primitifs de l'Amérique: essai d'une synthèse typologique et historique. SSCR 4.

1965a   The Study of North American Indian Religion: Retrospect, Present Trends and Future Tasks. Temenos 1: 87–121.

1965b   Type of Religion in the Arctic Hunting Cultures. Pp. 265–318 in Hunting and Fishing (ed. by H. Hvarfner). Luleå: Norrbottens Museum.

1966-67   North American Indian Religion in the History of Research: A General Survey. 4 parts. HR 6 (2): 91–107; 6 (3): 183–207; 7(1): 13–34; 7 (2): 112–148.

1967   Spirit Lodge: A North American Shamanistic Séance. Pp. 32–68 in Studies in Shamanism (ed. by C.-M. Edsman). Scripta Instituti Donneriani Aboensis, vol. 1. Uppsala.

1971   The Structure of Theistic Beliefs among North American Plains Indians. Temenos 7: 66–74.

1972a   An Ideological Dichotomy: Myths and Folk Beliefs among the Shoshoni Indians of Wyoming. HR 11 (4): 339–353.

1972b   The Elusive Totemism. Pp. 218–227 in Ex Orbe Religionum, Studies in the History of Religions, vol. 22. Leiden.

1973a   A Definition of Shamanism. Temenos 9: 25–37.

1973b   Prairie and Plains Indians. Iconography of Religions 10 (3). Leiden: E. J. Brill.

1974   Ecology of Religion: Its Scope and Methodology. Review of Ethnology 4 (1–2): 1–7, 9–12. Vienna.

1975   Conditions for the Spread of the Peyote Cult in North America. Pp. 70–83 in New Religions (ed. by H. Biezais). Scripta Instituti Donneriani Aboensis, vol. 7. Uppsala.

1976   The Contribution of the Study of North American Indian Religions to the History of Religions. Pp. 86–106 in Seeing with a Native Eye (ed. by W. H. Capps). New York: Harper and Row.

1977   Amerikanische Religionen. TRE 2: 402–450.

Hvidtfeldt, A.
1958   Teotl and *Ixiptlatli: Some Central Conceptions in Ancient Mexican Religion. Copenhagen: Munksgaard.
Ishida, E., et al.
1960   Andes: Report of the University of Tokyo Scientific Expedition to the Andes in 1958. Tokyo: University of Tokyo.
Johnson, F.
1972   (ed.) The Prehistory of the Tehuacan Valley, vol. 4. Austin and London: University of Texas Press.
Jones, W.
1905   The Algonkin Manitou. JAFL 18: 183–190.
1939   Ethnography of the Fox Indians (ed. by M. W. Fisher). BBAE 125.
Jones, W. T.
1972   World Views: Their Nature and Their Function. CA 13 (1): 79–109.
Joralemon, P. D.
1971   A Study of Olmec Iconography. Studies in Pre-Columbian Art and Archaeology no. 7. Washington, D.C.
Kaplan, D.
1963   Men, Monuments, and Political Systems. SWJA 19 (4): 397–410.
Karsten, R.
1926   The Civilization of the South American Indians. London: Kegan Paul.
1955   Zur Psychologie des indianischen Medizinmannes. ZE 80 (2): 170–177.
1964   Studies in the Religion of the South-American Indians East of the Andes (ed. by A. Runeberg and M. Webster). Finska vetenskapsakademiens handlingar 29 (1). Helsingfors.
Keen, B.
1971   The Aztec Image in Western Thought. New Brunswick, N.J.: Rutgers University Press.
Kehoe, Th. F., and A. B. Kehoe
1959   Boulder Effigy Monuments in the Northern Plains. JAFL 72: 115–127.
Kelley, D. H.
1960   Calendar Animals and Deities. SWJA 16 (3): 317–337.
Kelley, J. Ch.
1952   Factors Involved in the Abandonment of Certain Peripheral Southwestern Settlements. AA 54 (3): 356–387.
Kidder, A., II
1964   South American High Cultures. Pp. 451–486 in Prehistoric Man in the New World (ed. by J. D. Jennings and E. Norbeck). Chicago: University of Chicago Press.

Kirchhoff, P.
1955 Quetzalcoatl, Huemac y el fin de Tula. Cuadernos Americanos 14: 163–196.

Kloos, P.
1971 The Maroni River Caribs of Surinam. Studies of Developing Countries, no. 12. Assen.

Kluckhohn, C.
1942 Myths and Rituals: A General Theory. Harvard Theological Review 35 (1): 45–79.
1944 Navaho Witchcraft. PMP 22 (2).

Knorozov, Y. V.
1958 New Data on the Maya Written Language. ICA 32: 467–475.

Koch-Grünberg, Th.
1900 Zum Animismus der südamerikanischen Indianer. IAE, Supplement to vol. 13.
1909 Zwei Jahre unter den Indianern. Reisen in Nordwestbrasilien, vol. 1. Berlin.

Kock, G.
1956 Der Heilbringer: Ein Beitrag zur Aufklärung seiner religions-geschichtlichen Voraussetzungen. Ethnos 21 (1–2): 118–129.

Köngäs, E. K.
1960 The Earth-Diver (Th. A 812). Ethnohistory 7 (2): 151–180.

Krappe, A. H.
1930 Mythologie universelle. Paris.

Krause, A.
1956 The Tlingit Indians. Seattle: University of Washington Press.

Krickeberg, W.
1934 Das Schwitzbad der Indianer. Ciba-Zeitschrift.
1949 Felsplastick und Felsbilder bei den Kulturvölkern Altamerikas, vol. 1. Berlin.
1950 Bauform und Weltbild im alten Mexiko. Paideuma 4: 295–333.
1954 Ältere Ethnographica aus Nordamerika: Tabakspfeifen. Baessler-Archiv, Neue Folge, vol. 2. Berlin.
1956 Altmexikanische Kulturen. Berlin.
1961 Die Religionen der Kulturvölker Mesoamerikas. Pp. 1–89 in Die Religionen des alten Amerika (Die Religionen der Menschheit, ed. by C. M. Schröder, vol. 7). Stuttgart: Kohlhammer.

Kroeber, A. L.
1907 The Religion of the Indians of California. UCPAAE 4 (6): 319–356.
1925 Handbook of the Indians of California. BBAE 78.

1932   The Patwin and Their Neighbors. UCPAAE 29 (4): 253–423.
Kroeber, A. L., and E. W. Gifford
1949   World Renewal: A Cult System of Native Northwest California. AR 13.
Krusche, R.
1975   Zur Genese des Maskenwesens im östlichen Waldland Nordamerikas. Jahrbuch des Museums für Völkerkunde zu Leipzig 30: 137–190. Berlin.
Kubler, G.
1961   Chichén-Itzá y Tula. Estudios de cultura Maya, vol. 1. Mexico.
Kutscher, G.
1950   Chimu: eine altindianische Hochkultur. Berlin.
La Barre, W.
1938   The Peyote Cult. YUPA 19.
1964   Confession as Cathartic Therapy in American Indian Tribes. Pp. 36–49 in Magic, Faith, and Healing (ed. by A. Kiev). New York: Free Press.
1970   The Ghost Dance: Origins of Religion. Garden City, N.Y.: Doubleday.
Lafitau, J. F.
1724   Moeurs des sauvages amériquains, comparées aux moeurs des premiers temps. 2 vols. Paris.
Lambert, R. S.
1956   The Shaking Tent. Tomorrow 4 (3): 113–128.
Lamphere, L.
1969   Symbolic Elements in Navajo Ritual. SWJA 25 (3): 279–305.
Lanczkowski, G.
1962   Quetzalcoatl: Mythos und Geschichte. Numen 9: 17–36.
1970a   Aztekische Sprache und Überlieferung. Berlin, Heidelberg, and New York: Springer-Verlag.
1970b   Different Types of Redemption in Ancient Mexican Religion. Pp. 120–129 in Types of Redemption (ed. by R. J. Z. Werblowsky and C. J. Bleeker). Leiden: E. J. Brill.
Landa, D. de
1938   Relación de las cosas de Yucatán. Mérida.
Landes, R.
1959   Dakota Warfare. SWJA 15 (1): 43–52.
Lantis, M.
1938   The Alaskan Whale Cult and Its Affinities. AA 40 (3): 438–464.
1950   The Religion of the Eskimos. Pp. 309–339 in Forgotten Religions (ed. by V. Ferm). New York: Philosophical Library.
Larsen, H.
1937   Notes on the Volador and Its Associated Ceremonies and Superstitions. Ethnos 2 (4): 179–192.

Lathrap, D. W.
1971 The Tropical Forest and the Cultural Context of Chavín. Pp. 73–100 in Dumbarton Oaks Conference on Chavín (ed. by E. P. Benson). Washington, D.C.: Dumbarton Oaks Research Library and Collection.
1973 Summary or Model Building: How Does One Achieve a Meaningful Overview of a Continent's Prehistory? AA 75 (6): 1755–1767.

Lavallée, D.
1970 Les Représentations animales dans la céramique Mochica. Paris: Musée de l'homme.

Leander, B.
1971 La poesía Nahuatl: Función y carácter. ES 31.

Lee, Th. A., Jr.
1972 Jmetic Lubton: Some Modern and Pre-Hispanic Maya Ceremonial Customs in the Highlands of Chiapas, Mexico. Papers of the New World Archaeological Foundation vol. 29. Provo, Utah.

León-Portilla, M.
1956 La filosofía Nahuatl. Mexico.
1963 Aztec Thought and Culture: A Study of the Ancient Nahuatl Mind. Norman: University of Oklahoma Press.
1973 Time and Reality in the Thought of the Maya. Boston: Beacon Press.

Lévi-Strauss, C.
1948 La Vie familiale et sociale des Indiens Nambikwara. JSA 37: 1–131.
1965 Le Totémisme aujourd'hui. 2nd ed. Paris: Presses universitaires de France.

Lewis, O.
1942 The Effects of White Contact upon Blackfoot Culture. MAES 6.

Lid, N.
1933 Jolesveinar og grøderiksomsgudar. Det Norske Videnskaps-Akademi i Oslo, Historisk-Filosofisk Klasse, no. 5. Oslo.

Lindig, W. H.
1970 Geheimbünde und Männerbünde der Prärie- und der Waldlandindianer Nordamerikas. Studien zur Kulturkunde 23. Wiesbaden: Franz Steiner.

Lindig, W. H., and A. M. Dauer
1961 Prophetismus und Geistertanz-Bewegung bei nordamerikanischen Eingeborenen. Pp. 41–74 in Chiliasmus und Nativismus (ed. by W. E. Mühlmann). Berlin: Dietrich Reimer.

Linné, S.
1934   Archaeological Researches at Teotihuacan, Mexico. SEMNS
       1.
1938   Zapotecan Antiquities. SEMNS 4.
1941   Teotihuacan Symbols. Ethnos 6 (3–4): 174–186.
1942a Mexican Highland Culture. SEMNS 7.
1942b Pyramidstaden. Stockholm: Medéns.
1943   Humpbacks in Ancient America. Ethnos 8: 161–186.
1948   El valle y la ciudad de Mexico en 1550. SEMNS 9.
1954   Mayafolket i Mexico och pyramidgraven i Palenque. Ymer
       74 (3): 161–181.
1960   Die Kunst Mexikos und Zentralamerikas. Pp. 5–134 in Alt-
       Amerika, Die Hochkulturen der Neuen Welt (by H. D. Dis-
       selhoff and S. Linné). Baden-Baden: Holle.
Linton, R.
1926   The Origin of the Skidi Pawnee Sacrifice to the Morning
       Star. AA 28 (3): 457–466.
Lips, E.
1959–60 Formen der religiösen Verehrung des Maises bei indianis-
       chen Bodenbauern. Wissenschaftliche Zeitschrift der
       Karl-Marx Universität, Geschichts- und Sprachwis-
       senschaftliche Reihe, vol. 9 (2). Leipzig.
Locher, G. W.
1932   The Serpent in Kwakiutl Religion. Leiden: E. J. Brill
Loeb, E. M.
1926a Pomo Folkways. UCPAAE 19 (2): 149–405.
1926b The Creator Concept among the Indians of North Central
       California. AA 28 (3): 467–493.
1929   Tribal Initiations and Secret Societies. UCPAAE 25 (3):
       249–288.
1931   The Religious Organizations of North Central California
       and Tierra del Fuego. AA 33 (4): 517–556.
1932   The Western Kuksu Cult. UCPAAE 33 (1): 1–137.
1962   Staatsfeuer und Vestalinnen. Paideuma 8 (1): 1–24.
Loewenthal, J. W. J.
1913   Die Religion der Ostalgonkin. Berlin.
Long, J.
1791   Voyages and Travels of an Indian Interpreter and Trader,
       etc. London.
Lopatin, I. A.
1960   Origin of the Native American Steam Bath. AA 62 (6): 977–
       993.
Lou, D. W.
1957   Rain-Worship among the Ancient Chinese and the
       Nahua-Maya Indians. Institute of Ethnology (Nankang),
       Bulletin 4: 31–108.

Lowie, R. H.
1915 Ceremonialism in North America. Pp. 229–258 in Anthropology in North America (by F. Boas et al.). New York: Stechert.
1922 The Religion of the Crow Indians. APAMNH 25 (2): 309–444.
1935 The Crow Indians. New York: Farrar and Rinehart.
1937 The History of Ethnological Theory. New York: Rinehart and Co.
1949 Social and Political Organization of the Tropical Forest and Marginal Tribes. Pp. 313–350 in Handbook of South American Indians (ed. by J. H. Steward), vol. 5. BBAE 143.
1960 Some Aspects of Political Organization among the American Aborigines. Pp. 262–290 in Lowie's Selected Papers in Anthropology (ed. by C. DuBois). Berkeley and Los Angeles: University of California Press.

Luckert, K. W.
1976 Olmec Religion: A Key to Middle America and Beyond. Norman: University of Oklahoma Press.

Lumbreras, L. G.
1969 De los pueblos, las culturas y las artes del antiguo Perú. Lima: Moncloa-Campodonico.

McLean, J.
1849 Notes of a Twenty-Five Years' Service in the Hudson's Bay Territory. 2 vols. London.

Makarius, L.
1969 Le Mythe du "trickster." RHR 75: 17–46.
1970 Ritual Clowns and Symbolical Behaviour. Diogenes 69: 44–73.
1973 The Crime of Manabozo. AA 75 (3): 663–675.

Mariscotti, A. M.
1975 Die Stellung des Gewittergottes in den regionalen Pantheen der Zentralanden. Pp. 104–105 in Studies in the History of Religions, vol. 31. Leiden: E. J. Brill.

Mason, J. A.
1957 The Ancient Civilizations of Peru. London: Pelican.

Means, Ph. A.
1931 Ancient Civilizations of the Andes. New York.

Meggers, B. J.
1954 Environmental Limitation on the Development of Culture. AA 56 (5): 801–824.
1973 Prehistoric America. Chicago: Aldine.
1975 The Transpacific Origin of Mesoamerican Civilization. AA 77 (1): 1–27.

Meggers, B. J. C. Evans, and E. Estrada
1965   Early Formative Period of Coastal Ecuador: The Valdivia and Machalilla Phases. SCA 1.
Menghin, O. F. A.
1962   Grundprobleme der amerikanischen Urgeschichte. Homo 13 (1–2): 81–92.
Métraux, A.
1927   Les Migrations historiques des Tupí-Guaraní. JSA 19.
1928   La Religion des Tupinamba et ses rapports avec celle des autres tribus Tupí-Guaraní. Paris.
1942   Le Shamanisme araucan. Revista del Instituto de Antropologia de la Universidad Nacional de Tucumán, vol. 2 (10).
1943   The Social Organization and Religion of the Mojo and Manasi. PM 16 (1–2): 1–30.
1944   Le Shamanisme chez les Indiens de l'Amérique du Sud tropicale. Acta Americana 2 (3–4).
1946   Twin Heroes in South American Mythology. JAFL 59: 114–123.
1949   Religion and Shamanism. Pp. 559–599 in Handbook of South American Indians (ed. by J. H. Steward), vol. 5. BBAE 143.
1957   Les Messies de l'Amérique du Sud. Archives de sociologie des religions, no. 4. Paris.
1967   Religions et magies indiennes d'Amérique du Sud (ed. by S. Dreyfus). Paris: Éditions Gallimard.
Michelson, T.
1930   Contributions to Fox Ethnology, 2. BBAE 95.
Mitchell, W. P.
1976   Irrigation and Community in the Central Peruvian Highlands. AA 78 (1): 25–44.
Momaday, N. S.
1976   Native American Attitudes to the Environment. Pp. 79–85 in Seeing with a Native Eye (ed. by W. H. Capps). New York: Harper and Row.
Moon Conard, E. L.
1900   Les Idées des Indiens algonquins relatives à la vie d'outre-tombe. RHR 42: 9–49, 220–274.
Mooney, J.
1891   Sacred Formulas of the Cherokees. ARBAE 7: 301–397.
1896   The Ghost-Dance Religion and the Sioux Outbreak of 1890. ARBAE 14 (2): 640–1136.
Moreno, W. J.
1938   Fray Bernardino de Sahagún y su obra. Mexico.

Morley, S. G., and G. W. Brainerd
1956   The Ancient Maya. 3rd ed. Stanford: Stanford University Press.
Müller, J. G.
1855   Geschichte der Amerikanischen Urreligionen. Basel: Schweighausersche Verlagsbuchhandlung.
Müller, W.
1954   Die blaue Hütte. Wiesbaden: Franz Steiner.
1955   Weltbild und Kult der Kwakiutl-Indianer. Wiesbaden: Franz Steiner.
1956   Die Religionen der Waldlandindianer Nordamerikas. Berlin: Dietrich Reimer.
1961   Die Religionen der Indianervölker Nordamerikas. Pp. 171–267 in Die Religionen des alten Amerika (Die Religionen der Menschheit, ed. by C. M. Schröder). Stuttgart: Kohlhammer.
1970   Glauben und Denken der Sioux. Berlin: Dietrich Reimer.
Mundkur, B.
1976   The Cult of the Serpent in the Americas: Its Asian Background. CA 17 (3): 429–455.
Murphy, R. F.
1958   Mundurucú Religion. UCPAAE 49 (1): 1–154.
Nimuendajú, C.
1942   The Šerente. F. W. Hodge Anniversary Publication Fund, vol. 4. Los Angeles.
1952   The Tukuna. UCPAAE 45 (1): 1–209.
Nimuendajú, C., and R. H. Lowie
1937   The Dual Organizations of the Ramko'kamekra (Canella) of Northern Brazil. AA 39 (4): 565–582.
Noel, D.
1976   (ed.) Seeing Castaneda: Reactions to the "Don Juan" Writings of Carlos Castaneda. New York: Putnam's.
Nowotny, K. A.
1961   Tlacuilolli: Die mexikanischen Bilderhandschriften, Stil und Inhalt, mit einem Katalog der Codex Borgia-Gruppe. Monumenta Americana III. Berlin.
Oakes, M.
1951   The Two Crosses of Todos Santos. Bollingen Series 27. New York: Pantheon.
Ohlmarks, Å.
1939   Studien zum Problem des Schamanismus. Lund: Gleerup.
Olson, R. L.
1933   Clan and Moiety in Native America. UCPAAE 33 (4): 351–422.

Opler, M. E.
1972   Cause and Effect in Apachean Agriculture, Division of Labor, Residence Patterns, and Girls' Puberty Rites. AA 74 (5): 1133–1146.

Opler, M. K.
1946   The Creative Role of Shamanism in Mescalero Apache Mythology. JAFL 59: 268–281.

Ortiz, A.
1969   The Tewa World: Space, Time, Being, and Becoming in a Pueblo Society. Chicago and London: University of Chicago Press.

Overholt, Th. W.
1974   The Ghost Dance of 1890 and the Nature of the Prophetic Process. Ethnohistory 21 (1): 37–63.

Palerm, A.
1955   The Agricultural Basis of Urban Civilization. Pp. 28–42 in Irrigation Civilizations: A Comparative Study (ed. by J. H. Steward). Washington, D.C.: Pan American Union.

Park, W. Z.
1938   Shamanism in Western North America. Evanston and Chicago: Northwestern University.

Parrot, A.
1949   Ziggurats et "Tour de Babel." Paris: Albin Michel.

Parsons, E. C.
1939   Pueblo Indian Religion. 2 vols. Chicago: University of Chicago Press.

Parsons, E. C., and R. L. Beals
1934   The Sacred Clowns of the Pueblo and Mayo-Yaqui Indians. AA 36 (4): 491–514.

Parsons, M. H.
1972   Aztec Figurines from the Teotihuacán Valley. Miscellaneous Studies in Mexican Prehistory, Anthropological Papers of the Museum of Anthropology, University of Michigan, vol. 45. Ann Arbor.

Paulson, I.
1959   Zur Aufbewahrung der Tierknochen im nördlichen Nordamerika. Mitteilungen aus dem Museum für Völkerkunde in Hamburg 25: 182–188.
1962   Die Religionen der nordasiatischen (sibirischen) Völker. Pp. 1–144 in Die Religionen Nordeurasiens und der amerikanischen Arktis (Die Religionen der Menschheit, ed. by C. M. Schröder, vol. 3). Stuttgart: Kohlhammer.
1965   Die rituelle Erhebung des Bärenschädels bei arktischen und subarktischen Völkern. Temenos 1: 150–169.

Perry, W. J.
1927 The Children of the Sun. 2nd ed. London: Methuen.
Pettazzoni, R.
1931 La Confession des péchés. Paris.
1954 Essays on the History of Religions. Studies in the History of Religions, vol. 1. Leiden: E. J. Brill.
Pfister, F.
1927 Der Glaube an das "ausserordentlich Wirkungsvolle" (Orendismus). Blätter zur bayerischen Volkskunde 11: 24–48. Würzburg.
Pollock, H. E. D., et al.
1962 Mayapan, Yucatán, Mexico. Carnegie Institute of Washington, Publ. no. 619. Washington, D.C.
Ponce Sangines, C.
1969 Tunupa y Ekako: Estudio arqueológico acerca de las efigies pre-colombinas de dorso adunco. Academia Nacional de Ciencias de Bolivia no. 19. La Paz.
Powers, W. K.
1975 Oglala Religion. Lincoln: University of Nebraska Press.
Preuss, K. Th.
1901 Der Affe in der mexikanischen Mythologie. ZE 33: 1–11.
1903 Die Feuergötter als Ausgangspunkt zum Verständnis der mexikanischen Religion. Mitteilungen der Anthropologischen Gesellschaft in Wien 33: 129–233.
1921-23 Religion und Mythologie der Uitoto. 2 vols. Göttingen: Vandenhoeck und Ruprecht.
Radin, P.
1915 Religion of the North American Indians. Pp. 259–305 in Anthropology in North America (by F. Boas et al.). New York: Stechert.
1920 The Sources and Authenticity of the History of the Ancient Mexicans. UCPAAE 17 (1): 1–150.
1944 The Story of the American Indian. New York: Liveright.
1945 The Road of Life and Death. New York: Pantheon.
1948 Winnebago Hero Cycles: A Study in Aboriginal Literature. Indiana University Publications in Anthropology and Linguistics no. 1. Bloomington, Ind.
1950 The Basic Myth of the North American Indians. Eranos-Jarhbuch 17: 359–419.
1956 The Trickster: A Study in American Indian Mythology. New York: Philosophical Library.
1957 Primitive Man as Philosopher. 2nd ed. New York: Dover.
1959 The Sacral Chief among the American Indians. P. 83 in The Sacral Kingship, Studies in the History of Religions, vol. 4. Leiden.

Redfield, R.
1941 The Folk Culture of Yucatán. Chicago: University of Chicago Press.
Reichard, G. A.
1950 Navaho Religion. 2 vols. New York: Pantheon.
Reichel-Dolmatoff, G.
1951 Los Kogi, una tribu de la Sierra Nevada de Santa Marta, Colombia. Vol. 2. Bogota: Editorial Iquerima.
Ricketts, M. L.
1966 The North American Indian Trickster. HR 5 (4): 327–350.
Ridington, R., and T. Ridington
1970 The Inner Eye of Shamanism and Totemism. HR 10 (1): 49–61.
Riley, C. L., and J. Hobgood
1959 A Recent Nativistic Movement among the Southern Tepehuan Indians. SWJA 15 (4): 355–360.
Ritzenthaler, R.
1969 Iroquois False-Face Masks. Milwaukee: Milwaukee Public Museum.
Rivet, P.
1954 Mexique précolombien. Paris.
Rooth, A. B.
1957 The Creation Myths of the North American Indians. Anthropos 52: 497–508.
Roth, W. E.
1915 An Inquiry into the Animism and Folk-Lore of the Guiana Indians. ARBAE 30: 103–386.
Rowe, J. H.
1946 Inca Culture at the Time of the Spanish Conquest. Pp. 183–330 in Handbook of South American Indians (ed. by J. H. Steward), vol. 2. BBAE 143.
1948 The Kingdom of Chimor. Acta Americana 6 (1–2): 26–59.
1960 The Origins of Creator Worship among the Incas. Pp. 408–429 in Culture in History: Essays in Honor of Paul Radin (ed. by S. Diamond). New York: Columbia University Press.
Ruz Lhuillier, A.
1954 Exploraciones en Palenque: 1952. Anales del Instituto Nacional de Antropología e Historia 6: 79–110. Mexico.
1955 Exploraciones en Palenque. ICA 30: 5–22.
Sabloff, J. A.
1973 New Horizons in Mesoamerican Archaeology. AA 75 (6): 1768–1774.
Sabloff, J. A., and G. R. Willey
1967 The Collapse of Maya Civilization in the Southern Lowlands. SWJA 23 (4): 311–336.

Sahagún, Fray Bernardino de
1950-69 Florentine Codex, or General History of the Things of New
         Spain (ed. and trans. by A. J. O. Anderson and Ch. E.
         Dibble). 13 vols. Monographs of the School of American
         Research. Santa Fe and Salt Lake City.

Saler, B.
1962 Migration and Ceremonial Ties among the Maya. SWJA 18
      (4): 336–340.

Sanders, W. T.
1962 Cultural Ecology of Nuclear Mesoamerica. AA 64 (1): 34–44.

Sanders, W. T., and B. J. Price
1968 Mesoamerica: The Evolution of a Civilization. New York:
      Random House.

Sapper, C.
1897 Das nördliche Mittelamerika. Braunschweig.

Schaeffer, C. E.
1965 The Kutenai Female Berdache. Ethnohistory 12 (3): 193–236.
1969 Blackfoot Shaking Tent. Glenbow Institute, Occasional Pa-
      pers no. 5. Calgary, Alberta.

Schellhas, P.
1926 Der Ursprung der Mayahandschriften. ZE 58 (1–2).

Schmidt, W.
1929-35 Der Ursprung der Gottesidee, vols. II, V, VI. Münster in
        Westfalen: Aschendorffsche Verlagsbuchhandlung.
1933 High Gods in North America. Oxford: Oxford University
      Press.
1936 Donner und Regenbogen beim Höchsten Wesen der Yuki.
      Pp. 299–308 in Essays in Anthropology Presented to A. L.
      Kroeber (ed. by R. H. Lowie). Berkeley: University of
      California Press.

Schoolcraft, H. R.
1851-60 Historical and Statistical Information Respecting the His-
        tory, Condition and Prospects of the Indian Tribes of the
        United States. 6 vols. Philadelphia: J.B. Lippincott.
1956 See Williams, M. L.

Schuster, M.
1964 Zur Frage der Erste-Früchte-Riten in Nordamerika. Pp.
      611–619 in Festschrift für Ad. E. Jensen. Munich: Klaus
      Renner.

Séjourné, L.
1956 Burning Water: Thought and Religion in Ancient Mexico.
      London and New York: Thames and Hudson.

Sekaquaptewa, E.
1976 Hopi Indian Ceremonies. Pp. 35–43 in Seeing with a Native
      Eye (ed. by W. H. Capps). New York: Harper and Row.

Seler, E.
1902-23 Gesammelte Abhandlungen zur amerikanischen Sprach- und Alterthumskunde. 5 vols. Berlin.

Seler, E., et al.
1904 Mexican and Central American Antiquities, Calendar Systems, and History. BBAE 28.

Serrano, A.
1946 The Charrua. Pp. 191–196 in Handbook of South American Indians (ed. by J. H. Steward), vol. 1. BBAE 143.

Slotkin, J. S.
1956 The Peyote Religion. Glencoe, Ill.: The Free Press.

Soustelle, J.
1940 La Pensée cosmologique des anciens mexicains. Paris: Hermann.
1961 Daily Life of the Aztecs. London.
1966 Terrestrial and Celestial Gods in Mexican Antiquity. Diogenes 56: 20–50.

Speck, F. G.
1909 Ethnology of the Yuchi Indians. Anthropological Publications of the University Museum, University of Pennsylvania, vol. 1 (1). Philadelphia.
1931 A Study of the Delaware Indian Big House Ceremony. Publ. of the Pennsylvania Historical Commission. Harrisburg.
1935 Naskapi: The Savage Hunters of the Labrador Peninsula. Norman: University of Oklahoma Press.

Spence, L.
1914 Myths and Legends of the North American Indians. Boston: Nickerson.
1945 The Religion of Ancient Mexico. London.

Spinden, H. J.
1917 Ancient Civilizations of Mexico and Central America. American Museum of Natural History Handbook no. 3. New York.
1940 Sun Worship. SR 1939.

Spranz, B.
1964 Göttergestalten in den mexikanischen Bilderhandschriften der Codex Borgia-Gruppe. Acta Humboldtiana. Wiesbaden: Franz Steiner.

Stevenson, M. C.
1904 The Zuñi Indians: Their Mythology, Esoteric Fraternities, and Ceremonies. ARBAE 23.

Steward, J. H.
1931 The Ceremonial Buffoon of the American Indian. Papers of the Michigan Academy of Science, Arts and Letters, vol. 14: 187–207.

1946-59 (ed.) Handbook of South American Indians. 7 vols. BBAE 143.
 1947 American Culture History in the Light of South America. SWJA 3 (2): 85–107.
 1949 South American Cultures: An Interpretative Summary. Pp. 669–772 in Handbook of South American Indians (ed. by J. H. Steward), vol. 5. BBAE 143.
 1955 Theory of Culture Change. Urbana, Ill.: University of Illinois Press.

Steward, J. H., and L. C. Faron
 1959 Native Peoples of South America. New York: McGraw-Hill.

Stewart, K. M.
 1946 Spirit Possession in Native America. SWJA 2 (3): 323–339.
 1956 Spirit Possession. Tomorrow 4 (3): 41–49.

Stirling, M. W.
 1946 Concepts of the Sun among American Indians. SR 1945: 387–400.

Swadesh, M.
 1964 Linguistic Overview. Pp. 527–556 in Prehistoric Man in the New World (ed. by J. D. Jennings and E. Norbeck). Chicago: University of Chicago Press.

Swanton, J. R.
 1911 Indian Tribes of the Lower Mississippi Valley and Adjacent Coast of the Gulf of Mexico. BBAE 43.

Tatje, T., and F. L. K. Hsu
 1969 Variations in Ancestor Worship Beliefs and Their Relation to Kinship. SWJA 25 (2): 153–172.

Tegnaeus, H.
 1950 Le Héros civilisateur. Studia Ethnographica Upsaliensia, vol. 2. Uppsala.

Teicher, M. I.
 1960 Windigo Psychosis. PAES.

Tentori, T.
 1955 South American Ideas of the Other World. ICA 30: 199–201.

Tessmann, W.
 1928 Menschen ohne Gott. Stuttgart.

Thompson, J. E. S.
 1954a The Civilization of the Mayas. Field Columbian Museum of Natural History. Chicago.
 1954b The Rise and Fall of Maya Civilization. Norman: University of Oklahoma Press.
 1955 The Character of the Maya. ICA 30: 36–40.
 1960 Maya Hieroglyphic Writing: An Introduction. Norman: University of Oklahoma Press.

1970 Maya History and Religion. Norman: University of Okla-
      homa Press.
1972 A Commentary on the Dresden Codex: A Maya Hieroglyphic
      Book. Memoirs of the American Philosophical Society no. 93.
      Philadelphia.
Thompson, S.
1953 The Star Husband Tale. Studia Septentrionalia 4: 93–163.
Thurber, F., and V. Thurber
1959 Itzamna Cocahmut: The Possible "Spark-Bird" God of the
      Maya. SWJA 15 (2): 185–188.
Thwaites, R. G.
1896-1901(ed.) Jesuit Relations and Allied Documents. 73 vols. Cleve-
      land: Burrows Brothers.
Toelken, B.
1976 Seeing with a Native Eye: How Many Sheep Will It Hold?
      Pp. 9–24 in Seeing with a Native Eye (ed. by W. H. Capps).
      New York: Harper and Row.
Tooker, E.
1970 The Iroquois Ceremonial of Midwinter. Syracuse, N.Y.:
      Syracuse University Press.
Tozzer, A. M.
1940 (ed.) The Maya and Their Neighbors. New York: Apple-
      ton-Century.
1941 (ed.) Landa's "Relación de las cosas de Yucatán": A Transla-
      tion. PMP 18.
1957 Chichen Itza and Its Cenote of Sacrifice: A Comparative
      Study of Contemporaneous Maya and Toltec. Memoirs of
      the Peabody Museum nos. 11–12. Cambridge, Mass.: Har-
      vard University Press.
Trimborn, H.
1961 Die Religionen der Völkerschaften des südlichen Mit-
      telamerika und des nördlichen und mittleren Anden-
      raumes. Pp. 91–170 in Die Religionen des alten Amerika
      (Die Religionen der Menschheit, ed. by C. M. Schröder,
      vol. 7). Stuttgart: Kohlhammer.
Underhill, R. M.
1948 Ceremonial Patterns in the Greater Southwest. MAES 13.
1956 The Navajos. Norman: University of Oklahoma Press.
1957 Religion among American Indians. Annals of the American
      Academy of Political and Social Science no. 311: 127–136.
1965 Red Man's Religion: Beliefs and Practices of the Indians
      North of Mexico. Chicago and London: University of
      Chicago Press.
Vaillant, G. C.
1962 Aztecs of Mexico. Revised edition ed. by S. B. Vaillant.
      Garden City, N.Y.: Doubleday.

Voegelin, C. F., and E. W. Voegelin
1944 The Shawnee Female Deity in Historical Perspective. AA 46 (3): 370–375.
Vogt, E. Z.
1960 On the Concepts of Structure and Process in Cultural Anthropology. AA 62 (1): 18–33.
1961 Navaho. Pp. 278–336 in Perspectives in American Indian Culture Change, ed. by E. H. Spicer. Chicago: University of Chicago Press.
1963 (Conference on) The Cultural Development of the Maya. CA 4(3): 325–326.
Wachtmeister, A.
1956 Naming and Reincarnation among the Eskimos. Ethnos 21 (1–2); 130–142.
1957 Själavandringsföreställningar hos Nordamerikas indianer. Stockholm: Natur och Kultur.
Walker, D. E.
1966 The Nez Perce Sweat Bath Complex. SWJA (2): 133–171.
1969 New Light on the Prophet Dance Controversy. Ethnohistory 16 (3): 245–255.
Walker, J. R.
1917 The Sun Dance and Other Ceremonies of the Oglala Division of the Teton Dakota. APAMNH 16 (2): 51–221.
Wallace, A. F. C.
1958 Dreams and the Wishes of the Soul. AA 60 (2): 234–248.
Wallis, R. S., and W. D. Wallis
1953 The Sins of the Fathers: Concept of Disease among the Canadian Dakota. SWJA 9 (4): 431–436.
Wassén, S. H.
1949 Contributions to Cuna Ethnography. ES 16.
1960 A Comparative Reconstruction of the Post-Columbian Change in Certain Religious Concepts among the Cuna Indians of Panama. ICA 33: 502–509.
Wasson, R. G., et al.
1975 María Sabina and Her Mazatec Mushroom Velada. New York and London: Harcourt.
Weiss, G.
1972 Campa Cosmology. Ethnology 11 (2): 157–172.
1975 Campa Cosmology: The World of a Forest Tribe in South America. APAMNH 52 (5): 219–588.
Wheeler-Voegelin, E., and R. W. Moore
1957 The Emergence Myth in Native North America. Pp. 66–91 in Studies in Folklore (ed. by W. Edson Richmond). Bloomington: Indiana University Press.
Whiting, B. B.
1950 Paiute Sorcery. VFPA 15.

Wilbert, J.
1958   Kinship and Social Organization of the Yekuána and Goa-
       jiro. SWJA 14 (1): 51–60.
Wildschutz, W.
1960   Crow Medicine Bundles (ed. by J. C. Ewers). Contributions
       from the Museum of the American Indian vol. 17. New
       York.
Willey, G. R.
1955a The Interrelated Rise of the Native Cultures of Middle and
       South America. Pp. 28–45 in New Interpretations of
       Aboriginal American Culture History (ed. by B. Meggers).
       Anthropological Society of Washington, Washington, D.C.
1955b The Prehistoric Civilizations of Nuclear America. AA 57 (3):
       571–593.
1956   The Structure of Ancient Maya Society. AA 58 (5): 777–782.
1962   The Early Great Styles and the Rise of the Pre-Columbian
       Civilizations. AA 64 (1): 1–14.
1966-71 An Introduction to American Archaeology. 1: North and
       Middle America (1966); 2: South America (1971). Englewood
       Hills, N.J.: Prentice-Hall.
Willey, G. R., and D. B. Shimkin
1971   The Collapse of Classic Maya Civilization in the Southern
       Lowlands. SWJA 27 (1): 1–18.
Williams, M. L.
1956   (ed.) Schoolcraft's Indian Legends. East Lansing: Michigan
       State University Press.
Winning, H. von
1961   Teotihuacan Symbols: The Reptile's Eye Glyph. Ethnos 26
       (3): 121–166.
Wissler, C.
1912   Ceremonial Bundles of the Blackfoot Indians. APAMNH 7
       (2): 65–289.
Witthoft, J.
1949   Green Corn Ceremonialism in the Eastern Woodlands.
       OCMA 13: 31–77.
Wolf, E. R.
1958   The Virgin of Guadalupe: A Mexican National Symbol.
       JAFL 71: 34–39.
Zerries, O.
1952   Sternbilder als Ausdruck jägerischer Geisteshaltung in
       Südamerika. Paideuma 5 (5).
1954   Wilde- und Buschgeister in Südamerika. Wiesbaden: Franz
       Steiner.
1955   Krankheitsdämonen und Hilfsgeister des Medizinmannes
       in Südamerika. ICA 30: 162–178.

1961 Die Religionen der Naturvölker Südamerikas und West-indiens. Pp. 269–384 in Die Religionen des alten Amerika (Die Religionen der Menschheit, ed. by C. M. Schröder, vol. 7). Stuttgart: Kohlhammer.

1962 Die Vorstellung vom Zweiten Ich und die Rolle der Harpye in der Kultur der Naturvölker Südamerikas. Anthropos 57: 889–914.

1963-64 Dualorganisation und Weltbild bei brasilianischen In-dianern. Staden-Jahrbuch 11–12: 61-92. São Paulo.

Index

Designer: Dave Comstock
Compositor: Lehmann Graphics
Printer: Publishers Press
Binder: Mountain States Bindery
Text: VIP Palatino
Display: VIP Palatino & Headline Open
Cloth: Holliston Roxite B53538
Paper: 55 lb. P&S Offset A-69